KOSOVO DIARY

MY CIVILIAN POLICE MISSION IN KOSOVO

BY
CLAYTON L. COKER

INFINITY PUBLISHING

ISBN 978-0-7414-6644-0

Printed in the United States of America

Published August 2013

INFINITY PUBLISHING
1094 New DeHaven Street, Suite 100
West Conshohocken, PA 19428-2713
Toll-free (877) BUY BOOK
Local Phone (610) 941-9999
Fax (610) 941-9959
Info@buybooksontheweb.com
www.buybooksontheweb.com

Dedication

Dedicated to all the CivPol officers that have served in harm's way to bring order to chaos.

In memory of Ferdinand (Guam) Ibabao
KIA 10-14-2004
Baghdad, Iraq

PROLOGUE

Kosovo is the southernmost province of Serbia, which was the heart of Yugoslavia. Yugoslavia was a socialist state modeled after the Soviet Union and was led by Josip Broz, AKA Marshal Tito. Tito ruled Yugoslavia from 1953 until his death in 1980. His communist government repressed all ethnic and nationalist movements within Yugoslavia. He did not want any particular Yugoslav republic or nationality, especially Serbia, which was the largest and most powerful of the republics, to gain dominance over the others. Tito gave a semblance of autonomy to the Kosovo province of Serbia because of its predominantly ethnic Albanian population. Kosovo's position was bolstered in 1974 when the ethnic Albanian political status was improved by a new Yugoslav constitution which expanded political rights. The government was still communist, but in Kosovo the political power was held by the Albanian communists.

Kosovo's major problems began after the death of Tito in 1980. The whole of Yugoslavia began to unravel as nationalist movements began to pull the republics away. There began to be a breakdown of Tito's socialist order. Conversely, in 1981 there was a revolt in Kosovo where Albanian protesters demanded that Kosovo should become a formal republic, an Albanian republic, of Yugoslavia. Serbia would not stand for this. Ethnic tensions between Albanians and Serbs began to grow during the 1980s. In 1989, Slobodan Milosevic was elected president of Serbia. Because of demonstrations and ethnic tensions, he imposed curfews and a state of emergency in Kosovo and began to remove, by constitutional changes, the political autonomy the Albanian majority had enjoyed. Its political institutions and government were being formally disbanded. The Albanian language was banned from newspapers, television, and radio. Milosevic began to systematically oppress the ethnic Albanians.

The Albanian run security forces in Kosovo were replaced by the introduction of 40,000 Yugoslav troops. Kosovo effectively became a police state and eighty percent of the Albanian population became unemployed almost overnight. The communist party of Kosovo was effectively broken up, leaving the Democratic League of Kosovo (LDK) as the dominant political party. The LDK was led by an Albanian writer, Ibrahim Rugova. Rugova advocated a policy of peaceful resistance and believed that armed resistance against the powerful military of Serbia would lead only to a bloodbath in Kosovo. Rugova's passive resistance policy resulted in Kosovo staying relatively calm while the wars in Bosnia, Croatia, and Slovenia were playing out during the 1990s. However, the Albanian population of Kosovo became increasingly frustrated with the continued Serbian oppression.

On April 22, 1996, four simultaneous and coordinated attacks occurred across Kosovo. The targets were Serbian security forces and civilians. Responsibility for the attacks was claimed by an up until then unknown group calling itself the Kosovo Liberation Army. The Yugoslavian and Serbian governments saw the KLA as terrorists because they had targeted civilians. Most Kosovar Albanians looked at them as legitimate "freedom fighters." The KLA grew from a group of radicalized Albanian farmers and unemployed workers into a guerilla army. Fighting between the KLA and Yugoslav forces intensified over the next two years. These actions, as Rugova had predicted, cost the lives of many civilians; so much so that the conflict had now caught the attention of the world. Hundreds of thousands of Albanian refugees began to flee to the south, into Macedonia and Greece. By late 1998, the international community demanded an end to the fighting and that the Serbs stop offensive action against the KLA. It is interesting to note that at this time, the international community gave tacit approval to the KLA and made no demands that they stop making attacks. This would prove to be somewhat of an embarrassment in the future. On October 25, 1998, a ceasefire was agreed upon. However, within a matter of weeks the fighting resumed when KLA forces made movements to secure strategic bunkers overlooking the main highway into the capitol city of Pristina.

The KLA continued its attacks and the Serbs continued with reprisals against the civilian population. The culmination of this came on January 15, 1999 with the Racak Massacre where at least 45 Albanian civilians were murdered by Yugoslav forces. They claimed that the casualties were members of the KLA. The international community did not agree.

UK Prime Minister Tony Blair wrote in an article that *"It is no exaggeration to say what is happening in Kosovo is racial genocide. No exaggeration to brand the behavior of Milosevic's forces as evil. It is something we had hoped we would never experience again in Europe. Thousands murdered. One hundred thousand men missing. Hundreds of thousands of people forced to flee their homes and their country, robbed of anything of value at gun-point."* The international community and the United Nations Security Council condemned the Racak incident as a massacre. This would later be used as a basis for charges of war crimes against President Milosevic and others. It was apparent that the actions of the Yugoslav forces were now state sponsored terrorism. NATO decided that the only resolution to the conflict would involve the introduction of a peace keeping force into Kosovo to forcibly restrain both sides. On January 30, 1999 NATO announced diplomatic initiatives and issued a statement that it was prepared to launch air strikes against Yugoslavia *"to compel compliance with the demands of the international community and [to achieve] a political settlement."* A NATO spokesman summed up the goal of the operation as "Serbs out, peacekeepers in, refugees back." This was an historic and controversial move by NATO. The military intervention was seen by some to be incompatible with NATO's mission. They were not defending another NATO nation. However, it was apparent that the situation was in need of mediation by the international community.

After almost two months of failed negations NATO's bombing campaign against Serbia began on March 24, 1999. Over the next ten weeks more than 38,000 combat missions would be flown. During the war the Serbian forces continued to target the civilian Albanian population. As the Serb forces withdrew back into Serbia proper, they indiscriminately destroyed entire communities. Milosevic finally capitulated to NATO on June 12, 1999 and the NATO Kosovo peacekeeping force (KFOR) entered the province and began to restore order. By November of 1999, over 800,000 refugees had returned to Kosovo.

In November of 1999, I was in my twelfth year as a law enforcement officer and my fourth year as the Chief of Police of a small Northwest Montana police department. United States law enforcement was in the final years of the Clinton administration and the Community Oriented Policing (COPS) funding program was in full swing. President Clinton had vowed to put one hundred thousand more police officers on the streets of America. My small department had received funding for an additional police officer with one of these COPS grants in 1997. The grant funded the position for three years. My local city government was required to fund this position for at least one additional fiscal year. Continued funding was a problem with the economic conditions of our area at the turn of the century.

After surviving the end of the twentieth century and the Y2K scare I began the year 2000 with an ingenious plan. My wife and I had six children at home in a two bedroom house and I still had to find funding to comply with the conditions of the COPS grant. I had been receiving solicitations for overseas police missions from a company who was a subcontractor of the U. S. State Department. At the time, the company was paying around $90,000 for a one year contract to provide civilian police services and training of local police in war ravaged countries. This was about three times my annual salary. At the time, there were three missions available: Bosnia, East Timor, and Kosovo. If I took an overseas civilian police (CivPol) mission during the 2000/2001 fiscal year I could afford to buy a larger house for my family as well as enable my local city government to be able to fund the COPS grant position for the required time period. I would be on a leave of absence and my unused salary would be available to provide the funding for the grant requirement. My local government bought off on the idea and granted me a leave of absence from the police department. In the summer of 2000, I was hired by the company to participate in an international police mission.

In July of 2000, I travelled to my home state of Texas to complete a ten day orientation and selection process to participate in an overseas CivPol mission. My orientation class was composed of about one hundred police officers from all over the nation. We were housed and fed at the American Airlines flight attendant training center in Fort Worth. Our training was classified and the flight attendant candidates thought we were some kind of mercenaries, which was not really all that far from the truth.

We were bused daily to our training site at the Arlington, Texas Police Department's training center. We were trained by instructors from a company out of Fredericksburg, Virginia. We went through several classes to prepare for our missions, some of which were hand to hand combat, knife fighting, and firearms training. July in Texas can be very hot and the summer of 2000 was no exception. It was hot. The company provided unending coolers full of sports drinks and water. We drank copious bottles of fluid every day.

One of the requirements of the orientation was to pass a physical fitness test. The test consisted of several parts. There was an obstacle course that consisted of traversing a two, four, and six foot wall, crawling through a concrete tunnel, and running through a serpentine of wooden posts. There was also a quarter mile run inside a gym with two sets of stairs. When I was running the obstacle course I cut my forearm on one of the posts and had to be bandaged. One guy tripped while jumping over the two foot wall and face planted into the four foot wall. His head had to be bandaged also. There were a few more similar injuries on the day of our physical fitness test. When we got back to the American Airlines facility we looked as if we had really been put through the ringer. I think some of the single guys used this to their advantage with the female flight attendant candidates. Sympathy for warriors.

At the end of the ten day orientation there was an announcement that there were ten too many candidates that had passed and there was a request that ten of us volunteer to delay our departure for one month and deploy with the next group. I had taken vacation to attend the orientation and selection, just in case I did not pass, so I was free to delay my deployment. I volunteered for the delay. I went back home to Montana, having passed all requirements, and waited until the next group would be sent.

In August of 2000 I began a one year leave of absence from my agency to participate in an International Police Task Force mission. By this time the orientation class had been moved from Texas to Virginia. The ten of us who had already passed the orientation and had volunteered to delay our deployment for a month were flown to Fredericksburg, Virginia and were tasked with assisting in the training of the next class. We did not have to participate in any of the training but only had to issue equipment and uniforms and be runners. I made dog tags for the group. I made several extra sets for myself and a set for each of my kids. I sent them home as souvenirs. At the end of the ten days we were all set to deploy to Kosovo. I had been issued about one hundred pounds of gear. I was one to always travel light so I put all my personal gear in the one sea bag that I was issued. The only other bag I took was my laptop.

Our group was scheduled to fly out of Dulles Airport in D.C. We had a private chartered flight on East Line Air, a Russian commercial airliner. It was really old and worn out. Before we departed we had a group picture taken in front of the aircraft with the Russian flight attendants. All of the seats had been removed from the first class section to make room for extra gear storage. We were treated very well. Our first stop was at Gander, Newfoundland. We made a refueling stop and were allowed to get off the plane and go into the airport. I had a souvenir stamp placed in my passport. There was a U.S. Air Force C141 there also. We met and spoke with the crew in the terminal. They were curious about who we were. We were traveling in our U.S. CivPol uniforms. Speaking of our uniforms; I need to interject an explanation about our uniforms here. All of the other nations involved in the United Nations Mission in Kosovo (UNMIK) had a national police uniform. The United States, however, has 18,000 different law enforcement agencies, all with distinct and different uniforms. The company therefore had to develop a United States contingent uniform for our mission. We were issued a dark blue BDU uniform with an American flag on one shoulder and a United Nations patch on the other. We also had embroidered name tags with "U.S. CivPol" over one pocket and our name over the other. The C141 crew asked us who we were and what we were doing. We told them that we were all cops going over to Kosovo to help restore order and set up a police force. We let them know that we were being paid about $90,000 for a one year contract. After seeing our plane, the crew said that they would have to be paid a whole lot more than $90,000 just to fly across the Atlantic in that.

This did not make us feel much at ease but we continued on to our destination to fulfill our contracts.

I had contracted to deploy to the United Nations Mission in Kosovo (UNMIK) as a civilian police officer (CivPol). I would be part of the six hundred member United States contingent of police officers. The total CivPol strength in Kosovo at the time was approximately four thousand officers from fifty-three nations. The United States had the largest contingent in the mission. Under United Nations Security Council Resolution 1244, the UNMIK police had a twofold objective. The first was to establish and maintain civil law and order in Kosovo. The second was to build up a professional, credible and impartial Kosovo Police Service (KPS).

Upon my arrival in country I began keeping a daily diary. This book is a compilation of my diary entries, e-mails, and the daily UNMIK press releases. Kosovo is less than 3% the size of the state of Montana at an area of approximately 4,200 square miles. The population however is more than double that of Montana at almost two million people. Considerable editing, especially of the daily press updates, has gone into this book to reduce it to a comfortable length. The press updates, which are a daily account of the major incidents that occurred in Kosovo, would have taken over 1,000 pages alone. I have attempted to recount only those occurrences that were unique to the mission and were major criminal activity. The following is an account of my civilian police mission in Kosovo.

KOSOVO DIARY

UNMIK POLICE PRESS UPDATE
21 AUGUST, 2000
PRISTINA Region
GRENADE ATTACK/DEMONSTRATION/ASSAULT
Obilic - 1950 hrs. Unknown persons in a motor vehicle threw two to three hand grenades at a group of K-Serb children playing basketball. It was reported that ten kids were injured. In reaction to this incident approximately 100 K-Serbs attacked a police patrol unit in the area. The mob broke the window of the car and assaulted a UNMIK Police Officer and his K-Albanian KPS partner. The mob also stoned two other police vehicles that responded to the village to try and rescue their trapped colleagues. Police had to fire warning shots to contain the mob. Both police officers suffered minor injuries. Ten K-Serb children were treated at the hospital as a result of injuries sustained in the attack. The situation was later brought under control.
EXPLOSION
Stimlje, Lipjan – 20/08 – 2010 hrs. An explosion occurred in a K-Roma house causing minor damage. No injuries were reported.
MITROVICA Region
FIRST AID / LIFE SAVING
Mitrovica North – 19/08. A K-Serbian female, who sought assistance in the station to notify her relatives in Pristina about the death of her husband in Serbia, suddenly suffered a heart attack. She lost consciousness and started to convulse. An Egyptian UNMIK Police Officer and two female interpreters (K-Albanian, K-Bosnian) gave her the proper first aid to bring her back to consciousness. The K-Serbian female was transported to the Serbian Hospital. The quick and determined teamwork of the officer and the Language Assistants possibly saved her live.
INTIMIDATION
Leposavic – 19/08. A K-Roma male reported that a group of youths, ethnicity unknown, threw stones at him. No injuries reported.
PEC Region

GRENADE ATTACK
Cusk – 19/08 – 2230 hrs. A K-Bosnian male reported that unknown suspect(s) threw a grenade at his house resulting in damage to the roof. No injuries were reported.
IMPERSONATING AN OFFICER
Klina – 18/08 – 2345 hrs. A K-Albanian male wearing a KPS uniform was stopped by UNMIK Police for a traffic violation. Further investigation revealed that the suspect was not a KPS officer but had stolen the uniform and was posing as a KPS Commander. He was also collecting money from local businessmen. The suspect was subsequently arrested.
PRIZREN Region
SHOOTING
Orahovac – 19/08 – 2100 hrs. Unknown person(s) traveling in a car fired several shots towards the TMK main office. No injuries or damages were reported.

Monday, 21 August, 2000
ARRIVAL IN KOSOVO

We arrived at Prishtina airport, Kosovo via East Line Air (Russian Civilian Airliner). The plane landed hot and the pilot really had to stand on the brakes to get the plane stopped before we ran out of runway. When we unassed the plane we noticed that the ground crew was pouring water on the tires and drums to cool them down. I think they had caught on fire. The airport was under the control of the Russian military. We found out later that this was a touchy issue with the invading NATO forces last year. There were Russian Hind helicopters and BMP armored vehicles all around. There were a lot of sandbag bunkers with barbed wire all around. The air was very polluted and it was very hot. It occurred to me that if you would have told me back in the early 1980s that in the summer of 2000 I would be arriving in Yugoslavia, on a Russian plane, into an airport under Russian military control, my best guess then would have been that I would be a POW. We offloaded our gear from the plane and loaded into buses for the trip to the heart of city. The ride was about 30 minutes from the airfield to the Hotel Iliria. I immediately noticed that the county had a medieval look about it. The houses were little more than red brick huts. There were many old style haystacks in the area, animal draw carts and lots of garbage. These were quite contrasting with the presence of military vehicles and fortified checkpoints. We noticed right away that there was a lot of battle damage apparent. Many of the houses were burned out, bullet pocked, or completely destroyed. We were told there had been a grenade attack yesterday in the area where someone threw grenades at some kids who were playing, injuring many. There followed a riot where some cops were assaulted and injured. It sounds like this is going to be interesting duty. We arrived at the Iliria Hotel and met with a company representative. He lined us out on getting checked into the hotel and gave us an initial issue of drinking water. I got assigned to room 102 with Craig Martin. Martin was one of the two local Sheriff's deputies from the Lincoln County (Montana) Sheriff's Office that decided to participate in the mission. The other was Brent Faulkner. I had also been a deputy sheriff with them before I was the Libby, Montana Police Chief. They number the floors of buildings in Europe different than in the states. The ground level floor is not considered the "first" floor. Our "second" floor is their "first" floor, so room 102 was upstairs. The elevator did not work because of the erratic power issues. We had to lug our gear upstairs again. The room was very small. It had two small beds placed end to end, two small end tables and one dresser. There was a sink and what they considered a shower in a small closet size room. The "shower" was a water pipe coming out of the wall next to the sink and a drain in the floor. The bathroom, where the toilets were, was down the hall. There was one bathroom with two toilets for the entire floor. The bathroom was very dirty. We met with U.S. Contingent Commander Peter "Pete" Palmer at the hotel. He briefed us on what the next week to ten days would be like. This is Pete's 4th U.N. mission. Pete was in my Ft. Worth orientation class. We were released for the day. Some of the guys that were in our July orientation class in Ft. Worth came by and told us where the closest "safe" restaurants were located. "Safe" means that you can eat the food and not get sick. We were told not to wander too far from the hotel until we get issued our weapons. We ate pizza at Amaro's next to hotel. We settled into our rooms and tried to get some sleep. It was still very hot. I stopped by the Gunny's room to say hello. The Gunny was a Marine Gunnery Sergeant in Vietnam. He is one of the older members of our group. He was sitting on his bed drinking whiskey and sweating a lot. He seemed a bit shaken. He said that he felt like he was back in Nam. It was a little unnerving. There was a lot of gunfire in the city all night as well as the occasional explosion. There were also a lot of barking dogs. This is going to be a very long and interesting year.

UNMIK POLICE PRESS UPDATE
22 AUGUST, 2000
GNJILANE Region
DEMONSTRATION
Vitina – 1100 hrs. An Officer from the Civil Administration reported that an Albanian flag had been placed on the Civil Administration building. UNMIK Police and KFOR responded to the scene. Approximately 100 K-Albanians had gathered to demonstrate against the removal of the flag. After mediations with the opinion leaders of the crowd the flag was removed peacefully.
MITROVICA Region
SHOOTING/ASSAULT
Svinjare – 1845 hrs. A fight between a crowd of K-Albanians and KFOR started after two K-Albanian males mocked the soldiers at a KFOR checkpoint. During the fight KFOR shot at two K-Albanians attempted to assault KFOR soldiers. The suspects were taken to the Moroccan hospital where one died while the other is still under medical treatment.
ARSON / INTIMIDATION
Mitrovica North – 20/08 – 2315 hrs. After an abandoned K-Serbian house was set on fire by unknown person(s) a couple of K-Serbs threatened the occupants of a neighboring K-Albanian house to set this house on fire. The K-Serbs threw stones at the K-Albanian house.
PEC Region
ILLEGAL POSSESSION OF WEAPONS
Krusevac, Decani – 20/08 – 1730 hrs. A K-Albanian male was found in possession of a grenade by UNMIK Police and KFOR and was arrested.
GRENADE ATTACK
Dakovica – 0130 hrs. A K-Albanian male reported that an unidentified person threw a grenade into his shop causing damage to the property.
ARSON
Lubova, Istok – 20/08 – 2330 hrs. A K-Albanian male reported that unidentified person(s) had put hay bales in his home and set them on fire. The fire was extinguished. No injuries were reported.

MINE STRIKE
Ngucat, Suva Reka – 1100 hrs. A K-Albanian male stepped on a mine while cutting wood in a marked mine area. He died during the transport to the hospital.

Tuesday, 22 August, 2000
Prishtina, Kosovo

We met with other U.S. officers in the morning after breakfast. Breakfast was an omelet and bread. The omelet was an "air" omelet. What I mean is that it was just a folded egg with nothing else. No cheese, meat or anything. There is also no sliced bread here. The bread is a hunk torn from a large round loaf. I am very nervous about eating the food but we have to eat or we will starve. Two guys are already sick in bed. I did not drink the coffee or the orange juice. They are most likely made using the local water. It is a good thing I didn't drink them because I also saw the guy that was bussing the table pour the left over coffee and orange juice back into their pots to reuse. We have to use bottled water for teeth brushing. The local water is not fit to drink. You can wash your body but you have to keep the water out of your eyes and mouth. The company brought us more bottled water today. U.S. officers took us to the Induction Training Center (ITC) for orientation. The first thing we had to do was take the English test. We were waiting in line in the hallway and went into a room one at a time. When it was my turn I went in the room and was greeted by a Canadian RCMP officer. We introduced ourselves and started talking about where we were from. He was from British Columbia and was interested that I was from Montana. We talked for a few minutes and then I asked him what I was supposed to do for the English test. He said that I had just taken it and was free to leave. He said that I obviously speak English since we had a conversation. After this we got our U.N. I.D. cards made. We drew our weapons today. It feels good to be armed in this strange country. We were issued a Beretta M9, 9mm pistol. This is the current U.S. military sidearm. When I was in The Corps we still were issued the M1911A1, .45 ACP. I wish I had a .45 now. We only get 46 rounds plus 10 rounds for tomorrows' qualification. Ammunition is apparently in short supply. I went to the company office building. I got more water and found some computers to use. I set up an e-mail account. We can only use the company computers for

15 minutes per day. I e-mailed home to give them my address and let everyone know that I arrived OK. We tried another "safe" eatery tonight called Spaghetti Toni's. It was not bad.

E-mails home

My Dearest Wife and Children,

Things have been pretty hectic since I got in country. We landed at Prishtina airport on Monday the 21st. It is not much of an airport and is controlled by Russian troops. It was pretty weird to see all the Russian tanks and helicopters around. There were also many bunkers and stuff. It looks like the war zone that it is. We rode a bus to the Iliria Hotel here in Prishtina. It is quite a dump. There is a shower of sorts in a closet with a sink but the toilet is down the hall. You cannot drink the water so the company supplies us with bottled water to drink. You have to use the bottled water to brush your teeth also. The water goes off for several hours every day so you have to flush with buckets or bottles. So far we have been fortunate to have water every morning to shower off. The power has only gone off a couple of times. It is very, very dirty here. The air is very polluted and it is hard to breathe. It is supposed to be better outside of the city. It has been extremely hot and I have to drink a lot of water. We have been going through orientation. The first day we had to take an English test. It was a breeze for those of us from the USA. Then we went and got our I.D. cards made. Today we got to pick up our weapons from the armory. It feels better to be armed while walking the streets. In the morning we eat what they call an omelet. It is just like our omelets but with nothing inside. Only the eggs. This comes with a big piece of bread. The food here at the hotel is supposed to be safe. I haven't gotten sick yet so maybe it is. I have been taking my cayenne pepper and garlic every morning before breakfast. Maybe this is helping. We eat at a couple of restaurants near the hotel that are supposed to be safe. I've had pizza and spaghetti. I never drink anything that is not canned or bottled. Some are drinking the coffee and juice but I am not taking the chance. Tomorrow we have our firearms test of 10 rounds. It should be a breeze. For the U.S. cops it is a chance to function check our weapon and make sure it is sighted in. After that we take a driving test. We should get our first advance pay by Friday I hope. I am planning to get a cell phone. The way they work in Europe is you buy the phone and a chip for a certain number of minutes. No monthly bills or anything. When your minutes are used up you get another chip. I only get to use the company computer for 15 minutes so I am writing these e-mails with my laptop and then taking the disk to the company computer and sending it. This gives me time to read any e-mail that has come in from you. I am also sending pictures. The ones I sent tonight were a picture of me in Virginia the day before we left and a couple of bombed out buildings near the hotel. These were bombed a few months ago during the NATO air strikes. When I send this letter I will try and send you a picture of our group and a picture of Craig, Brent and I in front of one of the Headquarters buildings where we were waiting to get I.D. cards. I will try and mail a package home when I get assigned somewhere. We should get our assignments by Monday. Then maybe I can find a place, get to unpack and get settled in. I will send some stuff for the kids and some computer disks with pictures. This is going to be a pretty tough year. It is very difficult. I will be glad to take some time off and get to see you. It looks like we may not get any days off until about November because of the upcoming elections. They expect some trouble. Got to go for now. I'll write again soon. With all my love, Clay

UNMIK POLICE PRESS UPDATE
23 AUGUST, 2000
PRISTINA Region
Pristina – 23/08 – 0242 hrs. The radio operator of OSCE reported that an unknown caller using the Albanian language made bomb threats against the OSCE building. UNMIK Police and KFOR were dispatched to the scene.
DEAD BODY FOUND
Llapashtica, Podujevo – 22/08 – 1742 hrs. A K-Albanian male reported that he found a dead body.
GNJILANE Region
EXPLOSION
Vitina – 23/08 – 0150 hrs. An explosion destroyed a trailer near Niki village. No injuries were reported.
MITROVICA Region
ATTEMPTED SUICIDE
Mitrovica North – 22/08 – 1600 hrs. After a dispute with her boyfriend a K-Albanian female slashed her arms and took a

mixture of tablets. She was found by KFOR in Little Bosnia and was transported by UNMIK Police to a KFOR hospital where she was treated and released.

DEMONSTRATION

Mitrovica North – 22/08 – 1900 hrs. Approximately 200 persons demonstrated peacefully against the closure of Trepca.

PEC Region

SHOOTING / CRIMINAL DAMAGE

Vitomirica, Pec – 21/08 – 2230 hrs. A K-Bosniak reported that unknown person(s) shot several times at his house damaging a window. No injuries were reported.

Wednesday, 23 August, 2000

I woke up at the Iliria Hotel (room #102) to no water. I had to wash up from saved bottles of water. We save our empty drinking water bottles and fill them with local water so we can use them to wash and flush the toilet. We went to ITC and then took buses to the firing range. We shot 10 rounds to qualify. It was a piece of cake for the U.S. officers but others fail all the time. We had to show the instructors that we could disassemble and reassemble our weapons and then we had to place 8 out of 10 rounds on a paper plate sized target at 15 yards. The instructors said that a whole contingent from Egypt was sent back home last week for failing to qualify. Unbelievable! After shooting we went to the driving test area. We had to drive a Toyota 4x4 through cones at 19 mph. The Toyotas are Japan's contribution to the U.N. mission. They are called "Coca Colas" or "Cokes" because they are red and white. Again, it was a piece of cake for the U.S. officers. One of the female Swedish officers ran off the road into ditch and almost rolled it. We really had fun with the instructors with our driving abilities. We took the cones faster than any other contingent was able to. We even asked if they wanted us to drive through it backwards. We got off early and some of us went to KFOR PXs on KFOR hill. We shopped at Norwegian, French, German, Italian, and U.N. shops. We are not allowed in the U.S. or British PXs because of duty (tax) reasons. Military only allowed there.

I had supper at Spaghetti Toni's again. I had lasagna and a Beck's. I haven't gotten sick yet. Five guys are sick now. One is in the hospital. He has "the runs" bad and is really dehydrated.

I went to a get together for new arrivals at the ITC. I left early to get to bed. I still am not sleeping well. Barking dogs and gunfire keep you awake. It sounds like most of us will be sent to Mitrovica. This is the worst place to go. We should know for sure soon.

E-mail Home

Dearest Carn,

Hello again from "paradise". Another day has gone by and I thought I would tell you about it. I went to the company office building earlier in the day and sent you the e-mail I wrote last night. I hope it gets to you OK. Today we woke up to no water. I had to wash from bottles we had saved for just such an occasion. We went to the firing range and shot. Everyone passed. It was a piece of cake. The range instructor (a cop from Canada) told us that a group from Egypt had come through the training and that 40 out of the 42 of them failed the shooting course. They had to send them home. After shooting we went to the driving test. We had to drive through several cones going 40 kph (19mph) again a piece of cake. One of the Swedish female cops in the group before us had a wreck and got the vehicle stuck in the ditch. The Swedes live down the hall from us and they stay up late and are real loud. Craig and I haven't been getting very good sleep. It is very noisy here. Dogs bark and fight all night and there is gunfire, screams, explosions and all kinds of stuff. We finished pretty early today (about noon) and Brent and I went up on KFOR hill. KFOR means "Kosovo Forces", the multinational NATO forces. We checked out all the PXs. We went in the Norwegian, French, German, Italian, and U.N. shops. It was quit a sight to see all these nations together on one base. There was also a U.S. and British PX but we did not have the proper I.D. to get in. We came back and ate at Spaghetti Toni's. I had Lasagna and a Beck's beer. I have had pretty good luck at this location and still have not gotten sick. After that we went to a get together at the Induction Training Center for all the new arrivals. We had a couple of beers (made in Slovenia) and then went back to the Hotel. The Power went off for about an hour but I could still write this letter by battery power. I will send it tomorrow. We should know in a couple of days where we will be sent. It looks like most of us will be going up north to the Mitrovica region. This is the hot spot of Kosovo. We should see some action there. I will let you know how it goes. Well I better sign off for now. I need to get some sleep. I will send this tomorrow. Write soon. Tell all the children that I love and miss them and hug and kiss them for me. I love you very much. Love always, Clay

UNMIK POLICE PRESS UPDATE
24 AUGUST, 2000
GNJILANE Region
EXPLOSION
Pozaranje, Vitina – 23/08 – 0150 hrs. UNMIK Police responded to an explosion near NIKI gas station and found there a blown up gas truck.
MITROVICA Region
ILLEGAL HOUSE OCCUPATION
Mitrovica South – 22/08. A K-Albanian male reported that K-Serbs have occupied his flat in Mitrovica North.
PEC Region
SHOOTING
Vitomirica – 23/08 –0030 hrs. A K-Albanian male reported that two unknown persons fired several shots towards his house using a machine gun. No injuries or property damage were reported.
PRIZREN Region
MURDER
Studencane – 23/08 – 0930 hrs. A K-Albanian male shot another K-Albanian male in the chest. The victim died at Prizren Hospital. The suspect was arrested and an automatic rifle was seized.

Thursday, 24 August, 2000

No water again today. Bottle washing again. The sink and shower are in one small room. I have to brush my teeth with my bottled water. I try to keep the dirty tap water out of my eyes as much as possible. We had classes at ITC all day. It was very hard to stay awake. Most of the classes are very basic for U.S. officers but are mandatory. One thing that we disagree with is the U.N. policy allowing the firing of warning shots. The only "warning" shot I will ever fire will be an unintentional miss. I need to do laundry but don't know where yet. I wash out socks and underwear in the sink and let them dry on the balcony. No MSA (Mission

Subsistence Allowance) yet. Some guys are getting low on cash. Breakfast (the air omelet) is free with the room but is pretty awful. It is the same breakfast every morning. I am starting to hate this place. I hope this year goes fast. We still may be assigned to Mitrovica. They haven't issued deployment orders yet.

UNMIK POLICE PRESS UPDATE
25 AUGUST, 2000
PRISTINA Region
MURDER
Podujevo – 23/08 – 2325 hrs. During a fight in a restaurant between two K-Albanian males, one male pulled out a gun. In the struggle the weapon discharged and fatally wounded a third K-Albanian male sitting in the restaurant. Both suspects were arrested.
DEAD BODY FOUND
Lapastica, Podujevo – 24/08 – 1400 hrs. The remains of an adult male were found partially buried in an old infantry trench.
GNJILANE Region
ILLEGAL HOUSE OCCUPATION / THEFT
Gnjilane – 24/08 – 1330 hrs. A K-Serb male reported that a K-Albanian male had occupied his flat and stolen his household items.
DEMONSTRATION
Vitina – 24/08 – 1100 hrs. Approximately 150 K-Albanians protested peacefully against the prohibition of flying the Albanian flag freely in Kosovo and to be not allowed to put the flag on the Civil Administration building.
MINE STRIKE
Dakovica – 24/08 – 0700 hrs. An exploding mine injured three K-Albanians while they were cutting trees. One victim was seriously injured; the two others received minor injuries.

Friday, 25 August, 2000

Day five and I hate it. This hotel is really bad. I need to do laundry but don't know where. I am still washing in the sink and drying clothes on a chair on the balcony. Still not sick yet. A second guy in our group *(*Ferdinand Ibabao from Guam P.D. - KIA 10-14-2004 in Iraq)* is in the hospital. He may need colon surgery. I had dinner with him last night at Amaro's. He ate a lot of chicken. At least we think it was chicken. I remember eating some "chicken" in Okinawa that was actually dog meat. He ate a lot and I guess it really plugged him up. There are still rumors of at least half of us going to Mitrovica. This is the most dangerous spot. There is also a battery factory pumping lead into the air. They have pulled several officers out of there for high lead content. I really don't want to go there. We will find out soon. Still no MSA. Classes all day. I paid 20DM ($10.00) to talk to Carnita for 5 minutes. The currency we are using in mission is the German DM (Deutsche Mark). The exchange rate is about 2 to 1.

P.S. I am still not sleeping well. I am stuffed up from the pollution and it is still very noisy at night. (gunfire and barking dogs)

UNMIK POLICE PRESS UPDATE
26 AUGUST, 2000
PRISTINA Region
ATTEMPTED MURDER
Podujevo – 24/08 – 2225 hrs. A K-Albanian male was arrested for stabbing another K-Albanian male. The victim was hospitalized.
GNJILANE Region
THREATS/INTIMIDATION
Pozaranje, Vitina – 25/08 – 2230 hrs. A K-Albanian male reported that he had received a threatening phone call advising that his gas station would be blown up. His truck and trailer were blown up two days ago.
EXPLOSION
Cernica, Gnjilane – 25/08 – 2150 hrs. An unoccupied K-Serbian home was completely destroyed by an explosion.
MITROVICA Region
CRIMINAL DAMAGE/ASSAULT
Cabra – 25/08 – 0950 hrs. Four K-Serbs reported that they were stoned by a group of about 20 K-Albanians as they drove through the Albanian side of town. Windows of their vehicle were shattered and all four victims sustained injuries.
ABANDONED BABY
Mitrovica South – 25/08 – 2200 hrs. A K-Albanian male reported that he had found a newly born baby abandoned in the Islamic Community Mosque yard. The baby was handed over to the health center in Tavnik.
PRIZREN Region

ATTEMPTED MURDER

Prizren – 25/08 – 1635 hrs. A K-Albanian male received serious injuries after another K-Albanian male attacked him with a chainsaw.

DEMONSTRATION

General Jankovic – 25/08 – 1100 hrs. Approximately 500 K-Albanians demonstrated peacefully against the arrest of a high-ranking TMK member by KFOR.

Saturday, 26 August, 2000

We are still in the hotel. I hate this place! We call it "Hotel Hell". There are more classes today. We had classes on mines, use of force, etc., etc. We looked at examples of mines and markings. There was an area set up with a lot of dummy mines. We had to observe the area for a few minutes and then try to point out the hidden mines. I found the most mines out of my group but I still missed a few. There are a lot of mines and unexploded ordinance all over the area. The rule here is "Never leave the pavement!"

I went to the company building and got my polo shirts (finally). The BDU tops have been unbearably hot. I picked up body armor (entry type) that is not much good for everyday use and several small items like a traffic vest and cuff keys. I got more drinking water while I was there. I've been drinking 5-6 large (1.5 liter) bottles per day. I don't want to get dehydrated. I wish orientation would end. Still no MSA or deployment orders.

E-mail Home

2000 hrs. Prishtina, Kosovo
Internet Cafe

I just got your e-mail. It sounds like my last letter got through. Did you get the pictures? I am feeling better today. I got several hours of un-interrupted sleep last night. Things will be OK if I can take them one day at a time. I went back to the KFOR base today and bought each of the kids a small U.N. Civilian Police Badge. I wear one exactly like it on my I.D. neck pouch. Some of the other internationals wear this as their badge. I hope the kids like it. I will send them in a package in a few days. I will also send a few small souvenir items such as our dinner bill from the other night, a handy wipe pouch from the Russian airliner, some patches and hopefully a Kosovo flag. Make sure the kids take care of these things as they will be impossible to replace. I may not be able to get a phone this month if they don't get us enough of an advance on our pay. I will let you know. I don't think I want to use the other phone service I called you on the other night because it was really inconvenient, hot, crowded, delayed and expensive. I am at an "internet cafe" in Prishtina a couple of blocks from the hotel. I can be on the computer for 5DM ($2.50) per hour. Brent is on the chat thing with Cait right now. The chat is very good. It is like talking on the phone. Hopefully we can get everything worked out soon. We will be being deployed Tuesday. We don't know where yet but the rumor is up north in Mitrovica. If I get there and it is super awful I will ask for a transfer the first chance I get. I still want to get to Prizren or maybe stay here in Prishtina. I will let you know. I will try and come here to e-mail you every night until we leave. I will let you know about the phone also. I am going to sign off soon and write an e-mail to my folks. I will send a disk of pictures in the package also. Make sure you save all the disks in a safe place until I return. Just in case my laptop gets lost or stolen. Try and get the Instant Messenger set up so we can chat. I am looking forward to my first trip home. There are still some things that I cannot write or talk about but I will tell you when I see you. I will write soon. Clay

Sunday, 27 August, 2000

I still can't sleep. I'm also tired of Italian food. Especially Albanian made Italian food. I'm still not sick but losing my appetite. I need more variety in my diet. I wash my hands with anti-bacterial gel at least ten times per day. I even clean the silverware. I'm paranoid about this dirty place. I hope I will not be assigned to Mitrovica. I met two guys that got pulled out for high lead levels: Randy Wilson and Andy Margiota. They were only there for three months. The problem is supposed to be taken care of but I don't believe it. Some of the guys will quit if assigned there. We should know tomorrow.

UNMIK POLICE PRESS UPDATE
28 AUGUST, 2000
PRISTINA Region

DEAD BODY

Pristina – 27/08 – 0900 hrs. The body of a 25-year-old K-Albanian male who was reported abducted on 26/08 was found in a Muslim Graveyard.

MURDER

Obilic – 27/08 – 1850 hrs. The body of an 80-year-old K-Serbian male was found with gunshot wounds.

ATTACK ON UNMIK POLICE

Lipljan – 27/08 – 1330 hrs. After the hit and run incident in the K-Serb Village of Skulanevo a crowd of approximately 1,500 people gathered and blocked the road. When UNMIK Police arrived at the scene stones were thrown at UNMIK vehicles and one officer was assaulted. KFOR negotiated with the local people and the situation returned to normal.

EXPLOSION

Obillic – 25/08 - 2000 hrs. A K-Serbian male reported that unknown persons threw a Molotov cocktail at his house. It exploded without causing any property damage or injuries.

GNJILANE Region

ASSAULT ON A POLICE OFFICER

Urosevac – 27/08 – 1412 hrs. A K-Albanian male was arrested after he physically assaulted a KPS and a UNMIK police officer doing traffic duties. No injuries were reported.

SHOOTING

Vitina – 27/08 – 1245 hrs. The Macedonian Army shot at two K-Albanian males as they were driving their tractor to cut wood. The Macedonian Army personnel claimed that the two K-Albanians had crossed the border into Macedonia and failed to stop after being warned. None of the two were injured as a result of shooting but one of them received minor injuries when he jumped off the tractor to escape the firing.

EXPLOSION

Klokot, Gnjilane – 28/08 – 2341 hrs. An unoccupied Serbian house was completely destroyed as a result of an explosion.

DEMONSTRATION

Kacanik - 26/08 – 1115 hrs. Approximately 400 K-Albanians peacefully demonstrated against the previous arrest of a high-ranking TMK member.

MITROVICA Region

GRIEVOUS ASSAULT

Mitrovica South– 26/08 – 0140 hrs. A K-Albanian male who works as a security guard at an internet service shop reported that he was assaulted and stabbed with a knife by two unidentified persons. The victim suggests that the suspects wanted to steal computers from the shop.

PEC Region

ATTEMPTED MURDER

Pec – 26/08 - 1820 hrs. Two K-Albanian males reported that while they were sitting in a vehicle, unknown person(s) shot at them with an automatic weapon. UNMIK Police found the victim's vehicle riddled with 13 bullet holes. An automatic rifle and spent cartridges were found at the scene. Both victims received injuries. One was taken to hospital in a critical condition.

VEHICULAR HOMICIDE

Lipljan – 27/08 – 1325 hrs. Two K-Albanian males were arrested after the vehicle they were driving ran over three K-Serb children and one K-Serb juvenile as it was passing through a K-Serb village. One child was killed and the other three victims are listed in critical condition at a KFOR hospital. Immediately after the incident the driver and his passenger fled the area and were detained at a KFOR checkpoint.

PRIZREN Region

MURDER

Landovica, Prizren – 26/08 – 1040 hrs. The body of a K-Albanian male, who was missing since 25/08/00, was found by his son. The examination of the body revealed that he was physically assaulted to death.

GRENADE ATTACK / CRIMINAL DAMAGE

Orahovac – 27/08 – 0245 hrs. A K-Albanian male reported that unidentified person(s) threw a grenade into his back yard. The explosion caused damage to the house.

Monday, 28 August, 2000

No classes for us today. We finally got deployment orders. Craig, Brent, and I are all assigned to the Prishtina region. We are going to try and stay together and get assigned to station #2. The Station Commander is an American and the station is close to the hotel and the Internet café. We went to the Main H.Q. to try and get assigned to station #2. We still have no MSA. We are supposed to get it tomorrow at 1100. I'll believe it when I see it. We finally got the word that all three of us are assigned to station #2. Things are looking up. We will start looking for a house in the morning.

P.S. Cait finally got Carnita set up with Instant Messenger Chat. I was able to chat real time by computer. It was great to be able to talk to Carn.

UNMIK POLICE PRESS UPDATE
29 AUGUST, 2000
PRISTINA Region
BOMB THREATS
Pristina – 28/08 – 2143 hrs. UNMIK Police received two telephone calls from a male speaking Albanian who stated that a bomb had been planted at the Pristina hospital. UNMIK Police and KFOR responded to the hospital but no device was found.
UXO / MINE
Kosovo Polje – 28/08 – 1345 hrs. A KPS Officer found a hand grenade behind the old police station. KFOR EOD disposed of the item.
UXO / MINE
Kosovo Polje – 28/08 – 2143 hrs. A K-Serb male found a hand grenade in front of his residence. KFOR EOD disposed of the grenade.
GNJILANE Region
MURDER / SUICIDE
Kamenica – 28/08 – 0750 hrs. A K-Albanian male shot and killed a female family member and then killed himself with a hand grenade. Russian KFOR EOD disposed of another hand
grenade. No further details available.
CRIMINAL DAMAGE
Mitrovica – 28/08. The U.N. train was stoned by a K-Albanian youth outside the Mitrovica station. One window was broken.
PRIZREN Region
MURDER
Orahovac – 28/08 – 2230 hrs. Two K-Albanian male bodies were found on the road between Radoste and Gedza. The victims are supposed to be brothers from the village of Radore. They were shot to death.
GRIEVOUS ASSAULT
Zgatar Dragash, Prizren – 27/08 – 1030 hrs. A K-Albanian male was accused by an unknown man of being a Serbian informer

during the war. The suspect hit the victim with a stick on the head. The victim was hospitalized.

ILLEGAL POSSESSION OF WEAPONS

Prizren – 26/08 – 1530 hrs. Two K-Albanian males were arrested after three automatic rifles, a hand grenade, a homemade bomb and a sidearm were found during a search of their residences conducted by UNMIK Police and KFOR.

Tuesday, 29 August, 2000

I can't wait to get out of this hotel! We are supposed to get MSA at 1100. We can't afford to check out until we get our pay. I ate another yucky Iliria omelet and bread. I'm still afraid of food poisoning but I'm not sick. We reported to station #2. All three of us were checking in but then got jerked to Main H.Q. Personnel. Craig got reassigned to Kosovo Polje/ Obilic for 30 days. MSA draw was moved to 1400. What else is new! We met with a guy from our Ft. Worth class at lunch. He has a house for all of us to move into near station #2. It will cost us 500DM apiece per month for rent. One of the guys from the July Ft. Worth class is living there and his roommates got orders to another region. There will be six of us living in the house. Craig, Brent, and I, plus three other U.S. cops. We have to find our own places to live out in the community. The locals are willing to rent their houses to the internationals to make a big profit. Families are moving in with each other to make room to rent their houses out. We looked at the house and moved out of the hotel. It has three stories and is close to Station #2 where we will be working. Station #2 let a Turkish officer help us move. I went and had a cup of coffee with him. There are some safe places to drink the coffee. It was Turkish style coffee and was like drinking motor oil. Craig moved into our new house and will commute for now. We finally got our MSA today. 3,174DM. We had to pay a 450DM hotel bill. We got all of our gear moved to the house. This is our first night in country out of the Iliria hotel. Things are starting to get a little better.

UNMIK POLICE PRESS UPDATE

30 AUGUST, 2000

GNJILANE Region

ASSAULT

Livoc I Eperm – 28/08 – 2015 hrs. An UNMIK Police officer was assaulted as he tried to arrest a suspect from a previous case. The K-Albanian male hit the officer with a closed fist in the face and injured his nose. The suspect also tried to stab the officer with a knife. The suspect was arrested. The officer was brought to Camp Montheith hospital and released after treatment.

Wednesday, 30 August, 2000

First morning in the new house. It is just five minutes from station #2. We got today off to get settled in the house. I finally got to unpack my bags. I took a room on the third floor. It is a smaller room but has a large outside balcony that overlooks Prishtina. It is also safer from grenades. I spent the day shopping for food and other items for the house: Butt wipe, hangers, storage bins, etc. We have to fend for ourselves off the local economy. The company only supplies us with drinking water. I bought canned and packaged food items. I hope to get into a good eating routine.
I arraigned my room and got a uniform ready for work. We are supposed to report at 0800 to find out our assignments and finish checking in. The house is a six bedroom, two bath, and has one kitchen. It is pretty clean and has a gated entrance from the road. I will take some pictures to send home. More computer chatting with Carnita. It looks like we may be able to chat most every night.

P.S. The Internet Café is right at the end of the road we live on. It is about a 10 minute walk downhill, and a 15 minute walk back up hill. The internet chat costs only 5DM ($2.50 U.S.) per hour.

UNMIK POLICE PRESS UPDATE
31 AUGUST, 2000
MITROVICA Region
PLANNED HUNGER STRIKE
Mitrovica Detention Center – 30/08 – 1200 hrs. Nine K-Serb prisoners stated that they are beginning a hunger strike to protest against their long detention period. Negotiations with the President of the Mitrovica courts failed.
PRIZREN Region
GRENADE ATTACK

Musnikovo Village – 29/08 – 2100 hrs. An unknown person fired a rocket-propelled grenade at an unoccupied K-Serb house causing minor property damage.

Thursday, 31 August, 2000

First day of patrol- Station #2. Woke up at 0630. Showered and dressed. Brent and I reported in at 0800. I went on patrol with a CivPol officer from Kenya. His name is John Kariuki. We had a L.A. (Language Assistant) and a K.P.S. (Kosovo Police Service) officer. The Prishtina region, as well as the majority of Kosovo, is predominantly Kosovar Albanian in ethnicity. All of the Station #2 Language Assistants and KPS officers are Albanian. There is a small Serbian region in the city but the majority of the Kosovar Serbs are up north in Mitrovica. We patrolled the station #2 area. We were unit Alpha 2-3. We patrolled into a NATO bombing area and a minefield. We stopped and got out at the local pool, which is really a fish pond. I am told that it is the largest concrete swimming pool in Eastern Europe. It is filled from a local stream and is not chlorinated. We were warned not to swim in the pool. We went to an area east of Prishtina that the L.A. said was known as the area of "Jewish Graves". This is a very old area and name. I want to research this more. I got off shift at 1500. I will report tomorrow at 0700.

P.S. I was going to chat with Carnita by computer tonight but the power went off again. Brent called his wife and had her call Carnita and let her know.

UNMIK POLICE PRESS UPDATE
01 SEPTEMBER, 2000
PRISTINA Region
EXPLOSION
Lipljan – 31/08 – 0125 hrs. Two unknown persons fired a rocket at a K-Albanian owned mill. Workers were inside at the time of the attack but there were no injuries or serious damage caused.
GRENADE ATTACK
Podujevo – 01/08 – 2300 hrs. Unknown person(s) threw a hand grenade at a K-Albanian house. The explosion caused minor damage to the house, but none of the inhabitants were injured.
MITROVICA Region

ATTEMPTED MURDER/SUICIDE
Mitrovica South – 31/08 – 0650 hrs. A K-Albanian male shot and seriously wounded a K-Albanian female member of his family. The suspect later committed suicide by shooting himself. The victim was taken in very serious condition to the Morocco hospital.
PRIZREN Region
MURDER
Skorobishte – 30/08 – 2330 hrs. A K-Albanian male killed an identified K-Albanian male with two shots from automatic rifle to the head. The suspect fled the scene and is still at large.
ASSAULT
Selogradza – 31/08 – 1930 hrs. While on routine patrol, UNMIK Police attempted to stop a suspected wood thief who had a load of wood on his tractor. The K-Albanian male suspect released his load of wood into the path of the police vehicle in an attempt to escape. The suspect was arrested. The officers received no injuries.

Friday, 1 September, 2000

I woke up to no water this morning. I am also feeling bad today. I have stomach cramps and gas. I reported to station #2 at 0645 for the day shift briefing. I was assigned with the same unit: John Kariuki (Kenya), Bekim Gashi (KPS), B. Gashani (L.A.). We were assigned to area 2-3. Our call sign was Alpha 2-3. I spent the first two hours instructing the KPS officer, as well as the Kenyan officer, about Police Ethics. I told the feather pillow story. They liked my talk very much. We patrolled in a mountainous wooded area east of town. There are many land mines still in the area. The road was hard packed dirt but the L.A. said it was safe for us to patrol on. It started raining hard about 1100. The streets were flooded with muddy water and lots of trash. The rain caused traffic problems. I had to get out and direct traffic at a major intersection. Near the end of shift we had a kidnapping call. We looked for the suspect vehicle. Other CivPol units caught the suspect. I got off shift at 1500. I am scheduled to work three more day shifts and then I get assigned to another shift on the 5th.

P.S. I had a lunch of "Burek" at a local eatery. It is a kind of an Albanian egg roll. The KPS officer bought lunch. I hope I don't get sick.

P.P.S. I posted a warning sign on my bedroom door. I had one of the L.A.s print it in Albanian for me. It reads "Attention Burglars! This room belongs to an American Police Officer. If you steal from this room I will find you, cut your guts out, and strangle you with them! Have a nice day."

UNMIK POLICE PRESS UPDATE
02 SEPTEMBER, 2000
PEC Region
GRENADE ATTACK
Dakovica Town – 01/09 – 0150 hrs. A K-Albanian male reported that an unknown person(s) threw a hand grenade on his balcony. The explosion caused only minor property damage.

Saturday, 2 September, 2000

I woke up to no power this morning but had water. I feel much better after a good sleep. I reported for day shift at 0645 after a breakfast of O.J., a banana, and Physillium husks. I was assigned with John from Kenya again in section A 2-3. We had a different KPS officer and L.A. today. The L.A. was named "Loni", age 19, and KPS officer named Safed, age 28. He is former KLA. We had an assault call at Sunny Hill #2 that was reported to a British KFOR patrol. Two families were fighting about kids playing. Not much to it. We restored the peace. At 1415 we received a call of a man beating his family. We responded to area and were shown the apartment by a young girl. We had to take the stairs and climbed to the fifth floor. The elevator did not work as the power was off. I entered the apartment and found the 16 year old daughter unconscious with choke marks on her neck and the wife with a black eye. I immediately arrested the father who was very agitated and threatening the wife. The wife fainted when I made the arrest. John seemed not to know what to do and was impressed with my quick and decisive actions. I revived both victims and took statements using my L.A. We have to make one copy in Albanian and one in English. We transported the prisoner to the Prishtina detention center. The call took until 1800 to finish. I had to do most of the paper work myself because the Kenyan officer was too slow. After work I had a chat session with Carnita.

P.S. I turned in a request for my first CTO (Compensatory Time Off) for Sept. 23-28 (6 days). I will stay in country for my first CTO but I will try to go home on my next in November.

Sunday, 3 September, 2000

I had power and water this morning. I woke up to the Muslim call to prayer (very loud). There is a mosque very close by. I woke up to machine gun fire about midnight. The shots were very close to the house. I will check today to see what went on. I reported for day shift. There was no information about last night's gunfire. The British Marines who are billeted at our police station heard it also. I was assigned to section Alpha 2-3. I rode with an officer from Turkey, an L.A., and a female KPS officer. Not much going on for a Sunday. We patrolled up the mountain east of town. I took a different road through another minefield to the Swedish KFOR outpost. There was a great view of city from there. The air was also noticeably cleaner up there. We went to a vehicle registration post and visited with two Jordanian officers for about and hour. We had an interesting conversation about religion and politics. These are usually two subjects I avoid, but they insisted.
We heard a call on the radio about an officer who was out with an unconscious man. He called for an ambulance. The officer, from his accent, was apparently from some third world nation like Pakistan or India. About a half hour later the officer said, "ambulance says man is dead, send someone else." I thought this was very funny. You had to be there and hear it for yourself to appreciate the humor in it. We only had one call today, a burglary of a residence. Two internationals had their apartment broken into. I ended up doing the paperwork again so we could get off on time.

P.S. I found out that the two internationals from the burglary pay 2000DM each for rent. (Suckers!) Yesterday a lot of prisoners escaped from the detention center in Mitrovica. We were told that the jailers were CivPol officers from Africa (Nigeria, I think). The jailers got into a poker game with some of the prisoners and bet the jail keys. The jailers lost the keys and said they felt obligated to let them have them. There are U.S. CivPol running the jail today.

UNMIK POLICE PRESS UPDATE
04 SEPTEMBER, 2000
PRISTINA Region
DEAD BODY FOUND
Pristina – 03/09 – 0920 hrs. A K-Albanian male was found deceased in a stairwell. Initial investigation revealed that the subject died as a result of a drug overdose.
UXO/MINE
Pristina – 02/09 – 1545 hrs. A K-Albanian male reported that while demolishing some part of his house he discovered an object that looked like a bomb. KFOR EOD confirmed it was a hand grenade and it was disposed of.
UXO/MINE
Toplice-Milana Village, Obilic – 02/09 – 1900 hrs. A K-Albanian male reported that he found a hand grenade in a K-Serb house, which he has been asked to look after by the owner. KFOR EOD disposed of the grenade.
GNJILANE Region
GRIEVOUS ASSAULT
Gnjilane – 02/09 – 2115 hrs. One K-Albanian was arrested after he stabbed another K-Albanian in the back with a knife. The victim was taken to the hospital for treatment.
GRENADE EXPLOSION
Gnjilane – 03/09 – 2115 hrs. A grenade explosion on the ground floor of a K-Serb owned building caused minor property damage.
MITROVICA Region
PRISON ESCAPE
Mitrovica, Detention Center – 02/09 – 2045 hrs. Thirteen K-Serbian prisoners escaped from the Detention Center. Two prisoners were located and re-captured.
PEC Region
GRENADE ATTACK
Dakovica – 03/09 – 0015 hrs. Unknown person(s) threw a grenade at a K-Albanian shop. The explosion caused only minor property damage to the outer walls of the shop.
ARMED ROBBERY
Brekoc Village, Dakovica – 02/03 – 2300 hrs. A K-Albanian male reported that five unknown K-Albanian males, one of them armed

with a machine gun, entered into his shop. They took carved gravestones and other items worth 8000DM.
PRIZREN Region
EXPLOSION
Musnikovo Village, Orahovac – 01/09 – 2250 hrs. An explosion occurred in a Serbian graveyard causing minor damage to the door of the graveyard chapel.

Monday, 4 September, 2000

I had water this morning but only cold. I shaved and washed with cold water. I woke up early to the loud Muslim again. I was dreaming of being home. I didn't know where I was at first when I woke up. It was kind of weird. I worked day shift today. I rode with the officer from Turkey again. We had the same female KPS officer but a different L.A. We were assigned to area A 2-3. We towed an illegally parked vehicle with no registration. The Turkish officer wrote a ticket. It took him forever. I instructed the KPS officer about vehicle searches and contacting violators. The Turkish officer needed to listen too. We made a traffic stop and wrote a registration ticket. The stops are good training for the KPS officers and the other CivPol officers as well. We took a theft report. I still impress the others with my report writing skills.
I went to Supreme PX and then out to the Swedish PX for food. I had a chat session with Carnita at 1800. We got cut off by another power outage.

P.S. I got assigned to "C" shift. I report for work at 1500 tomorrow. I will work the 1500-2300 shift. The shifts rotate every week. I am getting into a routine and am feeling better about the mission. I am counting the days until leave in November.

UNMIK POLICE PRESS UPDATE
05 SEPTEMBER, 2000
PRISTINA Region
MURDER
Maticane – 04/09 – 1705 hrs. An unknown suspect killed a K-Albanian male and wounded the leg of another K-Albanian male with a sidearm. The suspect fled from the scene in a vehicle. The victims were transported to Pristina Hospital.
MITROVICA Region

ILLEGAL ROADBLOCK
Mitrovica North – 04/09 – 1445 hrs. A relocation of detainees from Mitrovica detention center to the detention center in Pec region had to be aborted because of the blocking of all bridges by the "Bridge Watchers". UNMIK officials started negotiations with them. No acts of violence were reported.
HUNGER STRIKE
Mitrovica North, Detention Center – 04/09 – 1600 hrs. Three detainees still continue with their hunger strike. Their condition is reported to be good.

Tuesday, 5 September, 2000

I woke up at 0900. I was able to sleep in because of the shift change. I ate and rinsed out some clothes. I dry them on a rack on the balcony. I reported to "C" Shift at 1500. During briefing a German officer came in to ask for volunteers for PFTO (Primary Field Training Officer). I volunteered. I will be working with Brent Faulkner. I start tomorrow on night shift. This will be good duty. I will be training 6-8 KPS officers. We will be doing foot patrols, vehicle patrols, and classroom training. It should be good duty. I finished shift on patrol in section A 2-5. I worked with a German CivPol officer named Ralph Karfmann, an L.A., and a 49-year-old KPS officer with 7 kids. We had a pretty good shift. We had an interesting conversation and pulled over 10-12 vehicles. We only issued one ticket. I made a trip to the company building for water. I got dropped off at the house by Ralph at about 2230. I missed my chat session with Carn tonight. I will call her in the morning.

P.S. The weather turned cool and rainy. My breath is fogging. I will have to wear warmer clothes tomorrow night.

UNMIK POLICE PRESS UPDATE
06 SEPTEMBER, 2000
MITROVICA Region
HUNGER STRIKE
Mitrovica North, Detention Center - 05/09. The hunger strike in which three detainees are involved is still ongoing. Their condition is reported to be good.
PRIZREN Region

GRIEVOUS ASSAULT
Prizren – 05/09 - 0730 hrs. A K-Roma male reported that during a dispute a K-Albanian male stabbed him with a knife in the leg. The victim was taken to a hospital and released after treatment.

Wednesday, 6 September, 2000

I'll be working the night shift tonight as a PFTO. I went to the Internet café and e-mailed home, my parents, and the police department. I sent some pictures. I set up a chat time with Carnita. I went back home and watched a movie. Later I went back to the Internet café and chatted with Carnita for an hour. I reported to work early to find out the plan of action. I took four KPS officers and a L.A. out on foot patrol. We walked our beat for about an hour and a half. I gave patrol technique instruction. The weather was kind of cold. I went back to the station and got a van for patrol. We drove around awhile and set up several Vehicle Check Points (VCPs) We stopped many vehicles and wrote one ticket. I took the team back to the station about 0530 to work on their daily report. I let the team go home about 0630. I got home and went right to bed. I slept until 1400.

E-mail home

Hi Hun,
I Just stopped by HQ to see one of my roommates and used his computer. I read your email. I am glad you liked the pictures. I will send you more tomorrow.
I've got to get back to work. I will tell you all about it tomorrow. It's 0415 right now. I will get off in a little bit. I will talk with you soon.
Yours always, Clay

UNMIK POLICE PRESS UPDATE
07 SEPTEMBER, 2000
PRISTINA Region
DEAD BODY FOUND
Pristina Town – 06/09 – 1420 hrs. Two K-Albanian males reported that they had found a dead body in a garbage area. UNMIK Police responded to the scene and found a plastic bag containing the dead body of a child.

UXO FOUND
Lipljan Village – 06/09 – 0745 hrs. A grenade was found at the gate of a K-Roma house. KFOR EOD disposed of the device.
GNJILANE Region
EXPLOSION
Pozaranje Village, Vitina – 06/09 – 2152 hrs. An explosion of unknown origin destroyed a coffee bar owned by K-Albanians. No injuries were reported.
EXPLOSION
Zitinje Village, Vitina – 06/09 – 2215 hrs. Explosions of unknown origin destroyed two unoccupied K-Serbian homes.
CRIMINAL DAMAGE
Berivojce Village, Kamenica - 06/09 – 1700 hrs. Three K-Albanian males damaged the headstones in a Serbian cemetery.
MITROVICA Region
POLITICAL ACTIVITY
Mitrovica North – 06/09 – 1245 hrs. At 1245 hrs a convoy of vehicles from Serbia crossed through Gate One into Kosovo. The convoy included the Serbian Deputy Head of Parliament
and the Minister of Information. Their first stop was at the Zvecan Cultural Center.

Thursday, 7 September, 2000

I'm on night shift again tonight. I woke up at 1400. I ate soup and canned chicken dogs. I got my uniform ready, watched a movie, and then went to chat with Carnita. Today is Josiah's birthday. I said hi to him on the chat session. John Hatchel (roommate) brought everyone a Whopper and onion rings from the Burger King at the U.S. base in Gnjilane (Camp Bondsteel). It was great! I reported to work at 2300. I was assigned five KPS officers and no L.A. One of the KPS officers speaks some English. We started out with a two-hour foot patrol. We walked about 3-4 miles. We set up a VCP at a couple of places and checked several vehicles. We walked foot patrol in three different housing project type areas. The KPS guys love to walk. Not much going on. It was a quiet night. The weather was a little warmer than last night. I gave basic police instruction to the KPS officers while walking. They are very interested in anything I have to tell them. Two more nights until shift change.

UNMIK POLICE PRESS UPDATE
08 SEPTEMBER, 2000
PRISTINA Region
UXO FOUND
Kosovo Polje – 07/09 – 1352 hrs. An UNMIK Police patrol located a rocket launcher and three grenades in the garden of an abandoned house. KFOR EOD disposed of the ordnance.
Kosovo Polje – 07/09 – 1352 hrs. Workers uncovered an unexploded rocket while digging. KFOR EOD disposed of the ordnance.
PRIZREN Region
Prizren - 07/09 – 1840 hrs. A K-Albanian male was arrested for assault on an UNMIK Police officer.
PROSTITUTION
Plava Village, Dragash – 07/09 – 2020 hrs. UNMIK Police assisted by KFOR arrested eight females and one male, the owner of a bar, after a search revealed that he was using his bar as a prostitution establishment.
MITROVICA Region
SHOOTING
Mitrovica - 07/09 – 0040 hrs. During an argument between K-Serbians near the bridge, several persons fired into the air to stop the disturbing noise. The shots caused minor damage to the surrounding buildings. One person received minor injuries from flying pieces of glass.

Friday, 8 September, 2000

I went to bed at 0730 and got up at 1300. I could not sleep any longer but I feel exhausted. I ate soup for breakfast and then went back to bed and read until time to chat with Carnita. Night shift again tonight. Me and four KPS officers. We walked too much last night so tonight we took the van and ran VCPs. We stopped several cars tonight and I let my KPS officers take turns writing citations. We wrote nine by the end of shift. The KPS officers were very pleased. Night shift wasn't so bad tonight. I started having more energy and staying busy made the time go by faster. I was back at the house at 0700 and into bed. I put my earplugs in to keep the noise from the construction next door bearable. One more night shift until I change shifts.

UNMIK POLICE PRESS UPDATE
09 SEPTEMBER, 2000
PRISTINA Region
UXO FOUND
Kosovo Polje Town – 08/09 – 1153 hrs. Four hand grenades and two rifle grenades were found in a ditch close to the power station. KFOR EOD disposed of the ordnance.
PRIZREN Region
MURDER
Llozice Village, Malishevo – 08/09 – 1130 hrs. A K-Albanian male clerk for the NGO "CARITAS" shot three K-Albanian males during an argument. Two of the victims died on the spot while the third died in the Pristina hospital. The suspect was arrested and the weapon seized.

Saturday, 9 September, 2000

I woke up about 1400. I ate and watched a movie. I went to chat with Carnita at 1800. We chatted for an hour. I walked back up the hill to the house. I ate noodles for supper. I went to work at 2300. This is my last night shift for a while. I have only three KPS officers tonight. We set up a VCP and wrote six tickets within the first two hours of shift. We patrolled the NGOs in our region. There have been a few robberies of NGOs lately so we perform extra patrol. Nothing much else happened the rest of the night. I got off at 0700. I went home and crashed. I have to get up about 1330 to get ready for work. Shift change time. I must report to work at 1500. I've got to get this stupid rotation changed.

Sunday, 10 September, 2000

I'm back into work at 1500. This is training week for my KPS officers. I didn't get much sleep since last shift. I get to work with a new partner tonight. An American officer named Randy Wilson. I met Randy a couple of weeks ago. He was reassigned from Mitrovica because of the lead problem. We worked with six KPS officers. We started our shift with some training in the briefing room. We instructed about traffic stops and officer safety. We went out on foot patrol and checked the taxi area downtown. We walked along doing vehicle checks. We wrote six citations during our shift then went back to the station and turned them in. Sundays here are the Albanian Wedding Day. Almost every Sunday there is a wedding celebration. It is a big deal now because the Serbs had not allowed it for many years. There is usually a large parade with lots of vehicles. The problem is that the Albanians like to fire weapons during the celebrations. UNMIK police and KFOR troops have to deal with it. We try not to make arrests for this but usually confiscate a lot of weapons. There was a wedding celebration in Prishtina today, with shooting, but it was not in our AOR. We had more classroom instruction with the KPS officers. They enjoy learning. They want to learn whatever American officers have to teach. We finished the shift by having the KPS officers do their daily report. We have to make a copy in Albanian and one in English. I went home at 2300.

P.S. I have to be back to work at 0800. I need more sleep.

UNMIK POLICE PRESS UPDATE
11 SEPTEMBER, 2000
PRISTINA Region
EXPLOSION/ILLEGAL POSSESSION OF WEAPONS
Hajvalia Village, Pristina – 09/09 – 0100 hrs. An explosion in a café caused minor damage to the glass doors. An investigation of the events surrounding the explosion led to the arrest of two K-Albanian males who were in possession of an AK-47 rifle.
BODY FOUND
Kisnica Village, Pristina – 09/09 – 1820 hrs. The body of an elderly K-Serbian female was found in the street. The woman had died from unknown causes.
ILLEGAL POSSESSION OF WEAPONS
Peran Village, Podujevo – 10/09 – 0020 hrs. Following a report of shots being fired during a wedding celebration, UNMIK Police in conjunction with KFOR recovered a total of nine pistols, over 1,000 rounds of ammunitions, knives, holsters and empty shell cases.
Caglavica Village, Pristine – 10/09 – 1830 hrs. UNMIK Police arrested three K-Serbs for possession of two AK-47 rifles, three rocket launchers, four grenades and one shotgun.
UXO/MINE
Obilic Village, Kosovo Polje – 10/09 – 0030 hrs. An UNMIK Police patrol located an air-launched missile that appeared to have

been tampered with and had its warhead removed. KFOR EOD responded to the location.

GNJILANE Region

SHOOTING

Lisacka Village, Kamenica – 09/09 – 1800 hrs. Heavy firing was reported into the village from across the Serbian border. The villagers left their houses.

UXO FOUND

Kabash Village, Vitina – 09/09 – 1800 hrs. Two K-Albanian males brought two mortar rounds, which they had found at their home to UNMIK Police. KFOR EOD disposed of the items.

PRIZREN Region

MURDER

Zrze Village, Orahovac – 10/09 – 2030 hrs. A K-Albanian male was shot and killed by two unknown suspects armed with AK-47s during a robbery at his gas station. The suspects fled the scene in a gray Opel Asconca.

MITROVICA Region

MURDER

Vucitrin Town – 10/09 – 2325 hrs. A K-Albanian journalist from *Rilindja News* was shot outside the Municipality building. Witnesses reported that two suspects fled on foot from the scene. The victim was transported to the hospital where he later died.

UXO FOUND

Srbica Village, Polac -10/09 – 1900 hrs. A K-Albanian male reported that he had found two mines. KFOR EOD disposed of the items.

Monday, 11 September, 2000

I woke up at 0630 after only five hours of sleep. I ate a pack of noodles for breakfast. I have only been eating about once every 12 hours for the past few days. I reported for work at 0800. I briefed the KPS officers about myself, and my partner (Wilson) and what to expect today. I gave instruction on traffic stops and officer safety. When we asked for questions one of the KPS asked if he could chamber a round. We were surprised that they had been taught to carry their weapon with an empty chamber. I asked the rest of the KPS officers who was carrying their weapon with an empty chamber and they all raised their hands. We took a minute and made sure everyone chambered a round and made it very clear that when they carry a weapon it must be loaded and ready. The KPS officers took great satisfaction in being able to "lock and load". It seemed to give them a new burst of confidence by trusting them to ready their weapons. I think they are beginning to feel like real cops. We walked to the Green Market and Taxi Loop area. We had to tow one vehicle for illegal parking. I got off at 1600.

UNMIK POLICE PRESS UPDATE
12 SEPTEMBER, 2000
PRISTINA Region
MURDER
Pristina – 11/09 – 1917 hrs. Unknown persons shot dead a K-Albanian male who was later identified as the Director of Planning, Reconstruction and Development.
ATTEMPTED MURDER
Gracanica Town – 11/09 – 1745 hrs. A K-Serb male attacked a K-Serbian female with an axe. She sustained head injuries and is being treated at a KFOR hospital. The suspect has been arrested.

Tuesday, 12 September, 2000

I got up at 0630, had noodles for breakfast, and off to work at 0745. This is the third day of training week. We started the day by walking to ITC to use one of their classrooms. I bought the four KPS officer's coffee and visited for a while to get them to open up. I gave a one hour lecture on Police Ethics. It went pretty well. Wilson gave a class on pat downs and handcuffing. We broke for lunch at noon. We were back at station #2 at 1300. We took the "Foot Patrol" van over to a school yard to practice vehicle stops. We worked on violator contacts and cover officers. We used toy guns for pat downs and searches. The KPS officers enjoyed our training very much. They really appreciate American cops helping teach them. I got off work at 1600. I went back to the house to eat. I ate ravioli with Ken McCarty.

P.S. My first CTO is in 10 days. I plan to stay in Prishtina. I need to plan the November trip and reserve plane tickets. The weather is cool this morning but turned off warm in the afternoon. I walked up the hill twice again today and broke a sweat.

UNMIK POLICE PRESS UPDATE
13 SEPTEMBER, 2000
PRISTINA Region
UXO FOUND
Urosevac – 12/09 – 2045 hrs. A 15 inch rocket was located in a field by children playing there. KFOR EOD was notified and disposed of the ordnance.
PRIZREN Region
KIDNAPPING
Prizren – 11/09 – 0840 hrs. A Swiss citizen was abducted and transported to Macedonia where he was forced to sign a check for a significant amount of money. Two suspects later tried to cash the check at a bank in Prizren.
MITROVICA Region
HAZARDOUS MATERIAL LEAK
Mitrovica South – 12/09 – 1615 hrs. A tank containing 40,000 liters of Sulfuric Acid located inside the battery factory started to leak and the Stinica river was contaminated. The Hazardous Material Team, KFOR, Fire department and UNMIK Police attended the scene. UNMIK Police sealed of the area and the population was notified with the help of *Radio Mitrovica* not to swim or fish in the river.
DEMONSTRATION
Mitrovica North – 12/09 – 1200 hrs. UNMIK Police monitored a peaceful demonstration outside the detention center. 35 persons demanded that a Serbian doctor should be allowed to examine the detainees.

Wednesday, 13 September, 2000

I reported for worked at 0800. Randy and I found that we had only two KPS officers and no L.A. Some of our KPS officers are in mandatory additional academy training. We took a Skoda (KPS police car) and went on patrol. We found an L.A. for the morning. We made traffic stops and wrote a few tickets. We ate lunch at Spaghetti Toni's. There was a big political demonstration downtown. There were at least a thousand vehicles involved and about five thousand people. We continued patrolling after lunch and had an English speaking KPS officer as our L.A. We pulled over a black Mercedes. The KPS officer asked the driver to get out of the vehicle. There were also two other passengers in the vehicle. The KPS officer was going to get everyone out of the vehicle for a search. The driver of the vehicle bolted and ran toward a local wooded park. Randy pursued on foot and I pursued in the Skoda. The KPS officer stayed with the Mercedes and the passengers. I jumped the curb with the Skoda and started to drive through the park to try and cut off the suspect. I suddenly remembered the rule to never leave the hard pack/pavement. I assumed that there were no mines left in the area because people were using the park. All of a sudden there was a loud bang and the Skoda almost flipped over. I was sure that I had just hit a land mine. The Skoda righted itself and came to a stop. There was no smoke or fire and I was not bleeding so I assumed I was OK. I got out of the vehicle and found that I had ran over an old engine block that was half buried in the ground and was hidden in the grass. The left front tire of the Skoda was blown and the rim was ripped up. I continued the pursuit on foot until the terrain became impassable. The area became a swamp. I slightly injured my hip in the swamp when I stepped on a buried stump. I got wet and messy up to my waist. We lost the suspect in the woods and swamp. Randy said that he thought the suspect had had a gun and appeared to be wearing body armor. When we finally got back to our KPS officer he was holding the passengers at gunpoint and had handcuffed them together because he only had one set of handcuffs. The passengers said that the driver was a wanted fugitive and was indeed armed and wearing body armor. We had the Mercedes towed and released the passengers after getting statements. After changing the tire on the Skoda, we returned to the station to write our report, get cleaned up, and find out more about our suspect.

UNMIK POLICE PRESS UPDATE
14 SEPTEMBER, 2000
PRISTINA Region
GRENADE ATTACK
Lipljan Town, 13/09 – 2241 hrs. An unknown person threw a hand grenade at an occupied UNMIK Police vehicle. No injuries were reported but there was minor damage to the vehicle.
POLITICAL RALLY
Pristina, 13/09 – 1500 hrs. Approximately 5,000 people attended a political rally organized by the PDK party. No incidents were reported.

GNJILANE Region
MURDER
Kamenica Town, 13/09 – 2245 hrs. A K-Serbian female was killed when an unknown person or persons fired into her home with automatic weapons.
PRIZREN Region
ROBBERY
Reshtan Village, 13/09 – 0825 hrs. A K-Albanian male reported that an unknown male robbed him of his vehicle after he gave the suspect a ride. The suspect threatened the victim with a hand grenade while on the road and took the vehicle.
MITROVICA Region
BURGLARY
Novolone Village, 13/09. Unknown persons broke into the offices of the Mother Theresa Society and stole 16 liters of cooking oil.
HUNGER STRIKE CONTINUES
Mitrovica Detention Center, 13/09. Three Serbian prisoners are continuing their hunger strike at the detention center. One is suffering from anemia and is under medical treatment.

Thursday, 14 September, 2000

I went in to work at 0800. Randy and I started working on the case from yesterday. We got paperwork together for arresting the driver of the Mercedes. No one wanted to go with us to arrest this guy because he was known as a "real bad actor". Some of the KPS and other internationals warned us not to go after him. We told them that was B.S. and we were going to arrest him and we were not afraid of anyone. One older KPS officer (in his fifties) said that he had worked in intelligence during the old Yugoslavia days and may be able to help us. He made a call and arranged for the suspect to surrender to us at a local café. He told us that he made it very clear to the suspect that he had two very determined and angry American police officers that were after him. Other KPS and internationals warned us not to go meet with the suspect because they thought it was a trap. The café was in an area of high criminal activity and they did not trust the older KPS officer and thought he was working both sides. We went anyway and took the suspect into custody without incident. We brought the suspect in for questioning. He said he was scared of the KPS because they are mostly former Kosovo Liberation Army (KLA). His story was mostly B.S. He said the KLA was trying to kill him. This was probably a true statement. We found he had collaborated with the Serbians during the war. He is known as a very bad criminal and is also a known serial rapist and murder suspect. We took the suspect to the detention center and jailed him. The jail was full and the African CivPol officer working the jail tried to turn us away at first but took our prisoner because we made it clear that we were not going to take no for an answer. Everyone back at the station was amazed that we had arrested such a bad criminal so easily. Randy and I have earned a reputation of being "Bad Ass American Cops" and a new and greater respect from the KPS officers. I got off on time. I plan to chat with Carn at 1800. Two more days of training day shift.

P.S. I went to the internet café to chat with Carnita. I got there and found the power was out and the Internet café was shut down.

UNMIK POLICE PRESS UPDATE
15 September, 2000
PRISTINA Region
MURDER
Pristina, 14/09 – 1950 hrs. An unknown K-Albanian male shot and killed one K-Albanian male and wounded another while the victims were sitting in their parked car. The injured victim was hospitalized with a wound to the leg.
GRENADE ATTACK
Mali Alas Village, 14/09 – 0700 hrs. An unknown person planted a hand grenade at the gate of a house occupied by a Roma (Gypsy) family. A male Roma was injured when he opened the gate causing the grenade to explode. The victim was hospitalized.
SUICIDE
Pristina, 14/09 – 1630 hrs. A male German national was found dead in his hotel room from an apparent suicide. The victim was with the organization "Arbeiter Samariter Bund".
DEMONSTRATION
Pristina, 14/09 – 1100 hrs. Approximately 300 people from Gjakove village gathered in front of the U.N. government building and demanded a meeting with Dr. Kouchner* to discuss issues concerning prisoners and missing persons. They dispersed peacefully after meeting with the Director of the OSCE.

(Dr. Bernard Kouchner- French Diplomat and the United Nations Special Representative of the Secretary General to Kosovo)*

GNJILANE Region

SHOOTING

Muciverce Village, 14/09. A K-Serbian male reported that shots were fired into a house belonging to a relative of an LDK candidate.

SHOOTING

Gornje Karacevo Village, 15/09 – 0211 hrs. KFOR reported they received information of mortar rounds exploding near checkpoint 131. Tracer rounds were also seen in the area.

PEC Region

DEAD BODY FOUND

Crkolez Village, 14/09 – 0745 hrs. The body of a 75 year-old K-Serbian male was found close to his home. The victim had been reported missing on the evening of 13/09. The cause of death has not yet been determined and the incident is under investigation.

MITROVICA Region

POLITICAL RALLY

Mitrovica North, 14/09 – 1310 hrs. A candidate of the "Serbian Democratic Party" held a political rally in Mitrovica North. The rally was marred by violence between rival political factions, and a hostile crowd attacked the entourage of the candidate.

Friday, 15 September, 2000

Today our group combined with Brent and Joe's group. Joe Massing is a German Police officer. We went to ITC. I gave a two hour lecture on Police Ethics. It went very well. At 1100 Brent, Randy, Joe and I met with the regional PFTO coordinator. We talked about rearranging the shift schedules and the KPS officer's days off to make training more efficient. We got the OK to make what changes we needed. We had lunch with two U.S. officers from Regional HQ. One of them was from Texas. We went back to ITC and gave a class on searching and handcuffing. It was a good class. We let everyone go a little early. I got home at 1530. I prepared an e-mail for Carn on my laptop explaining the last few days. I hope to find her on line but have the e-mail ready. I went to the Internet café and Carn was not on line. I sent a few e-mails home. I went back home and watched a movie before bed. My last day shift is tomorrow. I switch to evenings on Sunday.

P.S. It rained for about an hour today. The rain cleared the air. I sat on my balcony and listened to an Albanian party nearby. There were sounds of music and clapping. I need to get Courtni some Albanian folk music CDs to take home.

E-mail from Carnita

Hi Hon,
It sounds like you really got into a bad situation the other day. I'm so glad you didn't get hurt real bad. How’s the hip? That sounds gross, going into that stagnant water. What is going to happen to the guy you caught? Sounds like you did a good job. It sounds like the guy was real dangerous and I’m happy you didn't get hurt. I’m glad you are getting along better there and that you might make a difference with the shift changes.
Carn

UNMIK POLICE PRESS UPDATE
16 SEPTEMBER, 2000
PRISTINA Region
RAPE
Pristina, 15/09 – 1600 hrs. A K-Albanian female reported that three known K-Albanian males raped her.
GNJILANE Region
HIT & RUN ACCIDENT
Rogacica Village, 15/09 – 1645 hrs. A K-Albanian male struck a four year-old female child and then fled the scene. The victim was transported to hospital for treatment. UNMIK Police later located the suspect and arrested him.
RAPE/ABDUCTION
Pasjak Village, 15/09 – 1600 hrs. A K-Albanian female reported that she was raped and kidnapped by a known K-Albanian male.
PRIZREN Region
GRENADE ATTACK
Vitomiricia Village, 15/09 – 0030 hrs. A K-Albanian male reported that unknown persons threw a hand grenade at his house, causing damage to the roof.
MITROVICA Region

ARMED ROBBERY
Zubin Potok Town, 1509 – 2000 hrs. A Bosnian male truck driver reported that he was stopped by three men armed with a pistol who were standing in the road. The suspects took cash from the driver and then released him.

Saturday, 16 September, 2000

I started the day by helping the Station #2 Intelligence Unit get information about the suspect we arrested on the 14th. Intelligence and the British KFOR are very interested in him. He was definitely a Serb collaborator during the war. After I was done with the Intelligence Unit, we went to an area near the swimming pool on Germia Road and worked with the KPS officers on traffic stops and searches. It got a little hot today and I got a little sunburned from working outside. We found out that none of our four KPS have ever fired the weapon they are carrying. I let everyone fire one round to function check their weapons. Some of the KPS don't even have handcuffs yet. There is a serious lack of equipment and supplies. I loaned one of the younger KPS officers that had been with me on the 13th incident a pair of handcuffs. He had only one pair of handcuffs to arrest both suspects. I went to the Internet café and finally got in contact with Carnita after four days. It was good to chat with her. I am anxious for my November CTO. I will try and chat again tomorrow at 1400 before work (0600 Montana time). I go to swing shift (1500-2300) tomorrow.

P.S. The weather was sunny and clear today. It got fairly warm. It rained about an hour last night (about 0300).

Sunday, 17 September, 2000

I slept in until 0800. I ate, showered, and wrote e-mails. I went to the internet café at 1400 to chat with Carnita. (0600 Montana time). I got to chat for 45 minutes before work. It is hard for Carnita to chat this early so we will chat again on CTO. I went to work from the café. I started swing shift today. I had six KPS officers. We started the shift on foot patrol at the Green Market and Taxi Loop area. We wrote tickets and towed one unregistered vehicle. We moved to another spot and stopped several more vehicles. We wrote more tickets and towed another unregistered vehicle (probably stolen). We finished the shift by walking foot patrol through the park area near Station #2. The KPS said it was a very nice park about ten years ago. Now it is overgrown and unlighted. This will be a good C.O.P. project for Station #2. We ended the shift with seventeen tickets and two tows. We did more work in one night than the patrol shift does in two weeks. The KPS officers enjoy learning and working.

UNMIK POLICE PRESS UPDATE
18 SEPTEMBER, 2000
PRISTINA Region
GUNFIRE INCIDENT
Prapahtice Village, 17/09 – 1700 hrs. An off-duty KPS officer admitted firing eight rounds from his issued pistol into the air during a wedding ceremony. The officer was relieved of his duties and the pistol was confiscated. The case is under investigation both as a criminal incident and as an internal disciplinary matter.
GNJILANE Region
MURDER
Urosevac Town, 1709 – 2100 hrs. A K-Albanian male was killed and three others wounded in a shooting incident. A suspect is in custody.
MURDER
Gnjilane, 17/09 – 1135 hrs. A K-Serbian male died when an apparent hand grenade was thrown into the back yard of his house.
ATTEMPTED MURDER OF A POLICE OFFICER
Urosevac Town, 16/09 – 1745 hrs. A KPS officer returned fire and wounded his assailant after being shot in the leg. The suspect was arrested and both were transported to hospital for treatment.
PRIZREN Region
GRENADE ATTACK
Prizren, 16/09 – 2315 hrs. An unknown person threw a grenade at a house, causing minor damage to the building, a parked UNMIK vehicle and a parked civilian vehicle.
MITROVICA Region
HUNGER STRIKE CONTINUES
Mitrovica Detention Center, 17/09 – 1500 hrs. The three Serbian detainees continue their protest. They will be examined by the new Penal Management Doctor this week.
DEMONSTRATION

Mitrovica North, 16/09 – 1010 hrs. A group of approximately 50 people marched to the UNMIK police station to voice their concern about not being returned to their homes. The demonstration was peaceful.

Monday, 18 September, 2000

I ran out of food and money today. I had to dip into my savings stash. I only had 50DM notes so I had to walk all the way to the bank to get change. From there I walked to the market and bought 44DM worth of food stuff. Mostly packs of noodles and cans of tuna. I walked from there to the Internet café and checked my e-mail. I sent a note to Carn. I also read the RLT reunion site and sent a message about being in Kosovo. I hope to hear from some of my old classmates. I also read *The Western News*. I walked back home and got ready for work. I found some buckeyes on the way home and picked some up for the kids. I started patrol at 1500 with a VCP. The KPS officers wrote thirteen citations and towed one vehicle. I found some old Yugoslavian coins on the roadside. At 2030 we set up a trap to catch a band of highway robbers that have been working in our area. The robbers have been stopping vehicles at gunpoint and robbing the occupants. The robbers have fled on foot down a trail toward a ravine on the edge of town. The area is used as a dump and is full of wild dog packs. Two KPS officers and I were dropped off on the trail and stalked into the area. I taught them how to move quietly in the dark. We set up an ambush point along the trail that lead to the road that the robbers have been attacking. I had radio contact with a British Royal Marine reactionary team that was on standby as our backup about a kilometer down the main road. After about an hour we grabbed an Albanian male that was coming up the trail. We scared him so bad that he pissed himself. We ID'd him and searched him for weapons. He had none. His story was that he had been rummaging through the garbage heaps. We believed his story because he was in possession of some garbage. He was an Albanian "dumpster diver". We didn't find the robbers after two hours so we shut down the operation. The KPS officers learned a lot and really enjoyed it. I got off at 2300. I spent a couple of hours talking with one of my roommates, John Hatchel. I went to bed about 0130.

P.S. A thunder storm began about 0100. I sat on my balcony and watched it for awhile before going to bed.

UNMIK POLICE PRESS UPDATE
19 September, 2000
PRISTINA Region
ILLEGAL POSSESSION OF WEAPON/POLITICAL RALLY
Glogovac Town – 18/09 – 1545 hrs. Approximately 5,000 persons attended a political rally organized by the PDK party. During the rally 25 shots were fired into the air and one person, ethnicity unknown, was arrested for illegal possession of weapon/shooting.
GRIEVOUS ASSAULT
Kosovo Polje Town – 18/09 – 2230 hrs. An unknown person threw a hand grenade into a K-Serbian house. The grenade exploded inside the house causing injuries to the owner who was transported to the hospital.
PRIZREN Region
ILLEGAL POSSESSION OF WEAPON
Orahovac Town – 18/09 – 1415 hrs. Several children reported that an unknown male wearing a uniform threw a hand grenade, which did not explode, into a soccer field.

Tuesday, 19 September, 2000

The power and water were out most of the day. It rained early for about an hour. I was going to go to Mitrovica with Randy but felt sick today. I took a two hour nap before work at 1500. Randy and I started patrol on foot in the Green Market area. We worked our way back to the Taxi Loop. One of our KPS officers stopped a driver for trying to go the wrong way on Taxi Loop. He checked the driver's documents and found no proof of ownership. We decided to tow the vehicle. The driver was not happy. The tow truck took 20 minutes to arrive. The KPS officer was going to let the driver pull his vehicle onto the tow truck. The driver tried to flee and almost ran over the KPS officer. Randy had to break the driver's window with his ASP baton and pull him out. The driver tried to fight us but Randy and I took him down. We put the hurt to him. I skinned my elbow and banged my knee. He looked a lot worse. We thought we would have trouble with the crowd. We had been told that often if we have to use force making an arrest in public that the crowd may turn against us. We were surprised to find that the crowd was on our side. Our KPS officers said that everyone thought that the driver was a jerk and need his ass kicked. Randy and I again impressed our KPS officers. We are becoming almost legendary at our station. Since we were on foot patrol we did not have a vehicle to transport our prisoner. An American officer from station #3 was passing by and saw the commotion and stopped to assist. He offered to transport the prisoner for us. The American officer was from Boston. I rode with him and the prisoner and Randy took our KPS patrol back to station #2 on foot. The patrol vehicles have no cages for prisoners. I rode shotgun with the officer from Boston and the prisoner was in the back seat. He was bloodied up from our fight. We took the prisoner to station #2 for processing. As I was escorting the prisoner into the station we had to pass the British Royal Marine sentry that was on duty. I was banged up and the prisoner was bloodied and obviously beaten. The young sentry had a surprised and questioning look on his face. Without missing a beat I nodded toward the prisoner and said, "He got an American ass kicking!" The sentry acted like this was the funniest thing he had ever heard in his life and laughed his ass off. After the processing I took the prisoner to the detention center. It was full again but our American cop (a U.S. officer assigned to the detention center) friend made room for our prisoner. He needed to stay for fighting with us. No one fights with an American cop and avoids a cell. I went home at 2230. It rained hard for about an hour at 2200.

UNMIK POLICE PRESS UPDATE
20 September, 2000
PRISTINA Region
ARMED ROBBERY
Pristina – 19/09 – 0150 hrs. 5-6 unknown armed suspects entered a car rental office, took the security guards hostage and stole one safe.
MITROVICA Region
DEMONSTRATION
Mitrovica South – 19/09 – 1010 hrs. A peaceful demonstration took place at the KFOR base in which 150-200 K-Albanians held negotiations in reference to their homes and flats being reconstructed. The KFOR commander and the spokesperson for the K-Albanians came to a peaceful decision to hold further talks after the elections. The crowd dispersed peacefully.

HUNGER STRIKE
Mitrovica detention center – 19/09 – 1700 hrs. The hunger strike at the detention center has come to an end.

Wednesday, 20 September, 2000

I got up, ate, and went to the internet café. I was on line for about ten minutes and lost the network then the power. I had eight new messages to read but only got to read two. I left the internet café and walked to OSCE booking with Craig to check on free flights to Vienna. We determined there was too high a risk of getting bumped. I went to work at 1500. I had only five KPS officers and no L.A. We went to the Green Market and wrote a few tickets. We took a meal break and Randy and I went to the internet café to read e-mails and send some. I got an e-mail from two of my old high school classmates, Scott Sweet and Dana Yezak. We finished patrol on foot checking Station #2 area N.G.Os (Non-Governmental Organizations). One more shift until CTO. I plan to get a ticket home for November. I got off at 2300, went home and went to bed.

UNMIK POLICE PRESS UPDATE
21 SEPTEMBER, 2000
PRISTINA Region
RAPE/ABDUCTION
Perrori i Keq, 20/09 – 1430 hrs. A K-Albanian female reported that she was abducted by her ex-boyfriend, who assaulted and forcibly raped her. The victim was transported to hospital for treatment and examination.
GNJILANE Region
GRENADE ATTACKS
Gnjilane, 20/09. Grenades were thrown at two separate K-Serbian houses. No injuries were reported but minor damage was caused to both houses.
GRENADE ATTACK
Gnjilane, 20/09 – 2300 hrs. A K-Serbian home was damaged when an unknown person threw a grenade at it. The house was occupied but no injuries were reported.
PRIZREN Region
MURDER

Orahovac Village, 20/09 – 0845 hrs. A K-Albanian male was shot dead by an unknown gunman. The victim was a member of TMK.

Thursday, 21 September, 2000

Last shift before CTO. I went to work at 1500. I had seven KPS officers and no L.A. We did foot patrol at the Green Market area and wrote a few tickets. Not much going on tonight. It is kind of dangerous without an L.A. to interpret for us. We walked around town for awhile and checked our NGOs. We did a walk through of the park and caught some "parkers". We went in early to do paperwork. I let everyone go home about an hour early. I went home and watched movies until about 0300. I went to bed and slept pretty good.

P.S. Today is the third anniversary of the Wolf Creek Shootout.

UNMIK POLICE PRESS UPDATE
22 SEPTEMBER, 2000
PRISTINA Region
ATTEMPTED MURDER
Pristina, 21/09 – 1400 hrs. A K-Albanian male reported that during a meeting of the "Educational Council of Faculty of Sports" one of the persons in attendance became angry and fired a shot at him. The shot missed. UNMIK Police responded to the scene but the suspect was able to flee prior to their arrival.
GRENADE ATTACK
Ajvalia Village, 21/09 – 0510 hrs. An unknown person threw a hand grenade at a petrol station, causing minor damage.
POLITICAL DEMONSTRATION
Lipljan Town, 21/09 – 1000 hrs. A PDK political meeting involving 4,000 to 5,000 people was disrupted when numerous shots were fired. Two males and a female were taken into custody by KFOR in connection with the gunfire.
GNJILANE Region
GRENADE ATTACK
Gnjilane, 21/09 – 2300 hrs. A grenade was thrown at a K-Serbian house, reportedly by two K-Albanians.
PRIZREN Region
ATTEMPTED MURDER

Dragash Town, 21/09 – 2057 hrs. An unknown person threw an explosive device at a K-Goran house. Two elderly occupants of the house were transported to hospital for treatment of shock.
MITROVICA Region
SHOOTING AND ILLEGAL POSSESSION OF WEAPONS
Vucitrn Town, 21/09 – 1400 hrs. A K-Albanian male was arrested for firing an AK-47 rifle during a wedding. The weapon and ammunition were confiscated.
REQUEST FROM LOCAL TMK COMMANDER
Srbica Town, 20/09 – 1616 hrs. The local TMK commander appeared at the UNMIK Police station and advised that some shooting was planned during an engagement party scheduled for the next day. The TMK commander then requested that UNMIK and KFOR not "cause them any problems" with checkpoints and searches for weapons. UNMIK police officers advised him of the laws concerning shooting and illegal possession of weapons.

Friday, 22 September, 2000

This is my first day off on CTO. (Travel day). I walked down to the company building and turned in my time card. I checked my e-mail and regular mail. I went from the company building to the barber shop. I got a good short haircut. It took about forty-five minutes. I went from the barber shop to the travel agency. I checked on the price home and made reservations from Skopje, Macedonia to Spokane on October 31st. The price will be $1,270.00. I plan to check on prices on the internet. I went to the grocery store and bought a few days supply of food. I went to the internet café and made the 1600 chat date with Carnita. We chatted for 1 ½ hours. I went home and made a pack of noodles for supper. I sat around and B.S.'d with Ken, Craig, and Brent for a few hours and then went to bed to read. I plan to check on adoption for my brother Chris.

UNMIK POLICE PRESS UPDATE
23 SEPTEMBER, 2000
PRISTINA Region
GUNFIRE
Pristina, 22/09 – 2200 hrs. A K-Albanian male reported that he exchanged gunfire with three unknown persons who tried to forcibly enter his house.

POLITICAL RALLIES
Pristina, 22/09. Political rallies organized by various parties occurred around Pristina, with 350 to 2,500 persons in attendance.
PRIZREN Region
POLITICAL RALLY/DISTURBANCE
Suva Reka Town, 22/09 – 1100 hrs. Approximately 2,000 people attended a political rally held by the PDK party. Verbal confrontations between the participants escalated into an altercation with rock throwing. No injuries or arrests reported.

Saturday, 23 September, 2000

I got up early today to go with Randy Wilson to Mitrovica. Randy needs to get his blood drawn to check his lead level. We drove by a lot of war damaged houses. The fighting was heavy toward the north. I took a picture of an abandoned Serbian tank. We got to Mitrovica and the company "doc" was not in. We drove around and looked at the town and then went to the south police station. There were many war damaged buildings in town. From the south station you can see the bridge across the river that divides the town into the north and south sections. The Serbs live on the north side and the Albanians live on the south side. This is the French KFOR section. The French are known to be pro-Serb. Mitrovica also had a large battery factory during the communist days. There is a lot of chemical contamination caused by the factory and it has gotten into the river. I am told that the fish die often and the locals scoop them out of the river to eat. There are many people with birth defects in the community. I saw a lot of malformed and midget people. This has to be from the contamination. We ate lunch at a pizza restaurant in Mitrovica (supposedly safe according to the CivPol officers) and bought a couple of CDs at a local shop. They only cost about two to three dollars. We then drove back to Prishtina. I chatted with Carnita on the internet and then went to the house to eat and get settled. I watched part of *The Patriot* but went to bed early. I will try and check on adoption stuff during this CTO.

P.S. We took Randy's personal car, a BMW, to Mitrovica. The weather turned off cool and cloudy today with some late evening drizzle.

Sunday, 24 September, 2000

I got up early and ate breakfast. Noodles and coffee again. I was planning to go check with the NGOs about adoption but realized that they are not open on Sunday. I spent all day sitting around and watching movies or working on the laptop. I wrote a general update letter and sent it to all on my e-mail list. I made a chat date with Carnita at 1600. We chatted for an hour and a half. I came back to the house and sat around talking until after midnight. There is rumor we may get our MSA tomorrow. I will check it out and see.

P.S. I got all my clothes washed. I dry them on a clothes rack with a fan.

E-mail to Libby Press

24 September, 2000

Prishtina, Kosovo

Hello from Paradise. It's been a month now since I first arrived here and I thought it time to send an update. We spent the first ten days here in orientation. After that we were assigned to our regions and stations. I was assigned to the Prishtina Region, station #2, here in the city of Prishtina. The weather was hot here when we first arrived but the rainy season has begun now. Its only been a year since the war and things are not quite back to normal yet. The water here is off for several hours a day and is not drinkable at all. We have to use bottled water to cook and brush our teeth with. The power goes out every few days. The air quality here has much to be desired. The power plant just west of the city is powered by coal and puts out a continuous cloud of dirty smoke. The trash is dumped on the sides of the roads and is periodically burned making for more interesting aromas and more smoke. When it rains the water runs down the streets like a stream. The drainage system doesn't work well and the stream is full of trash and muddy water. The rain seems to be the only way to clean the city. The sewers back up and run out of the man-hole covers and join the stream. It is quite an interesting place to live.

I live in a three-story house with five other American officers. All of the houses here are constructed with concrete and a kind of red cinder block. There is a lot of construction going on here. There is a lot of rebuilding needed after the destruction of the war. There is building going on constantly, especially next door. They work from dawn till dusk, making it hard to sleep at times. At the moment I am training Kosovo police officers that have just completed the academy. They are very eager to learn about police work and learn quickly. It is very challenging work. The next big challenge on the horizon is going to be the winter. Most of the heat is wood or coal. Hopefully we will be able to stay warm enough.

UNMIK POLICE PRESS UPDATE
25 SEPTEMBER, 2000
ELECTION POLL INFORMATION
Mitrovica Region - 24/09. All polling stations in the region reported no incidents during the election process.
PRISTINA Region
ARMED ROBBERY
Pristina - 25/09 – 0100 hrs. A Norwegian male reported that two unknown suspects threatened him with a pistol and robbed him of his wallet. The victim sustained no injuries.
HAND GRENADE ATTACK
Kosovo Polje – 24/09 – 1815 hrs. Unknown person threw a hand grenade at a Serbian owned hotel resulting in minor property damage. No injuries were reported.

Monday, 25 September, 2000

I slept in until 1100. I got up and ate noodles again. I need to make a change. I trimmed my whiskers back. I haven't shaved for CTO. Ken, Craig, and I walked down to Main HQ and Ken got a vehicle. We went to the company building so Craig could see Doc. He wasn't in. We got our water for the week. Craig went to the UNMIK clinic while Ken and I checked on MSA and got some food at Arti's Market. Our MSA was not in today. Maybe the 27th. We picked up some new movies and went back to the house. I ate sauerkraut and sausage with mashed potatoes. We watched *The Rock*. I felt kind of bad and very sleepy. I missed my chat date tonight. Carn will understand. I went to bed early to read. I will contact Carn first thing tomorrow by e-mail. I found out the

Internet Café was closed. They were having trouble with the network.

UNMIK POLICE PRESS UPDATE
26 SEPTEMBER, 2000
PRISTINA Region
POLITICAL RALLY
Srbica - 24/09 – 1414 hrs. Approximately 2,000 people attended a political rally held by the PDK. Several times During the rally shots were fired into the air ("happy fire").
PEC Region
SUSPECTED MURDER
Pec – 25/09 – 1930 hrs. A K-Albanian female was found dead with gunshot wounds.
INTIMIDATION / ASSAULT
Decani Town – 25/09 – 1415 hrs. A K-Albanian male reported that he was threatened and assaulted by a known K-Albanian male and his four accomplices for supporting the LDK Party.
INTIMIDATION / ASSAULT
Decani Town – 25/09 – 1400 hrs. A K-Albanian male reported that while returning from a political meeting a group of supporters from another party stopped his vehicle and assaulted him. They further threatened him with bodily harm if he doesn't stop working for the LDK Party.
PRIZREN Region
POLITICAL RALLY
Zym - 25/09. Approximately 300 people attended a peaceful rally held by the "PSHDK" Party in the village of Zym.

Tuesday, 26 September, 2000

I got up early at 0700. I ate noodles again. Luckily I showered before the water and power went off. Craig, Ken, and I walked to town. We stopped at an NGO to check on adoption possibilities. I was told that no out of country adoptions were being allowed at this time. I went to the company building to e-mail Carn and let Craig see the doc. We went to Grecia's to eat lunch. I had chicken with mushroom sauce. We went back home to watch movies and I waited for chat time with Carn. The internet café has been down for a day and a half. I chatted with Carn at 1900. The internet went out four times during our chat. I arraigned for Carn to call Ken's cell phone at 2130. Carn called and we talked for fifteen minutes. It was good to hear her voice. I have no plans for tomorrow.

UNMIK POLICE PRESS UPDATE
27 SEPTEMBER, 2000
PRISTINA Region
HAND GRENADE ATTACK
Pristina – 26/09 – 2000 hrs. An unknown person threw a hand grenade at a K-Albanian owned shop.
MURDER
Kullec Village, Pristina – 26/09 – 2230 hrs. When two K-Albanians left after a visit at the house of their friends, they were shot dead by unknown person(s). Their friends found the bodies outside the house. A KFOR unit was first on the scene and conducted a search with dogs. Investigations by the UNMIK Police Murder Squad are continuing.
MITROVICA Region
ATTEMPTED MURDER
Vucitrn – 26/09 – 1100 hrs. A K-Serbian male reported that another K-Serbian male had stabbed him with a knife.

Wednesday, 27 September, 2000

I got up early. I have nothing planned for today. I got a ride down the hill. Ken, Craig, and I checked the bank for our MSA. Nothing today. It will probably be Friday as originally scheduled. We went to Arti's grocery and then to the "thieves" market. We walked around looking for clothes hangers for Craig. We went to the OSCE building for lunch. The restaurant is on the top floor of the building. It is a great view of the city. You can see our house from there. Craig and I walked home while Ken got a ride to the phone company to check on getting a phone line for the house. I watched movies, ate supper and went to bed early. Two more days off until I go back to work. I am counting the days until the trip home.

UNMIK POLICE PRESS UPDATE
28 SEPTEMBER, 2000
PRISTINA Region
GRENADE ATTACKS
Stimlje Village, Lipljan – 27/09 – 2215 hrs. Two grenade attacks were reported to have occurred in this village. One grenade was

thrown into the yard of a Gypsy family. A second grenade was thrown at a building where offices of the LDK are located. The attacks caused no injuries, only property damage in the second case.

POLITICAL RALLY

Pristina – 27/09 – 1530 hrs. Approximately 15,000 people attended an LDK Political rally, which was held at the Pristina Sports Center and addressed by Ibrahim Rugova. The event was peaceful.

MITROVICA Region

EXPLOSION

Roma Camp, South Mitrovica - 29/09 – 2330 hrs. KFOR reported an explosion in the vicinity of the Roma Camp. KFOR believes that the source was a stationary device.

ARREST OF A SUSPECT

Srbica - 28/09 - 0630 hrs. A joint UNMIK Police and KFOR operation resulted in the arrest of a wanted K-Albanian male who is suspected to be involved in the murder of a Russian soldier.

POLITICAL RALLY

Mitrovica South – 27/09 – 1600 hrs. Approximately 700 people attended a peaceful political rally of the AAK party in Mitrovica South.

PEC Region

SHOOTING

Decani – 27/09 – 2300 hrs. A K-Albanian male, Deputy President of the AAK Party, reported that an unknown person fired twice upon his vehicle when he was returning home. He escaped unhurt but the windscreen and the bonnet of his car were damaged.

Thursday, 28 September, 2000

I got up early and ate. I read until Craig and Ken got up. We cleaned up around the house and filled our water bottles. All of us walked to town to take some pictures and check our mail at the company building. Craig got a haircut while Ken and I waited. We went to lunch at OSCE. I took some pictures from the balcony of the 9th floor. We went home and sat around. A couple of guys from Mitrovica came over for a while and visited. I went to chat with Carn at 1800. I chatted for an hour. I tried to send some pictures but the computer was messing up. I came back to the house and watched *Gladiator.* I went to bed about 2200 and read some. Tomorrow is MSA day for sure.

UNMIK POLICE PRESS UPDATE
29 SEPTEMBER, 2000
PRISTINA Region
POLITICAL RALLY
Kosovo Polje – 28/09 – 1200 hrs. UNMIK Police and KFOR stopped a rally of about 100 PDK supporters who tried to march past the Y-junction towards the Kosovo Polje railway station.
POLITICAL RALLY
Obilic – 28/09 – 1800 hrs. Approximately 600 people attended a rally held by the LDK party.
PRIZREN Region
POLIITCAL RALLY
Prizren –28/09. A political rally was held by AAK in Malishevo Town from 1600 to 1700 hrs. The rally ended peacefully.
GNJILANE Region
ILLEGAL DISCHARGE OF FIREARM
Sadovina Village, Vitina – 28/09 – 1230 hrs. An unknown person fired several shots in the air from a crowd of about 5,000 K-Albanians who had gathered for the inauguration of a war memorial ceremony. No injuries were reported.
MITROVICA Region
ARMED ASSAULT / ARMED ROBBERY
Mitrovica South - 29/09 – 0351 hrs. UNMIK Police interrupted a robbery in progress at a K-Albanian pharmacy. Four suspects fled through the backyard of the building when the officers arrived. The officers attempted to pursue, but the suspects began firing their weapons and the officers were forced to escort the victims to cover. No UNMIK police officers discharged their weapons during the incident. Two of the victims were transported to local hospitals with varying injuries sustained prior to the arrival of the police. Two KPS officers assigned to the South Station returned to the scene this morning and searched the area. They recovered a handgun believed to have been abandoned by the fleeing suspects.
DEMONSTRATION
Rudnik – 28/09 – 1438 hrs. Approximately 200 people blocked the main road to Srbica while protesting against the arrest of a K-Albanian suspect wanted in the murder of a Russian soldier.
PEC Region

MURDER
Pec Town – 28/09 – 0630 hrs. A K-Albanian male was found shot dead inside his plumber shop.

Friday, 29 September, 2000

Today is my last day of CTO. I got up and ate and had coffee with Craig. When Ken woke up we went to the bank for our MSA. I got 4,987DM. We took a cab to the Maxi PX and bought some food. It was funny to see some of the signs on top of the cabs. Some were spelled "taksi". I spent 50DM at the PX. We took a "taksi" back to the house and watched a movie. I went to the internet café and sent some e-mails and pictures. I did not chat because we had to meet a new American contingent group of officers at the Iliria hotel. We met the new American offices and saw a few that we knew. We met Randy Wilson's sister, Shannon Leary. Randy was not around so we took her and her bags to his house. Randy was not there so we took her to our house until we could locate him. Randy finally showed up and we had coffee and beer. Randy stayed for about an hour and then took Shannon to his house. I went up to my room and went to bed. I have to be back to work tomorrow.

P.S. The water goes out on such a regular basis that I stopped noting it. It usually goes off around 1100 and stays off until sometime after 1800. The power is unpredictable and goes off at different times but is seldom off more than an hour or so at a time.

E-mail home

Hi Hun,
Just an e-mail to say hi and let you know I need to skip the chat tonight. I am going to the Iliria hotel to meet with the new American contingent that came in today. There are 102 cops in this group. I got my MSA today. Everything is going fine. I go back to work tomorrow at 0700. Just 32 days until I come home. I can't wait to see you and the kids. I couldn't get the pictures to send last night so I am sending them now. We probably need to cut the chatting to every other day so I can have food money and keep my savings. Let me know if this is ok with you. I can chat every day if you want but I will not be able to bring back quite as much money. I hope your trip to Kalispell was ok. I should know

in a couple of days if Craig is going to be able to come home at the same time with me so you and his wife can ride together. Hope you understand about chat tonight. I need to meet the cops and help them get settled and tell them safe places to go and eat and stuff and recruit some for my station. Tell the kids that I love them and will be home soon. I love and miss you so much. Talk to you tomorrow. Clay

E-mail from Carnita

Hi Hon,
I definitely understand about the chat and why you couldn't make it. I would have wanted someone to be there for you when you first got to Kosovo. I agree that we should chat every other day or so. It will be that much more exciting and we will have more to talk about. If we have something real important to say we could always e-mail. I hope you had a good rest on your CTO. We had a good trip to Kalispell. Courtni has three cavities that have to be fixed before getting her braces. I hope the roads won't be too bad. Thanks for the pictures. How about having our next chat on Monday. That way you can get into a routine again with work and have more to talk about. Love you forever, Carn

UNMIK POLICE PRESS UPDATE
30 SEPTEMBER, 2000
GNJILANE Region
UXO FOUND
Vitina Town – 29/09 – 1230 hrs. Two K-Albanian boys reported finding a hand grenade near the Vitina civil administration building. KFOR EOD was tasked for disposal.
MITROVICA Region
DEMONSTRATION
Rudnik Village – 29/09 – 1708 hrs. After the arrest of a homicide suspect, demonstrators blocked the main roadway. Negotiations lead to the dissolve of the blockade.
PEC Region
THEFT
Pec – 28/09– 1930 hrs. A Japanese female, working for the Japanese NGO “JEN” reported that an unknown person stole a bag containing a considerable amount of money belonging to the NGO.

Saturday, 30 September, 2000

Today is my first day back to work after CTO. I got up early at 0500. I shaved off my CTO beard. I had a small can of baked beans for breakfast. I reported for work at 0700. There are new schedules starting today. Some of the first KPS classes are going out on there own. The foot patrol is now called the Field Training Unit. The groups were reorganized into three units. My unit has nineteen KPS officers and will spend the next week on day shift. The notice of the new schedule didn't get out to everyone on time. Some of the KPS officers did not show up today because of no notice. Some showed up that now have Saturdays off and we sent them home. Out of my nineteen KPS officers I ended up with four at work today. I sent these four out with a Jordanian officer while the rest of us PFTOs (Primary Field Training Officers) tried to square away the scheduling. I got off work at 1500. I went to the internet café at 1800 and had a chat session with Carnita for an hour. I went back to the house and had a can of hot curry chicken over rice. I watched a movie (*Sleepy Hollow*) and then went up to bed to read. I should have thirteen KPS officers at work tomorrow. One month until leave at home.

P.S. I felt a little run down today. I started getting a headache about noon. It went away after my chat with Carn. The wind picked up tonight. Maybe a rain is coming.

Sunday, 1 October, 2000

I went in to work today at 0700. Randy was there for today but he goes on CTO tomorrow. I met a new American PFTO who will be working with us. His name is Jim Knudson. He is from Alaska. We wrote ten citations and towed four cars on our shift today. It was cloudy and cool. Not much else happened. I got off work at 1500 and went home. I ate noodles for supper and watched a couple of movies. I will have the whole shift alone for the next three days. Jim will be gone at training and Randy will be on CTO in Greece. I did not chat with Carnita tonight. We decided to chat every other night to save money to take home. I got to bed later than I wanted to (2300) and read for a while. I have to get up at 0530 to get ready for work. I have twenty-nine more days to work until my first trip home. I am counting down.

P.S. I talked with a buddy in Mitrovica. A new mass grave from the war (ethnic cleansing) was discovered there.

UNMIK POLICE PRESS UPDATE
02 OCTOBER, 2000
PRISTINA Region
ABANDONED BABY
Stimlje Village, Lipljan – 01/10 – 1645 hrs. A one-week-old baby girl with her mother's name on a hospital tag tied around her wrist was found alive in a closed bag by KFOR. The baby was taken to Pristina hospital.
GRENADE ATTACK/SHOOTING
Milosevo Village – 30/09 – 1900 hrs. Unknown persons threw a hand grenade that exploded in front of a K-Serb residence. The owner of the house reported having heard gunfire both before and after the explosion occurred.
RECOVERED AMMUNITION
Glogovac – 01/10 – 1350 hrs. One RPG7 anti-tank warhead was recovered partly buried just outside the Police station. KFOR EOD disposed of the device.
SUSPECTED MASS GRAVE SITE
Kosovo Polje-30/09-1600 hrs. KFOR found a small piece of bone, which is believed to be the upper part of a shinbone belonging to a child, at a location which is, according to the statements of locals, a suspected war grave site.
POLITICAL MEETING / RALLY
Lipljan – 30/09 – 1030 hrs. Approximately 250 people attended an unauthorized meeting, which was addressed by the President of the PDK party at the Civic Center. Prior requests to hold the meeting had been denied by OSCE.
Podujevo – 30/09 – 1700 hrs. Approximately 400 people attended a political rally held by the LDK at the local cinema hall.
GNJILANE Region
EXPLOSION
Mogilla – 01/10 – 2240 hrs. Two powerful explosions took place at two unoccupied homes believed to belong to K-Serbians.
POLITICAL RALLIES
01/10. A PDK political rally held at Koretin was attended by approximately 500 people. Another PDK political rally was held in Kopernica where approximately 250-300 people attended. The

last political rally was held in Terpeza Village where about 600 people attended.

FOUND UXO

Gnjilane – 29/09 – 2120 hrs. A K-Albanian male reported that he had found a hand grenade in his backyard after observing an unidentified person placing it there. KFOR EOD disposed of the grenade.

MITROVICA Region

ASSAULT

Mitrovica North, Trepca Factory – 01/10 – 0130 hrs. A K-Serbian male was arrested for throwing rocks at UNMIK Police officers.

FOUND HUMAN REMAINS

Zubin Potok – 01/10 – 1402 hrs. A phone call was received from an unknown caller giving the location of a dead body. UNMIK Police Officers recovered human remains of a man.

PEC Region

MURDER

Grabanica, Klina – 30/09 - 2100 hrs. A man was found shot dead in his vehicle. The ethnicity of the victim and the suspect(s) remain unknown at this time.

PRIZREN Region

CRIMINAL DAMAGE / EXPLOSIONS

Prizren – 02/10 – 0150-0200 hrs. An explosion took place in an unoccupied house that is under construction. As units from UNMIK Police and KFOR started to secure the crime scene a second minor detonation occurred in front of the units. This explosion was followed by a third, large one. This explosion damaged three UNMIK Police cars. The people living in the surrounding houses were evacuated and the area closed. According to the EOD Team, which investigated the scene, three explosives connected with time fuses were placed in the house. Two K-Albanians living in the neighborhood where slightly injured, 4 KFOR soldiers suffered a trauma of hearing. No UNMIK Police officers sustained injuries.

POLITICAL RALLIES

Ortakol, Prizren – 01/10 – 1600-1800 hrs. Approximately 1,000 people attended a peaceful political rally held by the LDK party.

Shaderban, Prizren – 01/10 – 1900-2100 hrs. Approximately 500 people attended a peaceful political rally held by the AAK party.

Village of Buce, Prizren 01/10 – 1720-1900 hrs. Approximately 100 people attended a peaceful political rally held by the LDK party.
GRENADE ATTACK
Dragash – 30/09 – 1940 hrs. Responding to a loud blast. UNMIK Police and KFOR found that an explosion of unknown source caused extensive damage to a house and destroyed the house owner's car which had been parked in front of the building.
HUMAN REMAINS FOUND
Gede – 30/09 –1320 hrs. Children found the remains of a human body which were later removed by UNMIK Police.

Monday, 2 October, 2000

I went to work at 0700. Brent left for his first CTO. Twenty eight days until my next CTO. I went out on patrol with three KPS officers and one L.A. We wrote seven tickets and worked two burglaries. One of the burglaries was of a hunting club. There were three large elk racks, one huge mule deer mount, a grizzly rug (the bear was killed in Peja) and two wolf rugs. It was very impressive. The second burglary was not much. An Italian NGO was broken into and apparently nothing was taken. I went to the house at 1500 and ate. I watched a movie and visited with Craig. I went to bed and read for a while.

P.S. I got my November CTO approved today. Craig should have his tomorrow so we can finalize our flight plans.

UNMIK POLICE PRESS UPDATE
03 OCTOBER, 2000
PRISTINA Region
ILLEGAL POSSESSION OF WEAPONS
Hajvalia Village, Pristina, 02/10 – 0600 hrs. Seven K-Albanian males were arrested after a joint search operation by UNMIK Police and KFOR resulted in the recovery of one light anti-tank weapon, six smoke grenades, one hand grenade, military diving equipment, and a large quantity of ammunition.
SHOOTING/CRIMINAL DAMAGE
Shtedim Village, Podujevo, 01/10 – 2240 hrs. Unknown person(s) shot at a truck driven by two Hungarian males as they drove through Kosovo to Serbia.

FOUND DEAD BODY

Obilic, 02/10 – 1150 hrs. The badly mutilated body of a K-Albanian male employee of the Kosovo Electric Power Company was discovered in the conveyer belt of a coal crushing machine at the power plant.

UXO/MINE

Obilic, 02/10 – 1203 hrs. A piece of unexploded ordinance, which was later confirmed to have been an 81mm high explosive mortar round, was found. KFOR EOD disposed of the item.

POLITICAL RALLIES

StimljeVillage, Lipljan, 02/10 – 1725 hrs. Approximately 200 persons attended a PDK political rally.

GNJILANE Region

GRENADE ATTACK / ARMED ASSAULT/ ATTEMPTED MURDER

Pasjan village, 2/10 – 1950 hrs. Five K-Serbians were injured as the result of a drive-by shooting and a grenade being thrown at the crowd in front of a local bar. All five K-Serbs were injured. Four where taken to hospital at Camp Monteith, and one was treated in the village clinic.

GRENADE ATTACK

Vitina, 2/10 – 2215 hrs. KFOR and UNMIK Police responded to the scene where two explosions had taken place. Upon arrival they found that explosions had destroyed two K-Serbian houses.

CRIMINAL DAMAGE

Karakovce, 02/10 – 1110 -1500 hrs. A K-Serbian male came to the UNMIK Police station and reported that unidentified suspects had fired shots at his home, causing damage. Further investigation revealed that ninety spent .45 caliber shell casings were found about one hundred meters from the victim's home.

POLITICAL RALLY

Strpce, Firaja, 02/10 - 1600 hrs. Approximately 150 persons were in attendance at an AAK political rally.

PRIZREN Region

EXPLOSIONS

Prizren, 02/10 – 0150 hrs. There was a large explosion behind UNMIK Police regional headquarters on Monday at approximately 0150 hrs. Upon arrival of UNMIK and German KFOR, there was another explosion at approximately 0156 hrs. A third explosion occurred shortly thereafter at approximately 0200 hrs. Residents in the surrounding area were evacuated by UNMIK and KFOR. EOD units advise that each explosive device contained approximately three kilos of TNT. The explosives were detonated with timers apparently set to victimize the responding UNMIK and KFOR personnel. Four German KFOR personnel were treated for concussion type injuries and two local residents were treated and released for shock. Three UNMIK Police vehicles were damaged in the explosions.

PEC Region

FOUND HUMAN REMAINS

Pec, 02/10 – 1630 hrs. A K-Albanian male found nylon bags of what appeared to be human bones near the Serbian Cemetery.

MITROVICA Region

MURDER

Leposavic, Kaljin, 02/10 – 1300 hrs. A conflict between two Serbian brothers resulted in the shooting death of the victim with a pistol. The pistol was confiscated and the suspect was arrested.

Tuesday, 3 October, 2000

I got up at 0530. I performed the three "Sierras" and then I was off to work. I skipped breakfast today. I took three KPS officers and a L.A. out on patrol. It was a slow day. There was not much traffic. We only wrote a few citations. I confiscated some fake Montana license tags off a vehicle while conducting a Vehicle Check Point (VCP). The driver tried to tell me that he had bought the vehicle from an American and that the plates were real. I called B.S. on him as said, "Guess where I'm from." I confiscated the plates and will keep them as a war souvenir. I found out later that novelty United States license plates were included in packs of CDs that were being sold in Macedonia. Craig had to guard a couple of newly discovered mass grave sites in Obilic. A farmer dug up some human bones while plowing a field. A couple of eye witnesses came forward to confirm that they were grave sites from the war. After I got off work I went with Craig to finalize our flight reservations for our next CTO. We are going to travel back home together. My ticket is going to cost $1,218. I went to the internet café and sent e-mails. I could not get on-line with Carnita tonight. I went to the Indian restaurant with Craig, Ken, and two Swedish cops. The food was very good and spicy. After eating I went home and went to bed and read for a while.

UNMIK POLICE PRESS UPDATE
04 OCTOBER, 2000
PRISTINA Region
Pristina – 03/10 – 1730 hrs. A hand grenade without a safety pin and nine empty artillery shells were discovered in the basement of a building, which is under construction. All the items were removed by a KFOR EOD unit.
UNIFORMS FOUND
Pristina – 03/10 – 1500 hrs. A K-Albanian male reported that he had found some old Serbian Police uniforms in the basement of his building that he suspected could be booby-trapped.
HUMAN REMAINS FOUND
Pristina – 03/10 – 1530 hrs. A security guard with the "US Office" reported that he had found a human skull and several other bones mixed with dirt at a construction site.
POLITICAL RALLY
Pristina – 03/10 – 1800 hrs. Approximately 100 people attended an AAK political rally, which was held at the Dardania Municipal building.
GNJILANE Region
MURDER
Vitina – 03/10 – 2020 hrs. An unidentified male suspect armed with a handgun fired two shots into a restaurant and fled. A K-Albanian male inside the restaurant was injured by the gunfire. Although the victim was rushed immediately to the Gnjilane Hospital, he died of the gunshot wounds.
Verbestica – 04/10 – 0148 hrs. A K-Serbian male shepherd was found dead in the hills near Verbestica Village. The victim had multiple gunshot wounds.
MITROVICA Region
U.N. BUS ATTACK
Mitrovica North – 03/10 – 1750 hrs. A U.N. bus transporting 12 Serbian KPS Officers and 10 language assistants was attacked near the Main bridge by approximately 40 - 50 persons. The attackers threw rocks at the bus damaging the windows and injuring three KPS officers.
UXO/MINE
PRIZREN Region
RAPE AND ROBBERY

Prizren - 02/10 – 2030 hrs. A K-Albanian female reported that she was forcibly dragged into a vehicle by two K-Albanian males. She was then taken to a room, raped and robbed of money.

Wednesday, 4 October, 2000

I got up at 0530 today. I had noodles for breakfast. I went in to work at 0645. I finished my KPS evaluation forms. What a pain. I took a patrol of three KPS officers and one L.A. out for the day. We started by driving to the top of the mountain east of Prishtina. The KPS loved the "mountain" ride. It was a great view. I let all of the KPS and the L.A. shoot one round into a mine field. I told them that I would buy dinner for anyone of them that could set off a mine with their shot. I also told them to aim far enough into the mine field that if they did hit a mine that it would be far enough away to keep from hurting us. I even took a shot. None of us were able to hit a mine. We went back into the city and made some traffic stops and wrote four citations. We had a robbery/homicide downtown. Someone shot and killed a man who was delivering a sack full of 100DM notes to a bank. We searched the area for the getaway vehicle. While searching we found an escaped mental patient. We took the patient back to the hospital. After lunch we were flagged down by a victim who had been car jacked by the robbery/homicide suspect. He took us to the original getaway vehicle in the Sunny Hill area. We called it in and spent the rest of the day assisting on the homicide. I got off work late at about 1700. I changed and went to chat with Carnita. We chatted for about one hour. I went home and ate some tacos that Ken had made. They were very good. I watched a movie and then went to bed.

P.S. The KPS had a great day. They love to work with me because we actually work and I make the day fun. I gave each one of them a 9mm cartridge to replace the one I let them fire into the mine field. They all wanted to keep it for a souvenir.

UNMIK POLICE PRESS UPDATE
05 OCTOBER, 2000
PRISTINA Region
ROBBERY / MURDER

Pristina – 04/10 – 1239 hrs. Two unidentified armed suspects attacked and robbed a cash delivery van. The K-Albanian driver, who was seriously injured, was evacuated to hospital where he eventually died from injuries that he had sustained during the robbery.

INTIMIDATION

Laniste Village, Lipljan – 04/10 – 1245 hrs. A K-Albanian male member of the LDK party reported that unknown people had sprayed graffiti, which says, "we will kill you" on his front gate.

DEAD BODY

Ade Village, Kosovo Polje – 04/10 – 1650 hrs. The body of a baby was discovered lying at the bottom of a well.

MINE/UXO

Qikatova, Gllogovac – 04/10 – 0830 hrs. One anti-personnel mine was discovered in an area that KFOR EOD advised could contain more mines. The area was safely secured and engineers have been tasked to clear the area in the next couple of days.

GNJILANE Region

MURDER

Urosevac – 04/10 – 2050 hrs. A K-Albanian male who owned a jewelry store was killed in an apparent robbery. The victim was reported to have been carrying 3Kg of gold.

EXPLOSIONS

Vitina – 04/10 – 2243 hrs. A powerful explosion occurred at an abandoned home owned by a K-Serb male.

Vitina – 04/10 – 0050 hrs. A second explosion occurred within 100 meters of the first explosion.

Thursday, 5 October, 2000

I got up again at 0530. I had instant oatmeal for breakfast. "Triple Sierra" and off to work. I started my shift at 0700. I finished the robbery/homicide report. It took me until about 0900. I went out on patrol with three KPS and no L.A. Jim took his patrol of three KPS and no L.A. along with me. We shared Visar Goxhufi (a KPS officer who speaks English) as our L.A. We set up a VCP and wrote six citations. I had a meeting with the KPS coordinator (Thommy Erdmenger from Germany) at 1030. I had lunch with him at the Turkish restaurant. I had chicken shish kabob. I got off work on time at 1500. I went home and ate instant chicken soup mix with garlic toast. I used my garlic capsules for the toast. I watched a movie with Craig until about 2200. I went to bed and read for a while. Two more days of day shift and early rising. I can't wait to go home on CTO.

P.S. There is a Station #2 BBQ planned for Sunday. There is a 10DM "donation" required from all UNMIK personnel. The KPS can come for free. They can't afford the 10DM. It should be fun.

UNMIK POLICE PRESS UPDATE
06 OCTOBER, 2000
PRISTINA Region
GRENADE ATTACK
Stimlje Village, Lipljan - 05/10 – 2230 hrs. A hand grenade was thrown in front of a K-Albanian house causing only minor damage to windows of the house. No injuries were reported.
SHOOTING / ILLEGAL POSSESSION OF WEAPON
Dubnica Village, Podujevo – 04/10 – 2245 hrs. Three K-Albanian males were arrested after they had driven to the Serbian border and provoked a cross border firefight. Three assault rifles and ammunition were confiscated.
POLITICAL RALLIES
Vranidoll Village, Pristina – 05/10 – 1630 hrs. Approximately 150 people attended an AAK political meeting that ended without incident.
Lukare Village, Pristina – 05/10 – 1840 hrs. Approximately 70 people attended an AAK political meeting that ended without incident.
GNJILANE Region
GRENADE ATTACK / SHOOTING
Bicevac - 06/10 – 0015 hrs. UNMIK Police responded to a report from a K-Albanian male that he heard gunfire near his house. The officers located an unexploded grenade inside the garage of the residence. The windows of the garage were damaged. Polish KFOR responded to the scene and will dispose of the device in the morning hours.
GRIEVOUS ASSAULT
Gnjilane – 05/10. A K-Albanian male robbed another K-Albanian male of his money. When UNMIK Police arrived at the scene the suspect attacked one officer with a chain saw. The officers overpowered the suspect and arrested him. The money was recovered.

PEC Region
MURDER
Pec Town – 05/10 – 1850 hrs. Three unknown suspects, who were driving in a vehicle, fired with an unknown type of weapon at two K-Albanian male pedestrians and injured them. Both victims were transported to hospital where one victim died. The extents of injuries of the second victim were not reported.
ARMED ROBBERY
Zajmovo, Klina – 05/10 - 0445 hrs. A Bosnian male was robbed at gunpoint by six unknown suspects (3 males and 3 females) of his truck and bananas worth of approx. 10,000DM.
PRIZREN Region
GRIEVOUS ASSAULT
Kursevo – 05/10 – 1350 hrs. A K-Goran male, who is with the Canadian de-mining team, was attacked from behind and struck with an unknown device by unidentified suspect(s) while working alone.

Friday, 6 October, 2000

I performed the same routine this morning, including breakfast. I went in to work at 0700. I patrolled the Station #2 area with four KPS officers. Not much going on today. Field Training Unit (FTU) "C" wrote twenty four citations. I hauled several boxes of KPS stuff (gun belts, batons, flashlights, etc.) from Regional Headquarters (RHQ) to Station #2. Because of a power outage I had to direct traffic at the Germia Road junction for over an hour. I went home and ate instant soup and a fresh garlic sandwich. I watched a movie and was going to go to the internet café but we had a huge thunder storm right at my chat time. I could not walk down the hill because of the storm. Craig got soaked walking back from an early chat with his wife. I watched another movie and then went to bed to read. One more day of morning shift. The Station #2 BBQ is on Sunday. I donated 30DM to the party. The Station Commander gave 200DM. The German NATO contingent is donating the beer.

UNMIK POLICE PRESS UPDATE
07 OCTOBER, 2000
GNJILANE Region
UXO

Kacanik – 06/10 – 0045 hrs. Unknown persons reported to UNMIK Police that they heard some shooting near their house. Upon further investigation UNMIK Police found an unexploded hand grenade. KFOR EOD was notified for disposal of the ordnance.

DEATH INVESTIGATION

Gornje Slakovsec – 06/10 – 1400 hrs. An eleven-year-old K-Albanian boy with a gunshot wound to the head was brought to KFOR checkpoint. The boy died during the transport to Camp Bondsteel.

MITROVICA Region

ABDUCTION / RAPE

Mitrovica South– Between 24/09 and 06/10. A K-Albanian female reported that two K-Albanian males abducted and raped her numerous times over a period of two weeks.

PEC Region

GRENADE ATTACK

Istok – 05/10 – 2300 hrs. A Bosnian male reported that unknown suspect(s) threw a hand grenade in front of his garage causing only property damage.

Saturday, 7 October, 2000

I performed the three "Sierras" and ate oatmeal for breakfast. Today is the last day of Day Shift this week. I have four KPS officers today. We patrolled our Area of Responsibility (AOR) and then I went to a meeting at Regional Headquarters (RHQ). I tried to get Ken and John assigned to Station #2. Any reassignments will have to wait until the elections are over. I finished the shift with more patrol and a VCP. I got off at 1500. Ken and I waited for Craig until 1630. We ran out of food today. All of us went to the Norwegian PX to buy some more supplies. Ken had a vehicle for us to use. I spent 95DM. The supplies should last until we get our next Mission Subsistence Allowance (MSA). We went home and I ate noodles for supper. I added a can of bean sprouts. It is raining again tonight. I did not want to walk to the internet café in the rain. I will get a ride to the company building to send an e-mail tomorrow. I went to bed and read. I watched part of an American movie on the satellite. I have a TV in my room and it is hooked up to a satellite dish on our house. Most of the programming is in German with some programs in Albanian.

Sunday, 8 October, 2000

I got up at 0700 this morning. I ate oatmeal again. It keeps you "regular". I wrote an e-mail to Carnita. I went to the internet café and read my e-mails. I sent the e-mail that I wrote to Carnita and made a chat appointment for 0900. I went to the Station #2 BBQ at noon. There were some problems with the cooking set up so the BBQ was delayed until 1400. The BBQ was pretty good after it got started. We hung out on the roof of Station #2 and the view of the city was pretty good. I had to work the night shift so I went home to sleep. I could not get to sleep so I made some "to do" lists for CTO. The weather is cool and cloudy today. I went in to work at 2300. It was cool and raining. We only wrote two citations. Not much was going on because of the weather. I dropped off my KPS officers at their homes at 0600. I got off shift at 0700. I went home and ate a can of beans with hot sauce. I went to bed and read for a while and finally went to sleep.

UNMIK POLICE PRESS UPDATE
09 OCTOBER, 2000
PRISTINA Region
FORCED PROSTITUTION
Kosovo Polje– 08/10 – 0100 hrs. Two K-Serb females were taken into police custody after they stated that they were forced into prostitution at a newly opened strip club.
POLITICAL RALLIES
Stimlje Village, Lipljan – 08/10 – 1720 hrs. Approximately 100 people attended a rally held by the PDK party.
Pristina – 08/10 – 1200 hrs. Approximately 250 persons attended a rally held by the PQLK party at the "ABC THEATRE".
GRENADE ATTACK
Shtime Village, Lipljan – 07/10 – 2030 hrs. Unknown person(s) threw a grenade, which exploded between a K-Roma residence and the KFOR Camp, causing minor damage to the front window of the house.
POLITICAL RALLIES
PDK RALLIES
Pristina – 07/10 – 1200 hrs. Approximately 300 persons attended a peaceful political rally at the Ismail Qemajli School.
Novo Rujce Village, Lipljan – 07/10 – 1700 hrs. Approximately 150 people attended an unauthorized meeting.

LDK RALLIES
Janjevo Village, Lipljan – 07/10 – 1200 hrs. Approximately 250 persons attended a political meeting.
Oklap Village, Lipljan - 07/10 – 1430 hrs. About 100 persons attended a political meeting.
Muzeqine Village, Lipljan – 07/10 – 1400 hrs. Approximately 150 people attended the meeting.
AAK RALLIES
Sharban Village, Pristina - 07/10 – 1500 hrs. About 35 people attended a political meeting.
Podujevo – 07/10 – 1200 hrs. Approximately 250 people attended a political meeting.
GNJILANE Region
POLITICAL RALLY
Vitina/Slatina – 07/10 – 1430 hrs. Approximately 500 members of the LDK party attended a political rally, which ended peacefully at 1650 hrs.
PRIZREN Region
HUMAN REMAINS FOUND
Dollovce – 07/10 – 1530 hrs. UNMIK Police found remains of human skeletons in the west part of Dollovce village.

Monday, 9 October, 2000

I got up at 1300. I ate some noodles and visited with Craig. I played a few games of solitaire. I went to the internet café with Craig and checked my e-mail. I went back to the house and watch a movie (in English this time) on the satellite. I went in to work at 2300. The weather was cool but there was no rain. We patrolled most of the shift. There was nothing going on tonight again. We only wrote a couple of citations. At about 0400 we noticed someone moving around in the darkness near a mosque. The mosque is one of the oldest in the area, about 400 years old. Places of worship have been the target of bombings. Serbian churches have been targeted the most and KFOR has static security on most of them. We made contact with the individuals and found them to be local bakers. They were getting water to make their morning bread. The problem is that they were getting the water from the mosque foot washing trough. I will never eat the local bread again! I got off work at 0700. I came home and ate oatmeal and then went to bed to read. Twenty days left to work until CTO.

P.S. Brent returned from his CTO in Greece.

UNMIK POLICE PRESS UPDATE
10 OCTOBER, 2000
PRISTINA Region
POLITICAL RALLY
Batllave Village, Podujevo – 09/10. Approximately 300 people attended a rally held by the PDK party.
GNJILANE Region
KIDNAPPING / RAPE
Kmetovee Village, Gnjilane – 05/10 – 1800 hrs. A 14 year old K-Albanian female reported being kidnapped and raped by a known K-Albanian male. The suspect was arrested by UNMIK Police.
LAND MINE
Kmetovee Village, Gnjilane – 09/10 – 1225 hrs. A K-Albanian male reported seeing some K-Serb boys planting a land mine on a road. UNMIK Police responded and observed a possible fuse. KFOR EOD was notified and disposed of the object.

Tuesday, 10 October, 2000

I fell asleep at 0800 but woke up at 1100. I ate a can of tuna with a cup of coffee. I talked with Craig for awhile. I went back to bed at 1400. I got up at 1600 and ate some noodles. I watched a movie with Craig. Ken and John made some soft shell tacos for everyone so I ate again. I went in to work at 2300. I had four KPS officers with me tonight. The weather was a little warmer tonight. I gave Ken and John a ride to work at Main HQ at 2330. There was absolutely nothing going on tonight. We wrote one citation. Ekrem Vlasa wanted to drive to get some practice for his U.N. driving test next week. I let him drive for a few hours. We caught some "parkers" on Germia Road. The male spoke English and had apparently been to the States. There have been many reports of rapes on Germia road so we checkout all "parkers" to make sure the females are there by there own choice. When we got this male out of the vehicle he said, in English, "This is Bullshit! This is a violation of my constitutional rights!" I said, "Oh, really?" He then said how he had been to the United States and knew that we were violating his rights. I made it very clear to him that we were NOT in the United States, he was NOT an American citizen, and that, as of yet, Kosovo had NO constitution for us to violate. He changed his tune pretty quick. After this stop there was a report of an armed robbery in the Station #1 area. We looked for the suspect vehicle for over an hour but never located it. I got off work at 0700. I ate a leftover taco and went to bed and read. Only nineteen shifts left to work until CTO.

P.S. Randy got back tonight from CTO. I am still working on getting Shannon, Ken, and John re-deployed to Station #2. There was also an explosion in Craig's area (Obilic/Kosovo Polje) at a little before 0500.

UNMIK POLICE PRESS UPDATE
11 OCTOBER, 2000
PRISTINA Region
EXPLOSION
Kosovo Polje, White Flats – 11/10 – 0455 hrs. An unknown person called UNMIK Police and reported an explosion at a nightclub. UNMIK Police officers responding to the scene observed minor property damages in the premises. At the time of the explosion the establishment was unoccupied, no injuries were reported.
GNJILANE Region
SOLICITING FOR PROSTITUTION
Radivojce Village, Vitina – 10/10 – 1920 hrs. A female of unknown ethnicity was arrested for solicitation of prostitution.
EXPLOSION
Kamenica – 10/10 – 2035 hrs. Unknown person(s) threw a hand grenade at a K-Serb residence. The grenade exploded on the front porch and caused minor property damage.
MITROVICA Region
CRIMINAL DAMAGE / ARSON
Mitrovica South – 10/10 – 1955 hrs. A British male national reported that while driving an NGO "Assemblies of God" motor vehicle, two unknown males stopped him, got inside and then directed him to a destination where they ordered him to leave the vehicle. Afterwards the suspects burned the car. While in the car the suspects told the victim that he should leave Kosovo as Christians are not needed.

Wednesday, 11 October, 2000

I woke up today at 1300. I ate noodles for breakfast. I sat around and talked with Craig for a while. I played many games of solitaire. I shaved and showered early just in case the water goes off. Thommy and Joe (The German Police Officers that we work with at Station #2) stopped by to visit. We discussed the PFTO program. I went in to work at 2300. I gave Ken and John a ride into work again. The KPS got new citation books issued but no accompanying code books. The KPS officers are upset about the new traffic code they are supposed to use on their citations. It reflects the old Yugoslavian law code numbers. The Albanian KPS officers do not want to have anything to do with Yugoslavia. It was a very, very quiet night. There was absolutely nothing going on. I stopped by Main HQ to see Ken and John. I took my KPS for a tour of Main HQ. Ken and John gave a quick class on defensive tactics. I got off work at 0700. I got a ride home from Ekrem.

UNMIK POLICE PRESS UPDATE
12 OCTOBER, 2000
PRISTINA Region
THEFT
Pristina – 11/10 – 2228 hrs. A female employee of the United Nations reported that unknown persons stole a U.N. 4WD vehicle while it was parked at her residence during the night.
POLITICAL RALLIES/MEETING
Pristina – 11/10. Approximately 60 people attended a peaceful LNDSH political meeting.
Sfeqel, Podujevo – 11/10. A group of about 250 people attended a peaceful PDK political rally
Bajqina, Podujevo – 11/10. Approximately 300 people attended a peaceful LDK political meeting.
GNJILANE Region
THREATS/INTIMIDATION
Vitina Town – 10/10 – 1730 hrs. The K-Albanian male Municipal President was threatened with a gun by another K-Albanian male, who was upset that he was not hired for a job with the municipality.

Thursday, 12 October, 2000

I got up today at 1630. I still feel tired. I ate noodles for breakfast. I played a game of solitaire again. The water was off so I washed

my hair with a bar of soap and a bottle of water. I went to the internet café to chat with Carnita and read the news. There is more fighting in Israel and Bush is in the lead in the Polls.
Reggie Godwin came back from CTO in Skopje, Macedonia. He bought two guitars. I asked him to pick one up for me. It was 270DM. I played my new guitar until 2200 and then had to get ready for work. I patrolled tonight with four KPS officers: Visar, Ekrem, Vjosa, and Rame. We towed one vehicle and wrote two citations. We had one call of vandalism to a vehicle. It was a very slow work load but I had a good time with the KPS. I got off at 0700. I went home and played a couple of games of solitaire and then played my guitar. I have to be at a PFTO meeting at 1500. I went to bed and read. I could not sleep so I got back up.

P.S. The weather is starting to cool off. It was a clear night with a full moon.

UNMIK POLICE PRESS UPDATE
13 OCTOBER, 2000
PRISTINA Region
ROCKET ATTACK
Mali Alas Village, Lipljan – 12/10 – 2050 hrs. Unknown person(s) attacked the third floor of a three-storied K-Roma house with a rocket launcher. Nobody was injured as the family was on the ground floor when the attack took place.
PUBLIC UNREST
Obilic, Kosovo Polje – 12/10 – 1100 hrs. Approximately 40 K-Serbs protested in front of the Police station against the arrest of two K-Serbs, who were earlier detained for trying to prevent efforts by UNMIK Police to accommodate a K-Serbian KPS Officer in a vacant apartment. The crowd only dispersed when the decision to accommodate the officer was reversed and the detainees released.
GNJILANE Region
UXO/MINE
Muzeqine Village, Urosevac – 12/10 – 0935 hrs. A K-Albanian male flagged down an UNMIK Police patrol unit and reported that he was in possession of a hand grenade which he had picked up on the roadside. KFOR EOD was notified and took possession of the ordnance.
MITROVICA Region

VIP VISIT
12/10. The King of Belgium visited the KFOR bases in the town of Leposavic and the surrounding area. The King arrived at 1140 hours and departed at 1450 hours.
PEC Region
MURDER
Batusa Village, Dakovica – 12/10 – 1215 hrs. During a dispute a K-Albanian male shot two other K-Albanian males, killing one and causing minor injury to the other. The suspect was arrested by UNMIK Police and the second victim was treated at the hospital.

Friday, 13 October, 2000

I stayed awake until my 1500 meeting. I am not feeling very well at all. I haven't been getting enough sleep. This schedule is a killer. I feel very run down. I went to the meeting and there was not much going on. I really could not get into the meeting because I felt so bad. I wish I could have a day off more often that every thirty days. I went back home and tried to sleep. I slept about three hours. I went in to work feeling awful. There was not much going on. During a traffic stop I had to intervene and handcuff an Albanian male for not obeying the KPS officers. I had to give a short lesson on taking and keeping control of the situation. The KPS were reluctant to be more aggressive with this guy because he was a former UCK soldier, apparently well known, and had been wounded. He was obviously still recovering from his wounds. I told the KPS that they could take the guy into custody or just cite and release him. I made it very clear that no matter who he was he had to give respect to them as the police. They decided to let him go with a citation and a warning. I felt sick so I had my KPS drop me off at the house at 0400. They will follow Randy for the rest of the shift. I went to bed and slept until noon but I still feel awful. One more night shift to go.

P.S. Craig went and paid for our plane tickets today. We are all set to go home. Tomorrow is my sixteenth wedding anniversary as well as Colt's thirteenth birthday.

UNMIK POLICE PRESS UPDATE
14 OCTOBER, 2000
PRISTINA Region

ATTEMPTED MURDER
Lipljan Town 13/10 – 1930 hrs. Unknown person(s) attacked a K-Serbian occupied residence with a rocket launcher. Remnants of the rocket were located inside the residence. The weapon was found approximately 100 meters away from the residence.
POLITICAL RALLY
Lipljan Football Stadium – 13/10 – 1300 hrs. Approximately 250 persons attended a peaceful rally held by the PRK Party.
Barilevo Village, Pristina – 1500 hrs. Approximately 175 persons attended a peaceful rally held by the AAK Party.
Lipljan Agriculture Building – 12/10 – 1400 hrs. Approximately 100 persons attended a peaceful rally held by the PLK Party.
Stimlje Village – 12/10 – 1400 hrs. Approximately 50 persons attended a peaceful rally held by the PQLK Party.
PRIZREN Region
EXPLOSION
Prizren – 13/10 – 0356 hrs. The sound of a loud explosion was heard near the UNMIK Police Station. KFOR and UNMIK Police responded to the area but nothing was found.
GNJILANE Region
UXO/FOUND
Urosevac Town – 12/10 – 2145 hrs. A K-Albanian male reported that children found an UXO while playing in the field. KFOR EOD confirmed it to be a mortar round and disposed of the ordnance.
MITROVICA Region
ABANDONED INFANT
Mitrovica South – 13/10 – 0725 hrs. A K-Albanian male found an abandoned infant of unknown ethnicity at a construction site. The infant was taken to Pristina hospital.

Saturday, 14 October, 2000

I got up at noon feeling like crap. I ate some rice and watched a movie. I need to get word to Carnita to be on the chat. Today is our sixteenth anniversary and Colter's thirteenth birthday. I went to the internet café and sent e-mails to Carnita for our anniversary and to Colter for his birthday. Carnita was not on line. I stayed for one hour. I used Brent's cell phone to call home but I got the answering machine. I went back to the house and went to bed at 1600. I slept until 2000 and then got up and went in to work at

2300. Nothing was happening at work tonight. It was very slow and quiet. We had no calls and wrote no citations. I dropped everyone off at 0600. I went home and went straight to bed. I have to be back at work by 1500. I am starting to feel a little better but am still exhausted. I got an e-mail from Carnita. She is worried about me being so worn out.

Sunday, 15 October, 2000

I got up at noon. I am feeling better. I am concerned about the U.N. operation of this mission and how we rotate shifts. I went to the internet café about one hour before work. I read my e-mails and sent some home. I went in to work at 1500. I had to help a new American officer get organized. Everything at the station was screwed up today. I patrolled our AOR and helped the traffic unit work an auto v. pedestrian accident. The victim is not expected to make it. It was a hit and run accident. The tag number of the suspect vehicle is 106KS700. It was a red Zastava car. There was blood and debris spread over a hundred yards. I got off shift at 2300. I went home and watched a movie with my roommates. I played my guitar until about 0300.

E-mail from Colter

Hey dad,
How are you? Well, I'm a teenager now and that's pretty cool. Me, Mom, Josiah and Levi went to Costco today and I bought a computer game with my birthday money. The game is called "Delta Force II". I haven't installed it yet because we have been waiting for you to come on line to chat with Mom. The game is like “Rainbow Six” and it’s a lot cooler because you can be under water and you can jump out of airplanes in parachutes and they have really cool weapons and they fight terrorists. That’s all. See you later dad.
Love, Colter

UNMIK POLICE PRESS UPDATE
16 OCTOBER, 2000
PRISTINA Region
ILLEGAL POSSESSION OF WEAPONS

Pristina – 14/10. A joint search conducted by UNMIK Police and KFOR of 13 homes in Pristina resulted in the arrest of twenty-seven individuals, sixteen of whom were female prostitutes and nine others related to high priority murder and serious crime cases. Also confiscated were eleven pistols, four rifles, one shotgun, detonators, rocket propelled grenade parts, silencers, ammunition, a computer, video equipment and a large amount of currency.

MINE EXPLOSION

Janina Voda Village, Kosovo Polje – 15/10 – 1945 hrs. A K-Serb male was instantly killed and another seriously injured, when the tractor they were driving ran over and detonated an anti-tank mine. The surviving victim was taken to a KFOR hospital in Pristina.

GRENADE ATTACK

Stimlje Village, Lipljan – 14/10 – 2055 hrs. Unknown person(s) threw two hand grenades at an occupied K-Roma residence.

MITROVICA Region

THREATS/INTIMIDATION

Mitrovica North – 15/10 – 1800 hrs. A Turkish female reported that three K-Albanians went to her residence in the Serb area and threatened to bomb her flat because she was living with K-Serbs.

Monday, 16 October, 2000

I got up today at 1100. The water is still on so I got shaved and a shower. I ate some oatmeal and watched a movie. I went back to bed for an hour and then in to work at 1500. I patrolled our AOR with three KPS officers. When it got dark I took them to the end of Germia Road and let them each fire two rounds by the light of our blue rotator and with flashlights. The KPS have had no practical firearms training and are not issued any practice ammo. I have to replace the rounds with my own. I can get replacement rounds off the "black market" in town. We found the suspect vehicle from yesterday's hit and run. The car was hidden and abandoned at the end of Ramiz- Zudiku Road. A passing British Royal Marine patrol stopped to assist. I found a small bag of what appeared to be cocaine inside the car. I notified the traffic unit and towed the vehicle. I went home and ate fresh garlic toast for supper. I played the guitar for a while and then went to bed and read. The power was out for about an hour or two. The internet has been down also. I need to chat with Carnita soon. I can't wait for CTO in Montana.

P.S. I forgot to tell you about the land mine casualties from 15 October. A tractor hit a land mine in Obilic and killed one and wounded another. This is in Craig's AOR. The mine was planted to stop the victim from stealing coal from the coal plant. It did!

UNMIK POLICE PRESS UPDATE
17 OCTOBER, 2000
PEC Region
MURDER
Piskota Village, Dakovica – 16/10 – 1820 hrs. Unknown person(s) shot a K-Albanian male in the chest while he was at the market. The victim was transported to the hospital where he was pronounced dead.
Rugova Village, Dakovica – 16/10 – 2130 hrs. An unknown person shot and killed a K-Albanian male.
HUMAN REMAINS FOUND
Croklez Village, Istok – 16/10 – 2200 hrs. The bones of a 28-year-old K-Albanian male, who was reported missing since 25/08/00, were discovered in a field approximately 300 meters away from his residence.

Tuesday, 17 October, 2000

Not much going on today. Same old thing again. I went into work at 1500. I had to wait for an hour to get a vehicle. We patrolled our AOR, wrote five citations, and towed a vehicle for having no documents. The vehicle was a dump truck. We had a new KPS officer with us tonight. He is not one of my usual KPS officers and is usually on another shift. We went out on Germia Road and made a traffic stop. My usual KPS officers have gotten to know that I have a sense of humor and wanted me to mess with the new guy. I told the new kid that it was his turn to make contact with the stopped driver. He asked what he was supposed to do. I told him, "Go kill him." The new officer never blinked. He turned around, unsnapped his holster and started toward the driver. I had to grab the kid and tell him I was just kidding. He was going to go shoot the driver. I will never make that mistake again! I took the opportunity for some remedial training. I got off work at 2300. I went home and ate some soup and watched a movie. I went to bed about 0200.

UNMIK POLICE PRESS UPDATE
18 OCTOBER, 2000
PRISTINA Region
POLITICAL RALLY / DISTURBANCE
Stimlje, Lipljan – 17/10 – 1320 hrs. Seven K-Albanians were arrested when a group of PDK supporters attempted to disrupt a LDK political rally (approx. 900 people) that was held near the Municipality building. KFOR and UNMIK Police had to use batons and pepper spray to contain the situation.
PRIZREN Region
DEMONSTRATION
Suva Reka Town – 17/10 – 1200 hrs. An unknown number of people attended a peaceful demonstration organized by the "Prisoner Association" against the ongoing detention of K-Albanians in Serbian prisons.
GNJILANE Region
ATTEMPTED MURDER
Shurdhan Village, Vitina – 17/10 – 1200 hrs. Four K-Albanian males reported that a K-Albanian male assaulted them by throwing two grenades at them. While UNMIK Police officers were investigating the case, another K-Albanian male shot at the officers and the victims with an automatic rifle without hitting or injuring anyone. Two K-Albanian male suspects were arrested by UNMIK Police.

Wednesday, 18 October, 2000

I got up at about 1100. I went to the internet café before work to check my e-mail. I sent a message to Carnita. I went in to work at 1500. Not much going on. I stopped a lot of vehicles but wrote no citations. There is a big problem brewing with the KPS. The new citations were issued and they have been instructed to write a statute code "SFRY 50/88" on all the citations. This is a Yugoslavian code number (SFRY-Socialist Federal Republic of Yugoslavia) and some of the Albanian KPS officers are refusing to use it. This is going to be a big problem for the U.N. It might even screw up this whole mission. Personally, I agree with the KPS. Kosovo does not want to be a part of Serbia or Yugoslavia. We should not force them to write citations using a communist law code that they do not want to be ruled by. If I voice my opinion to the wrong people I could be sent back to the U.S. It is going to be interesting to see how this turns out.

E-mail home

Hi Hun,
Sorry I haven't e-mailed in a few days. This shift is so hard to get anything done on. It is too early back home to chat before my shift and too late here for me to stay up. We are looking into getting a phone line at the house to use the Internet from there. It should be cheaper in the long run. This working every day is a killer, especially with the weekly rotation. I need more rest and some time off. Did you get your check on time? Craig's got sent to Chris Martin's account in Idaho. He just got it figured out with the company today. His wife still does not have her check. How is everything at home? I can't wait to get there. These last few days have been really dragging. It seems like CTO will never get here. All I do is work, eat and sleep. I still haven't gotten any e-mail from the office. Tell Brent to e-mail me with an update on what's going on. Is Darren still leaving? I know Scott is. How are they going to replace them? There are grant requirements to replace the officers in a timely manner. The City can't avoid replacing them. I need to be involved in what's going on but I refuse to spend my vacation at home doing work stuff. I am coming home to be with you and the kids. We are going to have to plan to be out of town most of the CTO to avoid people. Maybe we can stay a couple nights in Kalispell? Well, it's getting close to time for me to go to work. I came down the hill early to check the mail and send you a letter to let you know I am still alive. I don't know when we will be able to chat again. Probably not until I switch to days on Sunday. If we can't communicate until then let's set the date for Sunday at 1000 your time. Sorry it has been so hard for me to communicate this week. I need a day off. Only twelve more shifts until CTO. I am taking the 30th off to travel to Skopje with Craig. Our flight is at 0700 on the 31st. I can't wait. Well, I need to get going. Hug and kiss all the kids for me. I love and miss you so much. Write and let me know how you are. So long for now. Yours forever and always, Clay

Thursday, 19 October, 2000

I got up today at 1100. I ate rice and fruit cocktail from a can. I watched a movie and then went to work at 1500. I had a meeting with my shift of KPS officers about the statute code issue. They understand the issue and will write it in even though they oppose it. Some of the KPS officers that are out on their own are refusing to write the Yugoslavian code and are telling the other KPS officers to do the same. Most of the first groups of KPS officers are all former UCK (KLA). The weather was cold and rainy tonight. We only wrote two citations. Dennis Clark, one of the U.S. PFTOs on my shift got called to the company building for an emergency. His father-in-law had a heart attack and is not expected to live. He is leaving tomorrow on emergency leave to the U.S. That leaves only me on my shift as a PFTO. I got off at 2300. I went to the internet café and checked my e-mail.

P.S. The power went off around midnight. I had to make this entry by flashlight and candle. I can't wait to get home.

E-mail home

Hi Hun,
It's after 2300 and I just got off shift and came down to check the mail. I am counting the days until I can be with you. Not much new to tell over e-mail. I hope the kids are well and good. I will have souvenirs for all when I get home. I am glad to hear you got the check on time. It should be every 28 days like clockwork from now on. Craig's got screwed up. They sent his check to Chris Martin's account in Idaho by mistake. I think it is fixed now though. Well, I need to check and see if you might be on line and then go back up the hill to go to bed. Love and miss you very much. Yours always and forever, Clay

P.S. 12 days to go

UNMIK POLICE PRESS UPDATE
20 OCTOBER, 2000
PRISTINA Region
UNAUTHORIZED POLITICAL MEETING
Stimlje Village, Lipljan 19/10 – 1700 hrs. Approximately 110 people attended an unauthorized PK political meeting at the Municipality building. No incidents were reported.

LDK PARTY

Kosovo Polje Town – 19/10 – 1700 hrs. Approximately 70 people attended a peaceful meeting addressed by the local leader Rexhep Kelani.

GNJILANE Region

VEHICULAR HOMICIDE

Donja Gralica Village, Urosevac - 18/10 – 1130 hrs. A vehicle operated by a K-Albanian driver struck a pedestrian on the Pristina-Skopje highway. The pedestrian died because of his injuries. The driver was arrested and taken to Bondsteel Detention Center.

UXO FOUND

Kamenica Town – 20/10 – 0015 hrs. A K-Albanian male reported that he found a hand grenade lying on the ground beside his gas station. KFOR EOD was notified and disposed of the ordnance.

POLITICAL RALLY

The Republican Party of Kosovo, Vitina unit, held a political meeting in Vitina. 500 attended. The meeting was peaceful.

MITROVICA Region

MURDER

Mirace Village, Vucitrn – 19/10 – 1700 hrs. A K-Serbian male was found dead under a tree in an open field. The body was transported to Pristina hospital for an autopsy to determine the cause of death.

SUICIDE

Mitrovica North – 19/10 – 2200 hrs. A KFOR soldier fatally shot himself.

Friday, 20 October, 2000

I got up at 1100 again. I ate left over rice. I got the three "Sierras" out of the way while the water was still on. I watched a movie and then played a game of solitaire on my laptop. I actually won! I went in to work at 1500. There were changes again today. KPS class numbers 8 and 9 are going to training. I had three KPS officers and a L.A. today. The weather was rather cool at the beginning of the shift and turned off cold by the end. I assisted on an injury accident on Germia Road at about 2200. There was a cold wind blowing tonight. Earlier in the shift we saw a fox on Germia Road in the rubble of a bombed out hotel that had been used as a Serbian military HQ. Germia Road is the "make out" spot of Pristina. There are twenty to thirty “parkers” every night. I took all of my KPS officers home at the end of shift to save them the bus fare. I got home about 2330. I visited with the guys for a while and then went up to my room to read before going to sleep. I am counting down the days until CTO.

UNMIK POLICE PRESS UPDATE
21 OCTOBER, 2000
PRISTINA Region
ILLEGAL POSSESSION OF WEAPONS
Gornje Gadimlje – 20/10 – 1910 hrs. Two K-Albanian males were arrested after a combined team of UNMIK Police and KFOR discovered four hand grenades, six rifles, twelve shotguns, and 2,500 rounds of ammunition.
UXO FOUND
Terdeve Village, Glogovac – 20/10 – 0830 hrs. A K-Albanian male delivered an anti-personnel mine to the UNMIK Police Station. KFOR EOD disposed of the device.
GNJILANE Region
GRENADE ATTACK
Vitina Town, – 20/10 – 1900 hrs. A shop owned by a K-Serbian male was the target of a grenade attack. Three K-Serbs were injured by the explosion and transported to Camp Bondsteel for treatment. A K-Albanian male who was implicated in the attack was arrested.
PEC/PEJA Region
AUTO THEFT
Pec Town – 19/10. A Swedish national working for OSCE reported that unknown persons stole his vehicle overnight.
MITROVICA Region
SHOOTING
Serbica Town – 20/10 – 2000 to 2045 hrs. A KFOR commander reported that two of his checkpoints were fired upon.

Saturday, 21 October, 2000

Last swing shift this week. I went in to work at 1500. I set up a VCP on Ramiz-Zudiku Road near the student center. The first car we stopped had no documents and had to be towed. The driver was uncooperative and would not get out of the vehicle. The guy was giving the KPS officer a hard time and refused to exit his vehicle. I told the L.A. to tell the guy *exactly* what I was saying. I told the guy he could get out of the vehicle or I was going to pull him out through the wing vent and kick his ass. He got out. I assisted in the stop of a suspect vehicle that was supposed to have an armed and wanted subject. There were no bad guys on board. I got involved in an attempted rape on Germia Road. The guy tried to rape his "girl friend". He is married. He hit her in the face and she jumped out of a vehicle. I arrested the suspect and towed his vehicle. I got home about midnight. I have to be up at 0600 for day shift. I read until about 0100.

P.S. The weather has turned cold with a stiff, cold wind.

Sunday, 22 October, 2000

I got up at 0530. I washed my hair, brushed my teeth and made a breakfast of oatmeal and coffee. I went in to work at 0700. I went and washed the vehicle at a car wash owned by one of the KPS officer's family, Ekrem Vlasa. I assisted on a hit and run accident on Germia Road involving a U.N. vehicle. The U.N. vehicle fled the scene of the accident. The KPS found the vehicle at the restaurant near the end of the road. U.N. security was called. I went to turn in tomorrow's schedule and the KPS coordinator needed my vehicle. I got stuck with the jail van. It is worthless for patrol. I helped the shift leader get organized with manpower and vehicles. I got off work at 1500. I went to chat with Carnita but she was not on line. I went home and went to bed.

UNMIK POLICE PRESS UPDATE
23 OCTOBER, 2000
PRISTINA Region
SHOOTING
Pristina - 22 /10 – 0400 hrs. An apparent dispute resulted in numerous shots being fired at the Miami Beach Club. No injuries were reported. A patron's vehicle was slightly damaged as a result of the gunfire.
ILLEGAL POSSESSION OF WEAPONS
Pristina – 21/10 – 1420 hrs. A K-Albanian male was arrested after his vehicle was stopped at a checkpoint by KFOR. The suspect was found to be in possession of a 7.65 mm machine gun and two magazines containing 31 rounds of ammunition, one 7.62 caliber

pistol with two magazines containing thirteen rounds and one Sig Sauer 9 mm pistol with one magazine containing 9 rounds of ammunition. The suspect was arrested and the weapons were seized.

CHLORINE GAS LEAKAGE

Kosovo Polje Town – 22/10 – 0030 hrs. KFOR reported a chlorine gas leak at a factory located close to a barracks which houses refugees. Six refugees were taken to hospital for treatment of nausea and minor breathing problems.

POLITICAL MEETING

Pristina – 21/10 – 1400 hrs. Approximately 200 people attended a peaceful PDK party meeting at the movie theater.

POLITICAL RALLIES

Gadimlje Village - 22/10 - 1230 hrs. The PDK party held a political rally. No incidents reported.

Lipijan Football Stadium – 22/10 - 1500 hrs. The LDK party held a political rally. No incidents reported.

Petrova Village - 22/10 - 1700 hrs. The PDK party held a political rally. No incidents reported.

GNJILANE Region

ABDUCTI0N

Kacanik Town – 1400 hrs. A K-Albanian male was forced at gunpoint by another K-Albanian male to go to the village Vila. According to the witnesses the suspect was armed with an AK-47, several hand grenades and several mines. KFOR responded to the scene together with UNMIK Police and the hostage situation was resolved.

POLITICAL MEETINGS/RALLIES

Gnjilane Town - 22/10 – 1115 hrs. The LDK party held a political rally in Gnjilane. 13,000 people attended.

Kamenica Town - 22/10 – 0900 hrs. The LDK party held a political rally in Kamenica. 3,000 people attended.

Vitina Town - 20/10 – 1500 hrs. Approximately 80 people attended a peaceful LDK party meeting at the school compound.

PRIZREN Region

Globocica - 22/10. 1700-1835 hrs. SDK political party held a meeting. 20 people attended.

Globocica - 22/10. 1835-1900 hrs. GIG political party held a meeting. 20 people attended.

PEC Region

SHOOTING/GUNFIRE

Dakovica Town – 22/10 – 0050 hrs. Two K- Albanian males were arrested by UNMIK Police after they observed one of the suspects firing a handgun into the air. A second K-Albanian suspect was arrested after he attempted to intervene in the arrest of the first suspect. An UNMIK Officer received minor injuries to his left knee during the arrest.

GRENADE ATTACK

Dakovica Town 22/10 – 0230 hrs. A K-Albanian member of the LDK party reported that an unknown person threw a hand grenade at his home. Minor damage to the windows was reported. There were no injuries to the victim.

Dakovica Town 22/10 – 0130 hrs. A K-Albanian reported that an unknown person threw a hand grenade at his home damaging the door and telephone box.

UXO FOUND

Dakovica Town – 22/10 – 0230 hrs. A local leader of the LDK party found an unexploded hand grenade in the rear garden of his home. The device was defused by EOD.

Monday, 23 October, 2000

I got up at 0530. I feel awful. My left ear and throat are hurting again. I decided not to go into work today. I gargled with hot salt water. I kept cotton in my ear all day. I took a nap. I went to the company building to see "Doc". He was not in. I went to the store for some toothpaste and a little food. I went to chat with Carnita. We talked for an hour. They closed the street in front of the internet café because of a bomb threat. There was a suspicious package in the road. I went back home and went to bed at 2100.

P.S. I got woke up at 2200 by a big explosion. It really rocked the house. I wonder if the package down the street was a bomb after all.

UNMIK POLICE PRESS UPDATE

24 OCTOBER, 2000

PRISTINA Region

EXPLOSION

Pristina – 23/10 – 2215 hrs. A Serbian building was damaged by an apparent rocket attack by unknown persons. No injuries were reported. There was minor damage to the building.

SUDDEN DEATH
Pristina – 23/10 – 1800 hrs. A Swedish International was found dead in his vehicle of an apparent cardiac arrest.
GNJILANE Region
ATTEMPTED RAPE
Kamenica Town – 23/10 – 0800 hrs. It was reported that a K-Serbian male attempted to rape an eight-year old K-Serbian male juvenile.
PRIZREN Region
ASSAULT
Spinadja Village, Prizren 23/10 – 0745 hrs. A KPS cadet and his son were assaulted while enroute to the Prizren Police Station. There were two suspects, at least one of whom was armed with a weapon. The KPS cadet fired his service weapon, striking one suspect in the left leg. Minor injuries were reported to the son of the KPS cadet. The wounded suspect was transported to hospital for medical treatment and is reported in satisfactory condition. The incident is under investigation, but preliminary findings indicate the KPS cadet acted in self-defense.

Tuesday, 24 October, 2000

I got up at 0500. I still feel bad. I ate a pop tart with coffee. I went in to work at 0630. I had to reorganize the schedule. I found out that the explosion I heard last night was from an RPG (Rocket Propelled Grenade) that was fired at a Serb apartment a couple of blocks down the street from here. One of the Bulgarian officers at our station was living there with a Serb. No one was there at the time of the attack. I assisted on an auto v. pedestrian accident today. I also worked traffic control for an hour. I got off at 1500. I went home and ate. I used Ken's phone to call home. Carnita was not there. I talked to Courtni. I told her to tell Carnita that I would chat tomorrow. I am not feeling well enough to make the trip to the internet café. I got to bed a little after 1900. I read for a while and watched some TV. I only have five more shifts to work until CTO. I can't wait. I am ready to see my family.

UNMIK POLICE PRESS UPDATE
25 OCTOBER, 2000
PRISTINA Region
MURDER

Pristina - 24 /10 – 0040 hrs. A K-Albanian male was found lying in the roadway suffering from gunshot wounds. He was transported to hospital where he later died.
DEATH
Pristina – 24/10 – 1640 hrs. A K-Albanian female collapsed while walking on the street. She was transported to hospital where she was pronounced dead of apparent heart failure.
POLITICAL MEETING
Pristina – 21/10 – 1400 hrs. Approximately 200 people attended a peaceful PDK party meeting at the movie theater.
GNJILANE Region
EXPLOSION
Vitina Town - 24/10-2005 hrs. An explosion totally destroyed the home of a K-Albanian male.
PROSTITUTION
Urosevac Town – 24/10 – 1000 hrs. A Moldavian female was found to have been forced into prostitution by a K-Albanian male.

Wednesday, 25 October, 2000

I got up at 0500. Coffee, oatmeal, and off to work. The schedule is all screwed up today. Some KPS are in unscheduled training today and some are needed for the shift at the station. I ended up with one KPS officer and no L.A. We went out for a while but there was a political rally turned riot in Lipiljan. Station #2 got put on standby for the riot. We never got called to go. I got off on time at 1500. I went to the internet café and chatted with Carnita for an hour. I went home, ate, and went to bed. I can't wait to get home. Only four more shifts.

UNMIK POLICE PRESS UPDATE
26 OCTOBER, 2000
PRISTINA Region
CIVIL UNREST
Lipiljan Town – 25/10 - 1210 hrs. A PDK rally was held at the Lipiljan Stadium where members of the rally became unruly after being directed by police to use only one street for foot traffic. Party members assaulted officers and two "PDK" party members were arrested.
Lipiljan Town – 25/10 – 1100 hrs. The LDK party held a political rally at the Lipljan Stadium where approximately 2,200 people

attended. After receiving directions from police on foot traffic direction, the crowd became unruly and assaulted two police officers. Two party members were arrested.
GNJILANE Region
GRENADE ATTACKS
Urosevac Town – 25/10 – 0745 hrs. An inhabited K-Albanian residence was the target of a grenade attack. UNMIK Police responded to the scene and found a male victim unharmed. The home suffered extensive damage. The suspect is a known K-Albanian male.
Vitina Town – 25/10 – 0600 hrs. A K-Serbian home was damage by a grenade attack and gunfire. No injuries were reported and only minor damage was done to the home.
MITROVICA Region
ASSAULT
Mitrovica North – (Date/Time not reported). A K-Albanian male reported being attacked by six K-Serbian males. The victim was injured and stayed overnight at the hospital.

Thursday, 26 October, 2000

I'm counting down until CTO to home. I was off to work at 0700. We patrolled our AOR. I worked one accident and a burglary of a motor vehicle. There was a huge PDK rally in town today. About 35,000 people were there. Luckily it was not in our AOR but we were on standby again. The rally went OK. There were no major problems. It was a pretty slow shift. I took several pictures today. The pollution is really awful. I got my MSA today. 5,134DM. I got off work at 1500. I kind of got a headache from not eating enough. I only had two pop tarts all day. I made some noodles and ate. I watched a movie with John. I got to bed at 1930. I watched the last of a police movie on T.V., read for a while and then went to sleep. Three more shifts to pull until CTO. I can't wait.

P.S. We had a bomb threat in front of station #4. We had to evacuate and call EOD. There was a suspicious car that supposedly had a bomb in it. EOD blew up the car to be safe.

UNMIK POLICE PRESS UPDATE
27 OCTOBER, 2000
PRISTINA Region

GRENADE ATTACK

Vucitrn Village, Pristina – 26/10 – 2355 hrs. A building was damaged in a grenade attack by unknown person(s). Upon arrival of EOD, two unexploded grenades were found and disposed of.

BOMB THREATS

Pristina – 26/10 – 1258 hrs. An unknown male suspect called UNMIK Police Station #1 and stated that there was a bomb in the basement. The building was searched but no bomb was found.

Pristina – 26/10 – 1440 hrs. UNMIK Police located an abandoned vehicle where a bomb was located in the rear seat. EOD was called to the scene where a controlled explosion was conducted.

POLITICAL MEETINGS

Pristina – 26/10 – 1330 hrs. The PDK party held a political rally where approximately 35,000 people were in attendance.

GNJILANE Region

ATTEMPTED MURDER

Gnjilane – 25/10 – 2000 hrs. A K-Albanian male was assaulted and stabbed by two known K-Albanian males. The victim was reported in critical condition and has received blood donated by numerous KPS and UNMIK police officers.

THEFT

Pec – 25/10 – 1200 hrs. The NGO "Dutch Relief Rehabilitation Agency" reported the theft of a generator. The generator was located and a suspect was arrested.

POLITICAL RALLY

Klina Town – 26/10 – 1100 hrs. During a political rally, persons of the PDK Party threw stones and eggs at the stage. Minor injuries were reported.

MITROVICA Region

GRENADE ATTACK

Vucitrn Town – 26/10 – 2355 hrs. Unknown suspects threw grenades at a K-Albanian's residence. There was one person injured.

ASSAULT

Mitrovica North – 26/10 – 1200 hrs. A K-Albanian male was attacked by six K-Serbian males. The victim was transported to the hospital for treatment.

Friday, 27 October, 2000

I got up at 0530. I had instant decaf coffee and toast. We are out of bottled water. Tomorrow is water draw day. I have my own emergency stash, though. I went in to work at 0700. I have to take the Skoda today. I just had Visar and Ekrem with me today. We worked a false document case. A guy had a false Yugoslavian Driver's License. He gave a statement about how and where he got it. I did a report for the investigations division. I got off work at 1500. I have to be back in at 0600 for election detail. I went to eat with Craig at the Indian Inn restaurant. I had hot chicken curry and rice. It was very good. I went home and then to the internet café to chat but it was full. A very strong wind came up. I walked home and watched a western movie. I got into bed before 2100. I read for a while and then went to sleep. Two more shifts until CTO.

UNMIK POLICE PRESS UPDATE
28 OCTOBER, 2000
PRISTINA Region
ATTEMPTED MURDER/ROBBERY
Pollata Village, Podujevo - 27/10 - 2230 hrs. A K-Albanian male motorist reported being stopped on the roadway by two unknown males. The suspects forced the victim to drive to a remote location where he was robbed and his throat was slashed. The victim was transported to hospital for treatment.
GNJILANE Region
UXO MINE/GRENADE
Doganovic Village - 26/10 – 1815 hrs. A K-Albanian male found an anti-personnel mine in a field. EOD responded and disposed of the mine. No injuries were reported.
PRIZREN Region
EXPLOSION
Dushanova Village- 27/10 - 1430 hrs. An explosion injured three people who were clearing rubble. Damage to a vehicle was also reported. The nature of the incident has not been determined and is under investigation.

Saturday, 28 October, 2000

Today is election day. I got up at 0430. I ate a piece of cheese toast and coffee. There was no water this morning. I had a couple of bottles of saved water warming up on the electric heater to wash with. I went in to work at 0545. I had a one hour election briefing.

These are the first free elections for Kosovo. I was assigned to patrol with two KPS officers. Most of the others have been assigned static posts at the polling sites. I patrolled all the sites in my AOR. I had to go to one site for a VIP protection detail while one of the candidates voted. It was Ibrahim Rugova of the LDK party. He is expected to win the election for President of Kosovo. Today is the first time that I have worn my body armor. It is really heavy as it is a level IV with a heavy plate. There could be trouble because of the elections. I grabbed a passing British Royal Marine patrol and asked them to assist me with the VIP protection detail. They were more than happy to help. Rugova arrived in a big car and had several body guards as escorts. He went into the polling site, an elementary school, and cast his vote; I would assume for himself. I noticed a man come out of a top floor window of a nearby apartment building. He had something long and metallic in his hands that could have been a weapon. He was over a hundred yards away and it was difficult to make out what he had and what he was doing. I asked one of the British Royal Marines to take a closer look at him through the scope of his rifle. The Marine took a bead on the suspect and said that he had something that could be a rifle. He asked me if I wanted him to shoot the guy. I said if he could identify that he had a weapon and was pointing it in our direction that he could take him out. Just then the Marine said that it looked like the object was not a rifle but an antenna of some kind and the guy was trying to mount in on the building outside the window. We did not shoot him. As this conversation was taking place and the Marine was aiming his rifle at the guy, I noticed that all the civilians that had been standing around us waiting to vote were backing away from us. I guess we scared them. Rugova voted and left without incident. Thousands of people turned out to vote today. Some of them had to stand in line for two to three hours to vote. Election day went off without any major problems. We have the same schedule for tomorrow. Not everyone got to vote today. Tomorrow is my last shift until CTO. I came home after work, ate, and visited the guys for a while and went to bed early.

Sunday, 29 October, 2000

Today is my last shift before CTO! I got up at 0430. The water is off again. It was a good thing that I showered last night before bed. I ate noodles and onions for breakfast. I haven't been eating well lately. I went in to work at 0600. The election schedule was cancelled. I got to work regular patrol. I took Ekrem, Edona, Visar, and Berat. We patrolled our AOR. I took some pictures to take home for CTO. The KPS officers and the L.A. bought me some souvenirs for my family: a Kosovo "car hanger" and a plis (a traditional Kosovar Albanian hat). We call the hat the BRH (Brain Reducing Hat) or the "Brimless Stetson". They wanted me to wear the hat. We are supposed to wear our stupid, baby blue U.N. berets. I drove out to Germia Road to be sure that no one would see me wearing the plis. I put it on and all the KPS officers and L.A. cheered. Just then we passed a VIP procession coming down Germia Road. It was Bernard Kouchner, the U.N. head honcho of the Kosovo mission from France. He is the top dog of this mission. I wonder if he saw me in my CivPol uniform, driving my U.N. police vehicle, wearing my "Brimless Stetson". I guess if I get sent home in the next 24 hours I will know. Oh Well. I got off work at 1400. Randy picked me up at 1500 to go shopping. I bought some food and a switchblade knife up on KFOR hill. I went to Randy's house to eat and copy pictures off my laptop to a disk for him. I found out that Brent will have a U.N. vehicle to take me and Craig to Skopje instead of using Randy's car. We're going to leave at 0800. I went home and packed. I got to bed about midnight.

P.S. Brent called Cait with his cell phone. He told Cait to call Carnita and tell her that I would not be able to contact her before I leave.

UNMIK POLICE PRESS UPDATE
30 OCTOBER, 2000
GNJILANE Region
THREATS/INTIMIDATION
Gnjilane – 29/10 – 2315 hrs. A member of the LDK party reported that four unidentified males came to his privately owned TV station. The suspects fired numerous rounds into the air. It is suspected that this is because the owner of the TV station is now a member of the Gnjilane Municipal Council. No damage or injuries reported.
UXO FOUND

Vitina Town – 29/10 – 1530 hrs. A K-Serbian male informed a KFOR unit that he had found an anti-tank mine while working in his field. EOD disposed of the ordnance.

Monday, 30 October, 2000- Pristina, Kosovo/Skopje, Macedonia

I got up at 0600. No water again! I washed with a heated pitcher of water. The power is still on. We got on the road at 0800. Brent drove us in a white, U.N. 4x4. The road to Skopje was very scenic. The farther south we went the better the scenery. If it were not for the battle damaged houses you would never know a war had just been fought here. Almost every house we passed had machine gun or tank rounds in it. We got into a mountain range with terrain like Montana. We crossed the border without any problems and made it to Skopje, Macedonia about noon. We went straight to McDonald's and had a couple of Big Macs and fries. We had to exchange some DM for local money. The Macedonian money is called Dinar. It takes about 30 Dinar for one DM, which would be about 60 Dinars to a U.S. dollar. Our lunch cost about 250 Dinars. We met another CivPol officer at McDonald's who told us about a hotel close by for 50DM a night. We went there and got a room. The place is called hotel "Vuk". Craig and I walked over to McDonald's for supper. I had a Big Mac meal. We went to our room and watched T.V. It was hard to find anything in English. We got to bed about 2000. We plan to get up at 0400 and get a cab to the airport. The next time we sleep in a bed it will be in the U.S.A.

P.S. I bought Courtni a book, *Utopia,* in a store in Skopje. I also almost had to hurt a street vendor that would not leave me alone. A guy walked up to me and pulled out a switch blade. I took a step back and went for my own knife and was about to engage him. All of a sudden the guy says, "you want to by a knife?" I "went off" on the guy and told him to get lost. He was very persistent and tried to get me to buy a Zippo lighter. He put the lighter in my hand and said, "five dollars!" I threw the lighter into the passing traffic and he finally got the message.

UNMIK POLICE PRESS UPDATE
31 OCTOBER, 2000
PRISTINA Region

ARMED ASSAULT

Grace Village, Pristina – 30/10 – 0230 hrs. An UNMIK Police Officer and three KPS officers were slightly injured by a female suspect (ethnicity not reported), who attempted to stab them with a knife while they were serving a warrant on her husband. The husband used the opportunity to arm himself with a pitchfork and also attacked the officers. One KPS officer was forced to fire warning shots with his duty weapon. The female suspect and her husband were able to flee and are currently being sought.

PRIZREN Region

ATTEMPTED MURDER

Zjum Village, Prizren – 30/10 – 2330 hrs. Four unknown suspects attempted to enter the TMK compound and were discovered by the guard. A few minutes later, gunfire was exchanged and one TMK member was injured in the right arm. The suspects then fled the scene.

MITROVICA Region

PROTEST

Zvecan Town – 30/10 – 1900 hrs. A crowd of approximately 30 people came to the sub-station to protest the lack of electricity for the last twenty days.

Tuesday, 31 October, 2000- Skopje, Macedonia/Zurich, Switzerland/Spokane, Washington, U.S.A.

Craig and I got up at 0430. We got a ride with the hotel owner to Skopje airport. Everything went smooth. We had to walk out to the plane across the tarmac. There was no jet-way or stairs. Our plane was a jet but it must have been one of the first ones. It looked very old. We entered the plane through a stairwell at the rear of the plane. There were no seating assignments. It was seat yourself. After everyone was on board and seated, a crew member came through the cabin and had some of us move around. I assume this was to balance the plane. At least there were seat belts. The plane left for Zurich, Switzerland at 0740. The plane was very cramped. We had a two hour layover in Zurich. It was foggy and raining. We flew Swiss Air to JFK airport in New York. The plane was very big and comfortable. The flight across the Atlantic was eight hours long. I slept a couple of hours. I watched two movies on the screen on the back of the seat in front of me. The flight service was great. We had hot meals, free drinks, hot towels, etc. We arrived at JFK at 1530 local time. As we were landing, Craig and I were talking with an Albanian who was coming to the U.S. to go to school. When the plane touched down and started to taxi to the terminal, Craig and I unhooked our seat belts. The Albanian student did the same. Craig took the opportunity to mess with the guy. He told him that he better re-buckle his seat belt and keep it that way until the plane came to a complete stop or he could be deported. The Albanian asked why Craig and I had our seat belts unbuckled. Craig said that we were U.S. citizens and could not be deported. The kid put his seatbelt back on. Craig and I went to exchange our DM back to U.S. dollars. The booth where you change currency did not have a good rate of exchange. We complained that we were given a better exchange rate in Kosovo and asked to speak with a manager. The manager told us that for them to make a profit making exchanges they had to offer the lesser rate. He said he could give us a better rate only if we had a large amount to exchange. To his surprise we had over 7,000DM each. He gave us the rate we wanted. Our flight out of JFK to Salt Lake was a Delta flight. We left at 1830 local time. We changed planes in Salt Lake to Spokane, WA. We arrived in Spokane at 2300. We met our wives and went to the Ramada Inn near the airport. I was really worn out after over 25 hours of traveling. The only luggage we had was our backpacks and our coats. The weather in Spokane was cool. I took a hot shower (a real one) for the first time in months. I brushed my teeth with sink water and slept in a real bed. It is great to be back in the U.S.A.

UNMIK POLICE PRESS UPDATE
01 November, 2000
PRIZREN Region
ESCAPED PRISONER CAPTURED
Suva Reka Town – 31/10 – 1215 hrs. A KPS officer located a K-Albanian prison escapee. UNMIK Police and KPS officers apprehended the escapee after a foot pursuit.
PEC Region
MURDER
Klina Village, Pec – 31/00 – 1310 hrs. A K-Albanian male who was involved in an exchange of gunfire with two other unknown persons was struck and killed. The victim's AK-47 was recovered at the scene. The suspects fled the scene in a red Audi.

MINE EXPLOSION

Jasiqi Village, Decani – 31/10 – 0915 hrs. A K-Albanian male field supervisor of "ACT" demining organization was seriously wounded when he stepped on a mine.

MITROVICA Region

GRENADE EXPLOSION

Mitrovica North – 30/10 – 2203 hrs. An off-duty police officer reported hearing a loud explosion and KFOR responded to the scene. It was later confirmed by KFOR that a grenade explosion had occurred in the area of a local café.

GRENADE ATTACK

Vucitrn Town – 31/10 – 1830 hrs. A K-Albanian was threatened by another K-Albanian who then threw a hand grenade at him. The grenade did not explode and the suspect was arrested. The grenade was later recovered by EOD and disposed of. No injuries reported.

ASSAULT

Mitrovica North – 31/10 – 2002 hrs. An unknown male assaulted a uniformed UNMIK police officer in a marked patrol vehicle. The suspect punched the officer in the face while he was stopped. The officer sustained minor injuries.

Mitrovica South – 31/10 – 1115 hrs. A mentally handicapped K-Albanian male assaulted a KPS officer and attempted to take his weapon. The suspect was taken into custody and transported to a local hospital for mental evaluation.

UNMIK POLICE PRESS UPDATE

10 NOVEMBER, 2000

MITROVICA Region

MURDER

Dosevac Village – 09/11 – 1140 hrs. The dead bodies of four male Ashkalijas were found in the village of Dosevac. The four victims were taking part in an UNHCR relocation program. It appears the murders took place sometime during the evening hours on 08/11. French KFOR and UNMIK Police have secured the scene for further investigations. The bodies of the four victims were brought to Pristina hospital for post mortem examinations.

PRIZREN Region

DEMONSTRATION

Prizren Town – 08/11 – 1300 hrs. Approximately 3,000 persons attended a peaceful demonstration in connection with the release of the political prisoners in Serbia.

Friday, 10 November, 2000-Atlantic Ocean/Switzerland/Skopje, Macedonia

The flight to Zurich was long. I had in-flight movies to watch and ate two meals. I only slept about an hour. It was too hot and cramped to get any sleep. We arrived in Zurich and had a two hour layover. Craig and I went to a food court and ordered a cup of coffee each. A cup of coffee in Kosovo cost us 50 pfennig; which was about .25 cents. When we got our bill for the coffee in Zurich it was 5DM each. This is about $2.50. It was a good thing we did not order breakfast. We only had a few DM on us. We got on the plane to Skopje, Macedonia. The flight took about two hours. We got Craig's luggage and got through customs without any problems. I only travel with my backpack. Andy Margiota met us at the airport and drove us back to Pristina, Kosovo. We didn't have any problems at the border. Andy stayed for a movie and supper. Everything here in Kosovo is still the same.

P.S. Today is the 225th birthday of the U.S. Marine Corps.

UNMIK POLICE PRESS UPDATE
11 NOVEMBER, 2000
PRISTINA Region
GRENADE ATTACK
Musiqine Village, Lipljan – 10/11 – 2230 hrs. Unknown person(s) threw a hand grenade at a K-Albanian residence. The explosion caused only minor property damage.
BURGLARY
Pristina – 10/11 – 1600 hrs. Unknown person(s) broke into a parked OSCE vehicle and stole some documents together with a radio.
MISSING PERSON
Kishinareke Village, Glogovac – 10/11 – 1800 hrs. A K-Albanian male reported that his daughter who had gone to fetch water from a stream near his home had not returned since 1500 hrs.
MITROVICA Region
DEMONSTRATION
Mitrovica South 10/11 – 1100 –1300 hrs. Approximately 5,000 people attended a peaceful demonstration in Mitrovica South in connection with Albanian prisoners in Serbian jails.
PEC Region

MURDER

Vitomirica Village, Pec – 10/11 – 1630 hrs. Three K-Albanian suspects driving in a vehicle shot at three members of a K-Albanian family traveling in two vehicles. Two of the family members were struck with one later dying. During the incident the suspect's vehicle collided head on with an oncoming truck and burst into flames. All three suspects were injured in the crash with one later dying. All injured persons were transported to hospital for medical treatment. The two surviving suspects are being detained. The motive appears related to an ongoing feud between the parties and is not politically motivated.

GRENADE ATTACK

Dakovica Town – 10/11 – 0140 hrs. A K-Roma male reported that unknown suspects had thrown a grenade at his vehicle causing damage to the door and windscreen.

PRIZREN Region

HUNGER STRIKE / DEMONSTRATION

Dragash – 10/11. Three persons started a hunger strike in protest of Albanian prisoners in Serbian detention centers.

Prizren – 10/11. Approximately 350 persons held a peaceful demonstration concerning Albanian prisoners in Serbian detention centers.

Saturday, 11 November, 2000- Pristina, Kosovo

I slept in until about 1100. I am trying to avoid the jet lag. I got up and washed. It is a good thing that the water is still on. I had to wait until the landlord was done working on the kitchen sink before I could make some food. I made instant cream of wheat and cocoa. I went to work at 1500. Nothing has changed except Randy Wilson transferred to the traffic unit while I was on CTO. Dennis Clark is back from emergency leave. I had to wait for an hour to get a car. I patrolled with three KPS officers and a L.A. I gave out some souvenirs I brought back for some of the KPS officers. I let everyone go home around 2200. We have to be back in to work at 0700 in the morning. I went home and made some noodles. I think I will start looking for another assignment soon. I still have jet lag.

Map of Kosovo under UNMIK

Group photo- Departing for Kosovo

Iliria Hotel-AKA "Hotel Hell"

Clay, Craig and Brent at UNMIK Headquarters

Cruise Missile direct hit- Pristina

Clay on KFOR hill- Pristina in background

Pristina Internet Café

War graves in the park seen from Clay's room

Station #2 KPS Officers-Rame, Ekrem and Visar

Destroyed hotel in Germia-near Pristina

Hotel in Germia

Hotel in Germia

Clay with UNMIK "Coca Cola" in Germia

Welcome NATO

U.S. KFOR troops on patrol

U.S. KFOR soldier

Canadian KFOR

German KFOR boarding helicopter

British KFOR- Station #2- Pristina

French KFOR- Mitrovica

Russian Hind attack helicopter-Pristina

Russian Hind-Pristina airport

Pristina airport

UNMIK Police Station #2-Pristina

UNMIK Police Main Headquarters- Pristina

Clay on first CTO in Pristina

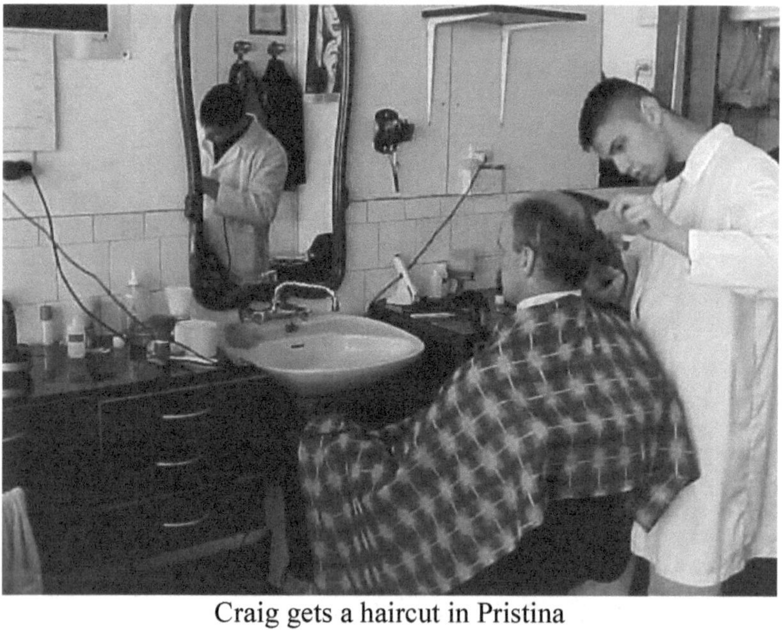

Craig gets a haircut in Pristina

Shannon Leary and Randy Wilson

The Ibar River bridge- Mitrovica

Abandoned Serbian tank

Map of the region

Aerial photos of probable mass grave site

Aerial photo of probable grave sites from the war

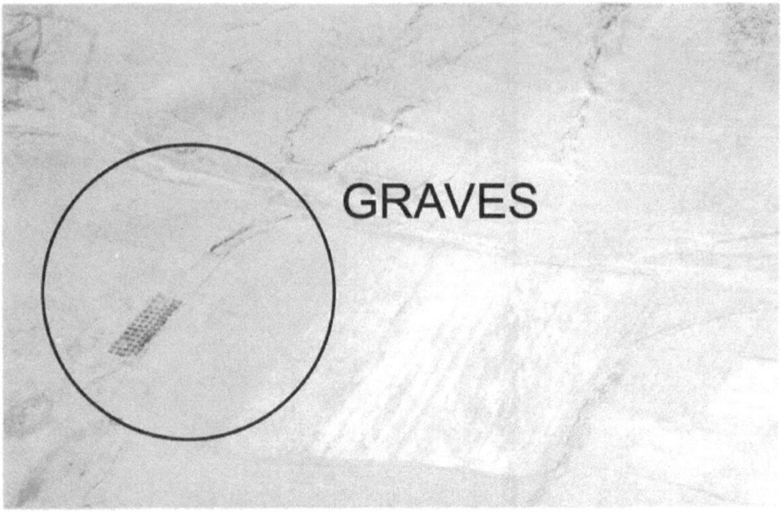

More war graves

Found body- Pristina region

Kosovar Albanian

Kosovar Albanians

TMK member

UNMIK POLICE PRESS UPDATE
13 NOVEMBER, 2000
PRISTINA Region
ASSAULT ON POLICE OFFICER
Pristina – 11/11 – 0200 hrs. Two K-Albanian males, one of whom was highly intoxicated, were arrested after assaulting UNMIK Police officers.
BOMB THREAT
Pristina – 11/11 – 1830 hrs. An anonymous person speaking Serbian stated, in two phone calls, that a bomb had been planted inside and outside the National Theatre on Mother Theresa Street. KFOR and UNMIK Police secured and searched the area, but no explosives were found.
PRIZREN Region
FOUND BODY
Brod Village, Dragash – 12/11 – 1615 hrs. A male dead body found by a shepherd on 04/11 was finally identified as that of a K-Albanian. The victim's remains were handed over to his relatives.
EXPLOSION
Orahovac – 11/11 – 1915 hrs. An explosion occurred at the borderline between the Albanian and the Serb area of the town. No injuries were reported. The exact place of the explosion has not been located yet.
GNJILANE Region
SUSPICIOUS DEATH
Urosevac Town – 11/11 – 1000 hrs. A thirteen-year-old K-Roma male was found burned to death. The boy had left the house of his family at approx. 1000 hrs. going into town. After two hours his brother became worried and began searching for the child. His remains were found in an abandoned house.
MITROVICA Region
DEAD BODY FOUND
Manasc Village, Leposavic – 12/11 – 0800 hrs. The body of a K-Albanian male was found outside a burning house. The circumstances of the incident, especially whether the death occurred accidentally, are under investigation.
SHOOTING
Srbica Town – 11/11 – 0030 hrs. Unknown person(s) fired upon an occupied K-Albanian shop damaging the windows and walls.
PEC Region
MURDER

Stupelj Village, Klina – 12/11 – 2030 hrs. Unknown person(s) shot and killed a K-Albanian male who went outside his house to investigate the sound of gunfire.
Kosare Village, Dakovica – 12/11 – 1600 hrs. Unknown person(s) shot and killed a K-Albanian male as he traveled in his vehicle. A second K-Albanian male in the vehicle was seriously injured.
ASSAULT
Pec – 11/11 – 1800 hrs. Two unknown K-Albanian males assaulted a K-Serbian male while he was going to the monastery. The victim was treated at the hospital and released.
MORTAR ATTACK
Grabanica Village, Klina – 11/11 – 0245 hrs. A K-Albanian business was damaged by mortar fire.

Monday, 13 November, 2000

I got up at 0500. I ate noodles for breakfast. I washed up and got to work at 0700. I worked patrol today with two KPS officers and one L.A. Not much happened until noon when we had a very large protest. The Albanians are protesting the holding of Albanian prisoners in Serbia. There was about fifty thousand people marching through the streets. A new American CivPol contingent arrived right in the middle of the protest and had to drive in among the protesters. It must have been "interesting" to the new arrivals. I bet they were wondering what they have gotten themselves into. I got off work late at about 1600 because we towed a car near the end of the shift and had to finish the reports.

UNMIK POLICE PRESS UPDATE
14 NOVEMBER, 2000
PRISTINA Region
ASSAULT
Janina Voda Village, Kosovo Polje – 13/11 – 1800 hrs. A K-Albanian male reported that a known K-Serb male, who demanded to know the identity of the persons responsible for the mine explosion that took place two months ago, assaulted him. The victim sustained minor injuries and was taken to hospital for treatment.
DEMONSTRATIONS
Pristina – 13/11. At approximately 1200 hrs. a large crowd of about 50,000 people assembled at the National Theatre joining

2,000 other people that are camped at the site to demonstrate against the continued imprisonment of K-Albanians in Serb prisons. The protest was peaceful and ended at 1600 hrs.
Lipljan Town – 13/11. At approximately 1200 hrs. a crowd of about 5,000 people marched through the town to demonstrate against the continued imprisonment of K-Albanians in Serbia. The demonstration was peaceful and ended at 1500 hrs. The demonstration is expected to be a daily event.
Stimlje Village, Lipljan – 13/11. Approximately 2,500 people attended a peaceful demonstration starting from 1200 and lasting until 1430 hrs. in connection with K-Albanian prisoners in Serbia.
Glogovac Town – 13/11. At 1200 hrs 2,500 people staged a peaceful protest march against the imprisonment of K-Albanians in Serbia. Approx. 1,000 other protesters blocked the road at the Kamoran junction. Both protests ended at 1500 hrs.
GNJILANE Region
ASSAULT
Vrbovac Village, Vitina – 12/11 – 2230 hrs. A K-Serb male was arrested by UNMIK Police after he assaulted a KFOR soldier.
EXPLOSION
Pozorange Village, Vitina – 13/11 – 0400 hrs. A K-Albanian male reported an explosion near his garage. UNMIK Police discovered that it was an improvised device that exploded.
DEMONSTRATIONS
Kacanik Town – 13/11. About 1,000 people gathered to demonstrate against the continued imprisonment of K-Albanians in Serb prisons. The demonstration ended at approximately 1500 hrs.
Gnjilane – 13/11. About 5,000 Albanian subjects gathered to demonstrate against the continued imprisonment of K-Albanians in Serb prisons. The demonstration ended at approximately 1500 hrs.
Kamenica Town– 13/11. About 300 Albanian subjects gathered to demonstrate against the continued imprisonment of K-Albanians in Serb prisons. The demonstration ended at approximately 1500 hrs.
MITROVICA Region
ASSAULT
Mitrovica North – 09/11. A KFOR soldier was assaulted by an unknown suspect while assisting in crowd control. The suspect fled the scene.

DEMONSTRATIONS

Vucitrn - 13/11 – 1200 hrs. A peaceful demonstration was held between the hours of 1200 – 1440 concerning the persons held in Serbian Detention centers.

Mitrovica South – 13/11 – 1130 hrs. A peaceful demonstration was held by approx. 2,000 people beginning at 1130 hours concerning the persons held in Serbian Detention centers.

PEC Region

DEMONSTRATIONS

Klina Town – 13/11 – 1230 – 1500 hrs. A peaceful demonstration was held by approximately 1,500 persons concerning the persons held in Serbian Detention centers.

Pec – 13/11 – 1230 – 1500 hrs. A peaceful demonstration was held by approximately 2,500 persons concerning the persons being held in Serbian Detention Centers.

Dakovica Town – 13/11 – 1100 hrs. A peaceful demonstration was held by approximately 1,000 persons concerning the persons being held in Serbian Detention Centers.

Istok Town – 13/11 – 1230 – 1500 hrs. A peaceful demonstration was held by approximately 600 persons concerning the persons being held in Serbian Detention Centers.

PRIZREN Region

THREATS/INTIMIDATION

Suva Reka Town – 13/11 – 1400 hrs. A K-Albanian male was arrested by UNMIK Police for threatening a KPS Officer with death after the officer wrote him a traffic citation.

DEMONSTRATIONS

Suva Reka Town - 13/11 - 1200 hrs. - 1500 hrs. Approximately 7,800 people attended a peaceful demonstration regarding K-Albanians being held in Serbian prisons.

Malisevo Town – 13/11 – 1200 – 1500 hrs. An unknown number of people attended a peaceful demonstration regarding K-Albanians being held in Serbian prisons.

Orahovac Town – 13/11 – 1200 – 1400 hrs. Approximately 3,000 people attended a peaceful demonstration regarding K-Albanian prisoners being held in Serbian prisons.

Tuesday, 14 November, 2000

I got up at 0530. “Triple Sierra” and a breakfast of instant oatmeal and cocoa. I went in to work at 0700. Nothing new today. I patrolled our AOR with four KPS officers. About 1000 I went to the company building and got a flu shot. "Doc" recommended that we all get the shot because of a really bad strain of flu this year. At about 1030 we drove about 25 km north of Prishtina to a big reservoir (lake). It kind of looked like Montana. We took some pictures on the beach. The KPS officers had a good time going there. I took us a little too close to the Serbian border than the KPS officers liked. They were a little uneasy and thought we may be shot at. We headed back into Pristina without incident. I got off work at 1500 and went to the internet café. I wrote an e-mail to Carnita to set up a chat time for tomorrow night. I went home and ate noodles. I watched a movie and then went to bed by 1900.

P.S. I had the landlord adjust or satellite dish to pick up the BBC. Now we have news in English.

E-mail home

Hi Hun,
I made it back OK. First time at the café. I have been working and fighting jet lag. I am going to have a day off on Thursday so we can chat tomorrow night. How about 1000, your time, Wednesday? I will be able to sleep late the next morning. Everything here is the same. Tell the kids I already miss them and that I had fun with them while I was home. Not much to write about yet. I will tell you all about things when we chat. I hope you get this message and the computer works on Wednesday morning. I just got off shift and walked down here from work. I am going to go home and eat and get to bed. Remember to be on line for our chat. Yours forever, Clay.

UNMIK POLICE PRESS UPDATE
15 NOVEMBER, 2000
PRISTINA Region
ASSAULT
Pristina – 14/11 – 1815 hrs. A K-Albanian male Correctional Officer sustained minor injuries when he was assaulted by a group of nine detainees. UNMIK Police and KFOR managed to bring the situation under control.
Obilic Village, Kosovo Polje – 14/11 – 0830 hrs. A K-Serb male reported that unknown person(s) damaged the windows of the

newly refurbished Serbian wing of the Civil Administration Authority offices.

DEMONSTRATIONS

Pristina – 14/11. Approximately 2,000 people held a peaceful demonstration against the continued imprisonment of K-Albanians in Serbia.

Lipljan Town – 14/11 - 1300 hrs. Approximately 1,000 people gathered and marched through the town to Pristina demonstrating against the continued imprisonment of K-Albanians in Serbia. The demonstration was peaceful.

Kamoran Village, Glogovac – 14/11 - 1430 hrs. Approximately 150 people blocked the road in protest against the imprisonment of K-Albanians in Serbia.

GNJILANE Region

ASSAULT

Gnjilane – 14/11 – 1100 hrs. Five K-Albanian male subjects were arrested by UNMIK Police for assault, after they pushed KFOR soldiers during the protest in Gnjilane.

DEMONSTRATIONS

General Jankovic – 14/11- 1222 hrs. Approximately 500 people protested against the continued imprisonment of K-Albanians in Serbia.

Kacanik Town – 14/11- 1306 hrs. Approximately 5,000 people protested against the continued imprisonment of K-Albanians in Serbia.

Gnjilane – 14/11 – 1200 hrs. Approximately 3,000 people in Gnjilane and about 13,000 people in Urosevac protested against the continued imprisonment of K-Albanians in Serbia.

MITROVICA Region

DEMONSTRATION

Mitrovica South – 14/11 – 1200 hrs. Approximately 1,500 persons held a peaceful demonstration concerning persons held in Serbian Detention centers.

Vucitrn Town – 14/11 – 1130 hrs. Approximately 1,000 persons held a peaceful demonstration concerning persons held in Serbian Detention centers.

Srbica Town – 14/11. Approximately 1,500 persons held a peaceful demonstration concerning persons held in Serbian Detention centers.

PEC Region

THREATS/INTIMIDATION

Pec – 13/11 – 1830 hrs. An unknown suspect threatened a K-Albanian female with a gun in an attempt to cause her to kiss him. The suspect fled the scene.
ASSAULT
Pec – 13/11 – 2130 hrs. A K-Bosnian male reported being assaulted by a K-Albanian male simply because of his ethnicity.
ILLEGAL POSSESSION OF A WEAPON
Smac Village, Dakovica – 14/11 – 1200 hrs. UNMIK Police conducted a search of several residences and as a result located a large cache of weapons and ammunition. One K-Albanian male was arrested.
DEMONSTRATIONS
Klina Town – 14/11 – 1300 – 1400 hrs. Approximately 1,000 persons held a peaceful demonstration concerning persons held in Serbian Detention centers.
Pec – 13/11 – 1200 – 1600 hrs. Approximately 3,000 persons held a peaceful demonstration concerning persons held in Serbian Detention centers.
PRIZREN Region
DEMONSTRATION
Suva Reka Town – 14/11 – 1130 – 1400 hrs. Approximately 2,000 people held a peaceful demonstration against the continued imprisonment of K-Albanians in Serbia.
Prizren – 14/11 – 1220 – 1430 hrs. Approximately 3,000 people held a peaceful demonstration against the continued imprisonment of K-Albanians in Serbia.
Malisevo Town – 14/11 – 1200 – 1300 hrs. Approximately 500 people held a peaceful demonstration against the continued imprisonment of K-Albanians in Serbia.

Wednesday, 15 November, 2000

I got up at 0530. Same routine as yesterday. I went in to work at 0700. I took three KPS officers and one L.A. out on patrol. We set up a VCP on Airport Road. We got fuel and washed the vehicle. We got assigned to regulate traffic at the World Food Program junction at 1100. There is a big demonstration again today. There was over one hundred thousand people. Some of them are going to sit on Mother Theresa Street all night long. We were supposed to get relieved from our position at 1430. Our relief did not arrive until almost 1600. Most of the businesses are closed for the protest, even the internet café. Language Assistant (L.A.) Bujar came by the house at 1800 to take me and Jim Knudson to his parent's house to eat. I had forgotten about the appointment and already had eaten a big meal of spaghetti. I did not say anything to Bujar and ate again at his parent's house. More spaghetti! I thought I was going to pop. I had a very good time and an interesting visit. His father is an attorney. We stayed until 2030. I came home and went to bed.

P.S. I am taking a day off tomorrow. I need to get a haircut and send some e-mails. The weather is still nice.

UNMIK POLICE PRESS UPDATE
16 NOVEMBER, 2000
PRISTINA Region
DEMONSTRATIONS
Pristina – 15/11 – 1100 hrs. Approximately 50,000 people held a peaceful demonstration against the continued imprisonment of K-Albanians in Serbia.
Lipljan Town – 15/11 - 1300 hrs. At 1000 hrs. Protesters marching from Urosevac were joined by a group of local villagers. Approximately 8,000 people marched through the town to Pristina demonstrating against the continued imprisonment of K-Albanians in Serbia. The demonstration was peaceful and passed Lipljan on their return journey at 1445 hrs.
GNJILANE Region
CONFISCATED ITEM
Kacanik Village, Gnjilane – 15/11 – 0010 hrs. A K-Albanian male was found to be in possession of CS tear gas. The item was seized by UNMIK Police.
MITROVICA Region
GRIEVOUS ASSAULT
Srbica Town – 15/11 – 1830 hrs. A K-Albanian female was transported to the hospital with a gunshot wound to the back. Further investigation revealed that she had been shot while parking at a service station. The condition of the victim was reported to be stable.
PEC Region
ATTEMPTED MURDER
Pec – 15/11 – 2145 hrs. An unknown male suspect, who forcibly entered the victim's home, shot a K-Albanian male one time in the

chest. The victim was transported to Pristina Hospital where his condition is unknown.

UXO FOUND

Dakovica Town – 15/11 – 0930 hrs. An unknown type of UXO was located near a school. The de-mining team was notified and the device was disposed of.

DEMONSTRATION

Pec – 13/11 1200 – 1600 hrs. Approximately 1,000 people attended a peaceful demonstration concerning K-Albanians being held in Serbian prisons.

PRIZREN Region

DEMONSTRATONS

Suva Reka Town - 15/11 – 0830 hrs. – 1045 hrs. Approximately 1,000 attended a peaceful demonstration concerning K- Albanians being held in Serbian prisons.

Prizren Town - 15/11 – 1200 hrs. – 1300 hrs. Approximately 900 people attended a peaceful demonstration concerning K-Albanian prisoners being held in Serbian prisons.

Orahovac Town - 15/11. Approximately 400 – 500 people attended a peaceful demonstration for approximately one hour, concerning K-Albanians being held in Serbian prisons.

Thursday, 16 November, 2000

I got up late today (0700) because I am not going in to work. I am taking an "administrative" day. We PFTOs agreed to create an administrative day and will cover for each other. I did the same morning routine. Ken was supposed to be in with a vehicle by 0900 but didn't get here until 1100. I shined my boots, arraigned my room, and washed a load of clothes before Ken got to the house. When Ken finally arrived, John and I went to town.

Our first stop was for my haircut. Then we went up to KFOR Hill to get some stuff for John's trip home. We ate lunch at the Norwegian PX. We went to the grocery store (Arti's) and got some food. We then went to the company building to turn in our time cards and draw our water supply. We got back home by 1500. We made prime rib, mashed potatoes, mac and cheese, and onion gravy with garlic bread for chow. I watched the BBC and then got to bed late at about 2200. I wrote in this diary, read for a while, and then lights out.

P.S. There is still no winner in the U.S. Presidential race. It could go on for weeks.

UNMIK POLICE PRESS UPDATE
17 NOVEMBER, 2000
PRISTINA Region
BOMB THREAT
Pristina – 16/11 – 1715 hrs. UNMIK Police Station #4 received an anonymous call stating that a bomb had been placed in a motor vehicle parked in front of the station. The motor vehicle was located but no explosive devices were found.
GNJILANE Region
DEAD BODIES FOUND
Kacanik Town – 15/11 – 1100 hrs. During a joint search for weapons UNMIK Police together with KFOR discovered the skeletal remains of four bodies in a mountain cave. Preliminary investigations revealed that the persons had probably been executed by shots in the head.
MITROVICA Region
ILLEGAL POSSESSION OF A WEAPON
Mitrovica North – 16/11 – 1900 hrs. UNMIK Police and KFOR responded to a Serb area of the town after hearing gunfire. A K-Serb family stated that they were threatened by K-Albanians who fired several shots and also had a grenade with them. During a follow up search of several houses a K-Bosnian male and a K-Albanian female were arrested after being found in possession of grenades. Later a further five K-Albanians were detained after being discovered hiding close to the crime scene.
Mitrovica South – 15/11 – 2345 hrs. During the arrest of a K-Albanian male for passing counterfeit currency UNMIK Police found him also in possession of a pistol. A search of the suspect's residence resulted in the seizure of a grenade and several land mines.
POSSIBLE MASS GRAVE
Drahova Village, Mitrovica – 16/11 – 1200 hrs. Information was received concerning a possible mass gravesite in the area of Drahova village. During the initial investigation of the site several bones were found. The site was secured for further investigations.
PEC Region
BURGLARY

Pec – 16/11 – 0730 hrs. An employee of the NGO "German Red Cross" reported that unknown person(s) had broken the windshield of a vehicle belonging to the organization and stolen a chain saw and welding equipment.

DEMONSTRATION

Pec – 16/11 – 1200-1600 hrs. A peaceful demonstration was conducted by approximately 1,000 persons concerning the K-Albanians prisoners being held in Serbia.

Friday, 17 November, 2000

I got up at 0500. Regular morning routine. Off to work at 0700. I wore a sweater (wooly pully) for the first time today. I went on patrol with four KPS officers. I had two English speakers (Visar and Makvire). We had a productive day today. We wrote seven citations and towed two vehicles. I had an interesting encounter today. We had a call where there was damage caused to a house because there was construction to build an additional floor to the building to house KLA veterans. The additional weight of the new construction was causing cracks in the ceiling and walls of the existing building. The residents were complaining that the addition was unsafe. An Albanian engineer that had made negative reports about the construction had been murdered so the residence did not know where to turn but to the U.N., i.e., the UNMIK CivPol. I took a report and went to the governmental offices to find out who to talk with about the issue. I was directed to talk with the Pristina TMK Commander. The TMK is the quasi Kosovo National Guard and is made up of former KLA veterans. The local commander was a man named Rrustem Mustafa. He is apparently a famous war figure here. He went by the KLA nom de guerre of "Commander Remi" during the war. Remi was a prominent figure during the war and was idolized by many of the former KLA. He held a high command position with the KLA during the war. I went to the TMK HQ building and asked to meet with Commander Remi. The security was tight and Visar, my KPS officer that I was going to use as my L.A., was quite nervous about the meeting. I was asked to leave my weapon at the front desk to be allowed in to see Remi. I could have refused because of my CivPol status but I complied to show that I respected the TMK and I had no fear of the meeting. I met with Remi and told him about my the concerns about the safety of the construction of the veteran's housing. He was very receptive. He was impressed with my concern for his people and especially impressed that I was a former U.S. Marine. I noticed that his office was decorated with many military items. I also noted during my conversations with him, though my interpreter, that he had a great respect for the United States Marines Corps. He showed me a USMC soft cover that a Marine officer had given him at the end of the war. I left with his assurance that he would look into the matter. I had a little paper work to finish at the end of the shift. I got off about 1530. I went to the internet café right from work to e-mail Carnita. I set up a chat for tomorrow night. I went home and ate noodles with veggie ground beef from home. I watched a movie with Brent, Craig, and John and went to bed about 2000.

E-mail home

Sorry about the chat. We had a big demonstration that day and all the businesses were closed. Craig went down to check if the internet café was going to open back up but before he got back home one of the Language Assistants (interpreters) came over to get me to take me to his parent's house for dinner. I had forgotten all about being invited over. It was very nice and interesting. His father is an attorney here and they thought it was great to be able to have an American over for dinner. I stayed until 2030. We are still working on getting a phone line at the house. We are trying to bootleg into a Serbian line. It is 1530 right now and I just got off work. I came here first instead of walking up the hill to the house. I wanted to e-mail you and let you know that I am still alive and OK. I need to go eat and go to bed after I send this. I checked to see if you were on line but you weren't. I would have chatted tonight if you had been there. 1800 has just been too late for me this time. I guess it was the long trip back. I will be here to chat tomorrow at 1800 (1000 your time unless something happens I can't control). I change to night shift on Sunday night. My next CTO starts on December 3rd. I will be staying here and catching up on e-mails and chats and saving my money. My next time home is going to be around mid February. I should be able to take a couple of more leave days than I did this time. I can't wait to see you again. I will write some e-mails on my laptop tonight in my room to send to you tomorrow before the chat. How is everything going with you? I hope it is not too cold there. It has been like spring here ever since I got back. Maybe it will be a mild winter here. Well, I better go walk up the hill back to the house. I am starving and need to eat and get in bed. All I do here is work, eat, and sleep. I will write you a longer letter tonight on the laptop. I need to go for now. If something happens to the chat time I will call you on Ken's phone or something. Talk to you tomorrow. Love, Clay

UNMIK POLICE PRESS UPDATE
18 NOVEMBER, 2000
PRISTINA Region
PROSTITUTION / ILLEGAL POSSESSION OF WEAPON
Kosovo Polje Town – 17/11 – 1130 hrs. UNMIK Police arrested five K-Serb males and seized four handguns during an operation into organized crime concerning prostitution. UNMIK Police detained twelve females suspected of involvement in prostitution.
ILLEGAL POSSESSION OF WEAPONS
Pristina – 18/11 – 0110 hrs. UNMIK Police and KFOR conducted a joint search operation of the "Miami Beach Club" and seized an automatic rifle and a pistol.
ARSON
Pristina – 17/11 – 0812 hrs. Two K-Serb males were arrested by UNMIK Police for burning down several K-Albanian houses during the war. The offences occurred on 03/04/1999. The suspects are being held in the Pristina Detention Center.
MITROVICA Region
MURDER
Pantin Village, Vucitrn – 17/11 – 1845 hrs. A doctor at the hospital reported that a K-Albanian female had been brought to the hospital by her father suffering from gunshot wounds to the chest. The victim was pronounced dead by the doctor.
PEC Region
DEAD BODY FOUND
Pec – 17/11 – 1500 hrs. The dead body of a man, later identified as a K-Albanian, was found in the Bistrica River. The cause of death is unknown at this time.
PRIZREN Region
SHOOTING
Plajnike Village, Prizren – 17/11 – 1830 hrs. Unknown person(s) shot with automatic weapons at three residences in the village. It is

believed that the shots were a result of an ongoing conflict between two families.

Saturday, 18 November, 2000

Up at 0530. I slept hard. This is the first morning that the alarm has gotten me up. I performed the same morning routine again. Craig also slept in today. He is usually up at the same time or a little before me. He got up at 0600. We usually have coffee and talk until time to leave for work. I had the same routine on patrol today. I started by fueling up and washing the vehicle. I worked a burglary and assisted on traffic at an accident where power lines were down. At about noon we went back to TMK HQ. I met with Commander Remi and we had coffee in his office. I presented Remi with a USMC KA-BAR fighting knife. Apparently in the Albanian culture, the giving of a knife as a gift is a high honor. Remi gave me an eagle sculpture and two plaques, one KLA and one TMK, in return. I had not expected any return gift as I had made the second contact in an effort to possibly foster a high level source of information within the TMK. After work I went home, ate, and then went to chat with Carnita. We chatted for two hours. It was really good to talk to her. We set up a chat for tomorrow night before I go to work. I start night shift tomorrow.

Sunday, 19 November, 2000

I got up about 0700. I ate rice for breakfast. I visited with Craig for a while. I went to the internet café to surf the net and check ticket prices for my upcoming CTO. After the internet café I went to the travel agency. It was closed on Sundays. I walked back up the hill to the house and ate some noodles for lunch. I went to bed and read until about 1300. I slept until about 1700. I got up, showered, and sat around with some of the guys. I went in to work for night shift at 2300. Things are screwed up tonight again as usual. I worked with four KPS officers. We only wrote one citation during the shift. I ate a burger at 0200. There is a restaurant that is safe to eat at that is open all night and used frequently by the police. A Kosovo hamburger is unique. The bun is a split open piece of bread, kind of like a leaven pita. The meat patty and fixings are stuffed inside, along with the fries. It is unusual but good. I got off work at 0700 and went home. I watched the BBC news and read and then I went to bed.

UNMIK POLICE PRESS UPDATE
20 NOVEMBER, 2000
PRISTINA Region
ILLEGAL POSSESSION OF WEAPONS
Kosovo Polje – 19/11 – 0230 hrs. A K-Albanian male was arrested by UNMIK Police when a search of his vehicle by KFOR revealed a hand grenade hidden behind the radio compartment of his motor vehicle.
ILLEGAL POSSESSION OF WEAPONS
Pristina – 18/11 – 0110 hrs. A routine joint KFOR and UNMIK Police search operation at a nightclub resulted in the recovery of an automatic rifle, two semi-automatic pistols and ammunition. UNMIK Police arrested one K-Albanian male.
GNJILANE Region
ATTEMPTED MURDER
Kacanik Town – 18/11 – 1500 hrs. A shooting incident between two K-Albanian males resulted in one subject receiving wounds to his right leg. The suspect was arrested by UNMIK Police and his residence searched resulting in the seizure of a large cache of weapons.
MITROVICA Region
GRENADE FOUND
Mitrovica North - 19/11 – 1320 hrs. One K-Bosnian and six K-Albanian males were detained by UNMIK Police after a search of their residences resulted in the seizure of two hand grenades.
THREATS
Mitrovica North – 17/11 – 1415 hrs. A K-Bosnian male reported that an unknown number of K-Serb males threatened to steal the roof from his mother's abandoned home.
PRIZREN Region
PROSTITUTION
Prizren – 19/11 – 0615 hrs. UNMIK Police arrested a Bulgarian female for prostitution.
GRENADE ATTACK
Orahovac City – 18/11 – 1905 hrs. An unknown person threw a hand grenade from the Albanian sector into a backyard of a K-Serbian home damaging a shed door.
THREAT

Prizren – 17/11 – 1900 hrs. A K-Albanian reported that his cousin threatened to blow up his home with a hand grenade.

Monday, 20 November, 2000

I got up at 1300. I ate noodles for lunch. I visited with Ken and Craig for awhile then Craig and I walked to the travel agency to make reservations for our February CTO. We got tickets into Kalispell for 13 February. After the travel agency we went to Ardi's market and bought some supplies. We then went to the internet café and checked e-mails. I sent a couple of e-mails home. I went in to work at 2300. I am all alone tonight with fifteen KPS officers. I am the only PFTO. This station is really screwed up. I sent most of the KPS officers to be disbursed by the shift leader. I took four KPS officers on patrol. It was a slow night. Nothing was going on. At about 0300 I noticed an obviously intoxicated male walking down the side of the road holding a bottle of whiskey. I stopped to make contact with the guy and found that he was a CivPol officer from Northern Ireland. The Royal Ulster Constabulary (RUC) contingent just got into country. He was the perfect, stereotypical "drunken Irishman." He had wandered away from a party and gotten lost. I gave him a ride back to his house and made sure he was with other officers. I got off work at 0700. I went straight to bed.

UNMIK POLICE PRESS UPDATE
21 NOVEMBER, 2000
PRISTINA Region
MURDER / ATTEMPTED MURDER
Peran Village, Podujevo – 20/11 – 1410 hrs. A K-Albanian male shot and killed another K-Albanian male and wounded the victim's daughter. The victim's daughter and the suspect, who was also injured, were taken to the hospital.
ASSAULT
Lipljan Town – 20/11 – 1632 hrs. A K-Serb male driver reported that K-Albanian students from a known secondary school damaged his motor vehicle by throwing stones at it. He managed to apprehend one of them and took him to a KFOR checkpoint where KFOR soldiers handed over the suspect to UNMIK Police. A large crowd of students later assembled in protest against the detention of their colleague.

MITROVICA Region
SWEARING IN CEREMONIES
Leposavic – 20/11 – 1030 hrs. Swearing in ceremonies for Municipal assemblies took place today in both Leposavic and Zubin Potok without incident.
PEC Region
MURDER
Dakovica Town – 20/11 – 1345 hrs. A K-Albanian male was found dead inside his vehicle with multiple gunshot wounds to the head and torso.
GRENADE ATTACK
Dakovica Town – 19/11 – 2145 hrs. A K-Roma male reported that unknown person(s) threw a hand grenade at his home resulting in the damage of one room and the destruction of the entire contents.

Tuesday, 21 November, 2000

I got up at 1400. I ate chicken "Spam" and sauerkraut. I performed my regular routine. I went in to work at 2300. It was a pretty slow night at first. I had four KPS officers with me: Ekrem Vllasa, Edona Demaj, Ejup Mehani, and Makvire Sveclla. We assisted with a DUI in the station #3 area. About 0430 we were called by the static post at the Serbian ambassador's residence. An Irish RUC CivPol officer had seen a couple of men moving around the complex. I arrived and spoke with the Irish officer (Barry Greene) and began to search the area. We were checking the rear of the ambassador's residence when a large bomb exploded. I was knocked down along with my KPS officers. I got up and ran to the ambassador's house and started helping get everyone out. One guy was trapped in the rubble at the rear of the house. Several officers and I dug him out. He was severely injured and later died at the British KFOR hospital. He was a Serbian driver for the ambassador. His name was Goran Jeftik. Barry Greene and I were taken to the British hospital also and checked out OK. No big holes, just some scrapes and some glass in my leg. My ears are ringing pretty bad though. We then had to see several people at Main HQ. I finally got home at about 1400. I have a bad headache, ears are ringing, and my right leg and shoulder are sore. I have small scrapes and scratches but I am alive!

P.S. I sat, and got myself composed after the blast, in a British KFOR ambulance. A Royal Marine Commando medic, Andy McCrum, stayed with me and kept an eye on me for a while.

The following is from my official UNMIK report No. 23638:

On Wednesday 22/11/2000 at about 0430 I was contacted by Unit Alpha 2-1 who was performing static security duty at the residence of the Serbian ambassador. Upon arrival at the location I spoke with the international officer, Sgt. Barry Greene, RUC, who advised me that he had observed at least two individuals in the housing area approximately two houses east of the ambassador's residence. He said that he had made contact with two U.N. security guards on the north side of the houses to see if it had been them that he saw. On the previous date he had challenged two individuals moving around in the same area and they turned out to be U.N. security guards assigned to the housing complex. They advised that they had not been in the area but that they had just seen three individuals leave the area running north toward another housing area.

Officer Greene and I decided to search the housing area before I left the area to search for the individuals. My call sign was Alpha 2-8 and I was accompanied by four KPS Officers: Ejup Mehani, Ekrem Vllasa, Edona Demaj, and Makvire Sveclla.

Officer Greene went up the street to the west of the houses and I took my team up a concrete path beside the house just east of the ambassador's residence. This is where Officer Greene had seen the two individuals. I searched the area with my flashlight. Each residence had a fenced in back yard and it was difficult to walk through the yards without crossing these fences. The KPS officers were walking ahead of me on the path and were to continue to search the area to the east. I was going to cross the fenced yard and search toward the rear of the ambassador's residence. I saw Officer Greene directly across from me to the west of my location. He was apparently going to cross through the yards also toward the ambassador's residence. He signaled me with his flashlight and I signaled in return. At that moment there was a bright flash that appeared to come from the rear of the ambassador's residence followed by a loud report. I was thrown to the ground by the force of the blast and there was debris falling around me. I then noticed that my team of KPS officers were also down. I remained prone and radioed Prishtina control to send back up to our location and advised that there had been an explosion.

After the blast had subsided I check my team of officers to see if they where injured. They appeared to be uninjured and I told them to return to the area of our patrol vehicle and set up a security perimeter. I went to the front of the ambassador's residence and made contact with Officer Greene. He appeared to be uninjured and we checked on the condition of his team that had been sitting in a patrol vehicle in front of the residence. His team members appeared uninjured.

The damage to the ambassador's residence was extensive. There was debris thrown into the street and surrounding residences also appeared damaged. Officer Greene began to call out to the occupants of the ambassador's residence. A man emerged on the second floor balcony. He identified himself as the ambassador and appeared to be uninjured. I entered the building with another officer that had arrived to assist to search for and evacuate any victims. I reminded the other officer to be aware of the possibility of any secondary devices. I could not locate anyone in the lower portion of the building. There was still a large amount of dust and it was difficult to see. I noticed what appeared to be the remains of a staircase leading to the second floor. It had been almost completely destroyed. I began to climb up to the second floor using the exposed rebar. Before I made it to the second floor I was advised that all the occupants from that floor had made it out and were accounted for.

I went to the rear of the residence and found that the damage there was extreme. The exterior wall was gone and there was a huge amount of debris. I noticed a man completely covered with dust walking in the debris. He was injured but apparently not seriously. I discovered a second individual trapped in the rubble with only his head and right shoulder exposed. The first injured man was Serbian and spoke English. He was asking me to help his trapped friend. I told him to stay with his friend and I would return with help. I went to the front of the residence and told Officer Greene that there was an injured man trapped in the rubble. Several international officers that had arrived on the scene came to the rear and we began to dig the injured man out.

We first had to lift a large concrete column off the man. I tried to assess his injuries. He said, through his English speaking friend, that he had pain in his abdomen and his right arm. I noticed that he had blood coming from around his eyes. I felt his abdomen and it felt as if he had some internal injuries and possible internal bleeding. As we removed the debris the first visible injury was his right hand. The bone from the man's right forearm was visible and the hand was partially amputated and hanging by a small amount of tissue. A British Royal Marine patrol had arrived on the scene and provided me with battle/wound dressings. I applied a dressing to the injured limb to protect the injury before we began to remove more debris. We continued to dig and were able to free his right leg. The condition of the leg was the same as the arm. The bone was exposed at the ankle and the foot was mutilated and attached only by a small amount of tissue. I dressed this wound, tying the foot to his leg, and continued to dig until we were able to uncover his left leg. His left leg was in the same condition as the right and was tangled in what appeared to be bedding. I considered cutting the tissue holding the foot, which was still trapped in the rubble, to expedite freeing the victim but decided against it as his friend was watching. We continued to dig until the foot was free. I dressed the wound as before and then began to extract the wounded man from the rubble. By this time there was a stretcher on the scene and we placed the victim onto it and carried him to a waiting ambulance.

After the injured were transported I began to check on the status of my KPS team and helped get the perimeter of the scene secured with police personnel. I was informed that one of my KPS officers, Ekrem Vllasa, had been slightly injured in the blast and had been transported to Prishtina Hospital. I remained at the scene until supervisory personnel and investigators arrived. Officer Greene and I were then directed to go to the British KFOR field hospital to be checked medically.

Addendum:

By the time that all the injured civilians had been transported out of the area the British Royal Marines had arrived in force to help secure the area. The British military were assigned the Pristina Region as there area of operation in the NATO Kosovo Force (KFOR). It had also finally begun to get light out and I could now better see the extent of the damage caused by the blast. I was taken to an ambulance and attended to. I was pretty shaken up by the blast and apparently had some signs of mild shock and a concussion. My ears were ringing and my head hurt. The only way I can describe the effect of the blast was that it was like being hit by an invisible car.

Now that the area of the blast was somewhat under control and the first response over, my adrenaline was spent and I realized that I felt exhausted. My clothes were full of debris and broken glass. I had a few shard of glass in my leg but the wounds were superficial. RUC officer Dedis had arrived back on the scene sometime during our rescue of the Serbian man from the residence. Dedis drove Sgt. Greene and myself to the British KFOR field hospital to be checked out. When we arrived we found that there was some kind of confrontation going on between the British Royal Marines and some Russian military troops that had arrived and were demanding entry to see the injured Serbian. Russia had not hidden there sympathies toward the now minority Serbian population.

While at the field hospital, the injured Serbian, Goran Jeftic, succumbed to his wounds and died. Jeftic had been Ambassador Vukicevic's driver and had been sleeping near the area of the seat of the blast. We were released from the hospital and returned to duty and were no longer involved in the investigation.

Further investigation revealed that the explosive device had contained and estimated ten kilos (22 pounds) of military explosives and was most likely placed by the Liberation Army for Presevo, Medvedja and Bujanovac (UCPMB), a spin off of the former Kosovo Liberation Army (KLA/UCK). The commander of the British forces in the Pristina region, Brigadier General Robert Fry, called the bombing a "ruthless and determined act of terrorism".

UNMIK POLICE PRESS UPDATE
22 NOVEMBER, 2000
PRISTINA Region
EXPLOSION
Pristina – 22/11 – 0451 hrs. An explosion occurred next to an apartment building containing the residence of the Yugoslav Representative in Kosovo. One 35 year-old Serbian male sustained critical injuries and later died at hospital. Another sustained serious injuries and was transported to hospital for treatment. The five other occupants of the apartment were uninjured. One UNMIK Police Officer, resident of another apartment, received minor injuries.
SHOOTING
Podujevo – 21/11 – 1835 hrs. Unknown persons shot several times at a Serb truck driver. One shot struck him in the shoulder. The incident happened just after he left gate three headed towards Pristina. His injuries were not serious.
RAILWAY ACCIDENT
Obilic Village, Kosovo Polje – 21/11 – 0705 hrs. A vehicle driven by a K-Albanian male was involved in an accident with the U.N. train in front of Power Plant B.

Wednesday, 22 November, 2000

I did not make it back home from the bombing until about 1400. I could not sleep and stayed up and watched movies. I tried to call Carnita. The line was busy so I called Carnita's sister, Peggy, and gave her Ken's cell phone number. I went next door to the Red Lion bar for about 45 minutes to say goodbye to an Italian CivPol officer (Renzo) who is leaving the mission. I came home and tried to lie down. Carnita finally got through and we talked for a few minutes. I told her that I was OK. I finally got to bed about 2300. I only slept until about 0200 before waking up. I finally got back to sleep at 0400 and slept until 0900. My head still hurts and my ears are still ringing.

P.S. We had an officer involved shooting in our region this morning. A U.S. officer shot an Albanian male three times in the chest when he attached his KPS officer with a knife during a domestic call. This 9mm hardball ammo is crap.

Reuters - 22 November, 2000

P R I S T I N A, Yugoslavia, - One person died from injuries sustained in a bomb attack today at the residence of Yugoslavia's chief representative in Kosovo, the U.N.-led administration of the province said. One man died from injuries suffered in the blast at the home of Stanimir Vukicevic, the head of the Yugoslav government. The early morning blast was at the Pristina home of Stanimir Vukicevic, the head of the Yugoslav government's liaison committee with the international administration in Kosovo - still legally part of Yugoslavia. A U.N. spokeswoman said Vukicevic had been among seven people in the house when the bomb exploded, but that he was not injured. The head of the U.N.-led administration in Kosovo (UNMIK), Bernard Kouchner, initially said at least two people had been injured, one of them seriously. He later said one man who had lived in the house had died from his injuries, but gave no further details. "This was not a random act of violence; it was well-prepared and very carefully executed," he said in his statement. "This was a professional job, and the perpetrators were willing to take enormous risks to achieve their ends." (Buza, 2000)

AP - 22 November, 2000

PRISTINA, Yugoslavia -- A bomb explosion rocked a building used by the Yugoslav representative in Kosovo early Wednesday, killing one staff member and injuring another. Top NATO and U.N. officials in the province condemned the attack. NATO peacekeepers believed the blast, which sent glass and debris flying up to 150 yards away, may have been caused by up to 22 pounds of explosives attached to the side of the building. Two Serb staffers were seriously injured and transported to the British hospital, where one later died, according to a statement from Bernard Kouchner, chief U.N. administrator in Kosovo. Speaking to the local Serb SRNA news agency, Vukicevic called the blast a "pure terrorist attack on the staff of the Yugoslav Committee," which serves as the liaison between Belgrade and NATO missions to Kosovo. (*Associated Press*, 2000)

NY Times - 22 November, 2000

BELGRADE, Serbia, Nov. 22 - Yugoslav authorities warned today that the region could be facing the risk of a new war after violence grew with attacks on Serbian targets in Kosovo and southern Serbia. The head of Kosovo's United Nations administration, Bernard Kouchner, also expressed concern in a statement reading in part: "As I have repeatedly said, Kosovo remains in crisis. The conflict between the two communities is not over." The warnings came after a bomb exploded in Pristina on Tuesday night, half demolishing the home of the Serbian representative in Kosovo, killing one man and injuring several others. (Gall, 2000)

AP - 22 November, 2000

WASHINGTON-- Secretary of State Madeleine Albright condemned the bombing of a building used by the Yugoslav representative in Kosovo and attacks by Albanian insurgents against Serbian police in southern Serbia. (*Associated Press*, 2000)

The Guardian - 23 November, 2000

A senior member of Yugoslavia's government warned yesterday that war could start once again in the Balkans, after renewed fighting on the boundary between Kosovo and Serbia. The warning coincided with a bomb attack on the home of the Yugoslav representative in Kosovo which killed one person. The blast early yesterday tore through the ground floor of the official residence, where Stanimir Vukicevic and his staff were living. An RUC sergeant and an American police officer, on secondment to the UN, were searching the area when the bomb went off. Both were thrown back by the explosion. The residence's driver, Goran Jeftic, a Kosovo Serb, suffered arm and leg injuries in the blast. He was driven to the British military field hospital in Pristina, where he died. A second person was injured in the attack, which was described by Dr. Kouchner as "well prepared and carefully executed".

UNMIK POLICE PRESS UPDATE
23 NOVEMBER, 2000
PRISTINA Region
POLICE SHOOTING

Podujevo – 22/11 – 1125 hrs. UNMIK Police and KPS officers responded to the residence of a K-Albanian male after a complaint was made by the suspect's wife concerning domestic abuse. The suspect armed himself with a "hunting" knife when the officers approached and attacked the KPS officer with the weapon. An UNMIK police officer fired his pistol, striking the suspect in the chest. The suspect was transported to hospital for treatment. The investigation into the complaint of domestic abuse will continue, and the suspect also faces charges involving the attack on the KPS officer. UNMIK Police Internal Affairs will investigate the police shooting, but initial reports indicate the action was justified.

GNJILANE Region

ATTEMPTED MURDER

Urosevac – 21/11 – 1945 hrs. A K-Albanian male was taken to the hospital after being shot by unknown person(s) while he was driving a truck. The victim received a gunshot wound to the back and is listed in serious condition.

EXPLOSION

Vitina/Klokot – 22/11 – 1940 hrs. Two explosions occurred at a vacant home owned by a Serbian male. No injuries were reported. The explosion caused a fire in the yard of the neighboring residence.

DEMONSTRATION

Kamenica – 22/11 – 0115 hrs. Approximately twenty K-Albanian males blocked the road while protesting being evicted from their homes. Two subjects were arrested during the demonstration when they became hostile towards UNMIK Police.

MISSING PERSONS

Gnjilane – 21/11 – 1345 hrs. A K-Albanian female reported that her three sisters have been missing for three weeks.

PRIZREN Region

PROSTITUTION

Prizren – 22/11 - 0130 hrs. Two K-Albanian males along with one K-Albanian male juvenile were arrested in connection with the trafficking of five Moldavian females in prostitution. The prostitution operation was carried out at a coffee bar where suspected narcotics and a weapon were located by investigators. The suspects were also found to be in possession of the victims' passports.

Thursday, 23 November, 2000- Thanksgiving Day

I finally got out of bed at 1000. I ate and showered. I walked down to the internet café. It was full so I went over to the new phone café. I called Carnita and talked to her for awhile. I walked down to the company building to check my e-mail and to turn in my injury report. My left ear is still ringing and I am sore all over. The offices were closed for Thanksgiving. I went to the travel agency to check on air fare home. I was going to surprise Carnita by coming home in December (after almost getting killed) but a ticket for December's CTO was too much ($2,800). I went with all the guys to the company Thanksgiving dinner at the Parliament Restaurant. It was pretty good but I did not have much of an appetite. I went home to rest before work. I had a stress/anxiety attack of some kind but got through it OK. I felt like throwing up. I went to work at 2300. Nothing happened. I got off work at 0700.

P.S. This afternoon a top aid to the newly elected President (Ibrahim Rugova) was assassinated near our AOR (Dardania). He was shot once in the chest and twice in the head while coming out of a restaurant.

UNMIK POLICE PRESS UPDATE
24 NOVEMBER, 2000
PRISTINA Region
MURDER
Pristina - 23/11 - 1520 hrs. A K-Albanian male, Xhemajl Mustafa, was murdered near his residence by an unknown male who shot him three times with a handgun. The victim died shortly after being transported to hospital. Mr. Mustafa was a high ranking member of the of the LDK party and described as "key associate of the leader of the party."
ABDUCTION
Dumnica Village, Podujevo - 23/11- 1930 hrs. A K-Albanian male reported that his girlfriend, an Albanian, was forcibly taken at gunpoint by a K-Albanian male who was on foot. UNMIK Police and KFOR responded to the scene and only managed to locate the victim's clothes and shoes after searching the area.
UXO FOUND
Orllat Village, Glogovac - 23/11 - 1625 hrs. A K-Albanian male reported an item of unexploded ordinance near a school. The area was secured and KFOR EOD was notified.
DEMONSTRATION

Lipljan Town - 23/11 - 1400 hrs. Approximately 300 K-Serbs gathered on the grounds of the church protesting against the ongoing ethnic violence in Lipljan and throughout the province of Kosovo. A speech was delivered by one of the leaders and the crowd dispersed peacefully.

GNJILANE Region

GREIVOUS ASSAULT

Serbia - 23/11 (Time not reported). A male subject, ethnicity unknown, was brought to the Kamenica Hospital with gunshot wounds to the right arm and left elbow. The injuries were allegedly sustained in Serbia during a fight. The subject was treated at the hospital but he departed prior to the arrival of UNMIK Police and without advising hospital personnel or the attending doctor.

ASSAULT

Klokot Village - 22/11 - 2000 hrs. A KFOR Soldier was assaulted when a K-Serbian male attempted to throw rocks at him while the soldier investigated an explosion. The suspect was arrested.

PRIZREN Region

PROSTITUTION

Suva Reka - 23/11 - 1200 hrs. Two K-Albanian males were arrested for patronizing a prostitute and two Moldavian females were arrested for solicitation of prostitution. A routine check by UNMIK Police located the four suspects in a vehicle.

RECOVERED WEAPON

Suva Reka - 22/11 - 1630 hrs. A K-Albanian male found a Karabiner 7.9 mm rifle with 71 rounds of ammunition in his home and handed the weapon over to KFOR.

MITROVICA Region

EXPLOSION

Zitkovac Village, Mitrovica North - 22/11 - 1830 hrs. Unknown subject(s) threw two grenades into the Danish KFOR camp. No injuries were reported but two vehicles were damaged.

Friday, 24 November, 2000

I got off work at 0700. I ate and changed clothes. Craig and I walked down to station #2 and got a vehicle. We drove to the bank and got our MSA (5,216DM). We then drove to the site of the bombing. I took a full disk of pictures. I went home to sleep. I got a call from Brent about a job as the KPS/PFTO Coordinator at

Station #1. He set up a meeting with the Regional Coordinator for 1600. I got to bed at 1100 and slept until 1500. Brent picked me up for the meeting. I stayed until 1800. I should start on Monday. It is a straight days, office job. I am still not feeling very well from the explosion. My ears are still ringing and I have a constant headache. I kind of feel dizzy and fuzzy in the head. I took a nap before work. I went in at 2300. There was not much going on. Our station is manning several static positions in our AOR. We have to keep an eye on the LDK party members. There have been death threats. I got off work at 0700.

P.S. *(Post Script entry made here on 1 December, 2000) *I can tell by looking back at some of these entries that my concussion affected my handwriting somewhat.

E-mail from Carnita

Hi my honey,
I can't stand how much I miss you. I have been so anxious ever since I dropped you off at the airport last time. I'm having a hard time just relaxing. I know it is because I miss you so bad. I'm scared to have you over there now since the bomb incident. Also I heard in the news that four Serbian cops were killed a few days before your incident. We had a nice Thanksgiving, but I was wishing you were here too. How was your company dinner? Well I need to go and check on kids. Love you, Carn

UNMIK POLICE PRESS UPDATE
25 NOVEMBER, 2000
PRISTINA Region
THEFT
Pristina - 24/11 - 1510 hrs. Unknown persons broke into a locked and parked motor vehicle belonging to a KPS Officer and stole several items that included a KPS uniform, yellow traffic vest, handcuffs, baton, holster, whistle and a magazine with 15 rounds of ammunition.
BOMB THREAT
Pristina - 24/11 - 1955 hrs. An unknown Albanian-speaking male called UNMIK Police and stated that a bomb had been placed on the 1st floor of a gymnasium where the Miss Kosova contest was

being organized. KFOR EOD together with UNMIK Police searched the area but nothing was found.

GNJILANE Region

BOMB THREAT

Gnjilane - 24/11 - 1525 hrs. An unknown person phoned the UNMIK Police Duty Officer to report that there was a bomb in the Police Building Complex. The Police Station, Regional Offices and the Courts were evacuated. The building was cleared by American KFOR without incident. Normal operations were resumed at approximately 1705 hrs.

UXO FOUND

Gnjilane - 24/11 - 1130 hrs. A K-Albanian female reported a suspicious package on the front steps of her residence. KFOR EOD responded and found an unexploded grenade, which was disposed of.

MITROVICA Region

GRIEVIOUS ASSAULT

Srbica - 24/11 - 1530 hrs. A K-Albanian male was found by his brother on a roadside bleeding from the head after being assaulted by another K-Albanian male. The suspect, who is believed to be a member of the TMK, was arrested.

Saturday, 25 November, 2000- Hannah's 9th Birthday

I didn't sleep very well. I still have a headache and ringing ears. I got up around 0200. I watched a movie and ate some noodles and cabbage. I went back to work at 2300. Not much going on tonight. We still have static positions at LDK party member's homes. I talked to Pete Anderson (British). He is the new station #2 commander. He was at the station to get a ride to Skopje to go on CTO. Pete said that I could have a few extra days off with my CTO. He also said that he was putting me in for some U.N. award or recognition. I decided to go home on CTO and will try and get reservations on Monday.

P.S. I am starting to feel better. Getting to go home again sure helps. The British medic, Andy McCrum, checked on me again.

E-mail home

I'm here at the cafe checking to see if you are on line. You are not. I will try for an hour or so before I leave. I sent you the pics from the bombing and my report. I had one of those anxiety episodes Thursday night. First one in a couple of years. It went away though. I can't wait to talk to you again. Tonight is my last night shift. Tomorrow I go to the 1500 shift. I don't know when we can connect on the chat so I will just give you a call. Tell Hannah happy birthday for me. I love you so much. Yours forever, Clay

UNMIK POLICE PRESS UPDATE
26 NOVEMBER, 2000
PRISTINA Region
ILLEGAL POSSESSION OF WEAPON
Mali Alas Village, Lipljan - 25/11- 0820 hrs. A local Ashkali resident reported finding a booby trap at the gate of his house, which was set to detonate as soon as the gate opened. KFOR EOD responded to the location and confirmed the device was a M75 hand grenade with approximately 600 grams of high explosives glued to it. A search operation in the village following the incident resulted in the recovery of eleven hand grenades, two rifles, one belt-fed machine gun and two pistols.
GNJILANE Region
MURDER
Pozarane Village, Gnjilane - 25/11 - 1145 hrs. UNMIK Police arrested a K-Albanian male who shot his brother in law with a 7 mm pistol. The victim was pronounced dead at the Gnjilane Hospital. The weapon was also confiscated.
BOMB THREAT
Gnjilane - 25/11 - 2046 hrs. An unknown male called the Gnjilane Police Station and stated that there was a bomb inside the building. The building was checked by KFOR and nothing was found.
UXO FOUND
Kamenica - 25/11 - 0855 hrs. A hand grenade was found under a local vehicle. The area was secured and KFOR responded and disposed of the device.
PRIZREN Region
THREATS
Prizren - 25/11 - 2146 hrs. On the above-mentioned time and date, Prizren Headquarters received a telephone call by an unknown caller who stated that a high-ranking member of the LDK political

party would be assassinated. Immediate safety measures were taken for the protection of all party members.
PROSTITUTION/PIMPING
Prizren - 25/11 - 0015 hrs. Four female suspects, two Moldavians, one Bulgarian and one K -Albanian, were arrested for suspected prostitution. Two males, one Macedonian and one K-Albanian, were arrested for suspected pimping.
MITROVICA Region
ATTEMPTED MURDER
Mitrovica South - 25/11 - 2300 hrs. A K-Albanian male employed as a security guard at a local bar was shot and wounded in the left thigh by six to ten unknown suspects who were trying to enter the bar. The victim's condition was reported as stable.
ASSAULT
Vucitrn - 25/11 - 0110 hrs. A K-Albanian male PDK member who is employed as a journalist was found unconscious and lying in the middle of the street. The victim had apparently been beaten and then dumped by unknown person(s).
FALSE DOCUMENTS
Srbica - 25/11 - 1630 hrs. Three K-Albanian males were arrested for possessing both false documents and inkpads used in producing false documents.

Sunday, 26 November, 2000

Back into work at 1500. I didn't get much sleep. Sundays are always hard because of the shift change. I talked to Brent at the station. He said that many people had talked to him about me. Everyone said that I was acting strange. Randy Wilson said that he thinks I have a concussion. I talked with British medic Andy McCrum again. He also said that he thought I had a concussion and had been keeping an eye on me. I told Brent about talking with the station commander. We worked out how to take the extra days for CTO off the record. Not much happened on shift today. I have been trying to take it easy and get my head back together.

P.S. The weather is still very mild.

UNMIK POLICE PRESS UPDATE
27 NOVEMBER, 2000
PRISTINA Region

POSSIBLE MURDER OF A MISSING PERSON
Grashtic Village, Pristina - 26/11 - 0930 hrs. A K-Albanian male reported that a motor vehicle with a shattered window and blood stains on the driver's seat was parked in his village. The ownership of the vehicle was traced to a K-Albanian male who has been missing since 1100 hrs. on 25/11. Further investigation discovered bullet holes and empty cartridges in the car's interior.

PRIZREN Region

ILLEGAL POSSESSION OF WEAPON
Danjane Village, Orahovac - 26/11 - 0830 hrs. A K-Albanian female surrendered her AK-47 and 29 rounds of ammunition at the UNMIK Police station.

MITROVICA Region

SHOOTING
Srbica Town - 26/11 - 1115 hrs. Persons identified as TMK members fired several pistol and AK-47 rounds into the air. TMK General Shala met with UNMIK Police and KFOR, promising that the guilty persons would be disciplined and this type of incident would never happen again.

UXO FOUND
Vucitrn Town - 26/11 - 1530 hrs. A K-Albanian male delivered a hand grenade to KFOR for disposal. The grenade was disposed of by EOD and a check of the subject's residence revealed no weapons or explosives.

Monday, 27 November, 2000

I got up today at 0900. I washed and ate. I went to the company building to see Doc and to fill out my injury report. I am also going to see the travel agent about tickets home. Doc filled out the injury form and told me to go to Prizren to see the German KFOR Docs for a hearing test. The travel agent took my info and said to check back tomorrow about tickets. I went home and ate lunch. I had noodles and cabbage. I watched a movie and went to a Critical Incident Stress Debriefing (CISD) meeting at 1500. It was a good session. All the CivPol officers that were involved in the bombing were required to be there. I found out from Brent that the station #1 job is not going to happen. Instead I will be going to straight days at station #2 to do the KPS officer in-service training. I won't start until after my CTO. Just a few more days to go.

P.S. I did not go into work today because of the CISD. After the CISD I went out to eat at the Indian Inn with the RUC officers from Northern Ireland. We had a good meal and drinks. After the meal we went to the Kukri bar.

UNMIK POLICE PRESS UPDATE
28 NOVEMBER, 2000
PRISTINA Region
THREATS AGAINST UNMIK POLICE
Glogovac Town - 27/11 - 1805 hrs. Three UNMIK Police Officers received a call at their residence from a male voice speaking in English that advised them not to report for work the following day as something was going to happen. The caller went on to say that he knew were they stayed and that they had no business in this country.
ATTEMPTED MURDER
Kosovo Polje Town - 27/11- 0235 hrs. Unknown persons shot and injured a K-Bosnian female in her right leg when she opened the door of her house after hearing a knock at the door. The victim was taken to the hospital were she was released after treatment.
FLAG DAY CELEBRATIONS
Obilic Village, Kosovo Polje - 27/11 - 1700 hrs. Approximately 400 persons attended peaceful Flag Day celebrations that included a variety of dancing acts, music and speeches. A fire caused by an electric short circuit occurred just after the function closed. An evacuation was carried out, the fire was controlled and no further incidents were reported.
PEC Region
MURDER
Bardasne Village, Dakovica - 27/11 - 0915 hrs. Gunfire erupted during an argument between neighboring K-Albanian families. Two K-Albanian males were shot dead and three K-Albanian males were critically wounded as a result of the gunfire. House searches after the shooting revealed one AK-47 and 2 magazines, which were seized.
SUICIDE
Pec - 27/11 - 0820 hrs. The body of a K-Albanian male was found hanging in a cell at the Pec Detention Center. It was apparently a suicide.

Tuesday, 28 November, 2000

I got up at 1000. I went straight to the company building to find out about my flight home. The travel agent got reservations from Skopje to Kalispell for only $1,223 (2,800DM). I paid for the tickets with my MSA and still had enough for the rent and extra CTO money. The tickets won't be ready for a couple of days. I have to come back to the company travel agent to pick them up. I am scheduled to arrive in Kalispell at 2355 on December 3rd. Today is Kosovo Flag Day. We are working a twelve hour shift until 0300. Operations is expecting trouble. I got called to assist at the gym where they were having a concert. They oversold the event by about 8,000 tickets. The crowd was very angry. It took about an hour but we got them to disburse. We had a bomb threat at the youth center but nothing happened. Other than sporadic automatic "celebration" gunfire, nothing major happened. We stood down at 0200.

P.S. There was a large parade earlier in the day and the dedication of a large UCK memorial statue.

UNMIK POLICE PRESS UPDATE
29 NOVEMBER, 2000
PRISTINA Region
ATTEMPTED MURDER
Majaci Village, Podujevo - 28/11 - 1400 hrs. A K-Albanian male reported that he was shot and wounded in the right elbow by his neighbor when he went to draw water from a communal spring. The victim was taken to hospital for treatment and was later discharged.
FLAG DAY PARADE
Pristina - 28/11 - 1230 hrs. A parade organized by the TMK including 250 unarmed members, marched from TMK headquarters to the Grand Hotel on Mother Theresa Street where a statue of Zahir Pajaziti was unveiled. Cultural ceremonies followed thereafter. Approximately 10,000 persons attended the event, which was peaceful.
UXO FOUND
Obrea Village, Glogovac - 28/11 - 1015 hrs. An M75 hand grenade was located. KFOR EOD was notified and disposed of the device.
GNJILANE Region
EXPLOSION

Urosevac Town - 28/11 - 2200 hrs. A K-Albanian male was holding a hand grenade when it accidentally exploded in the man's hand. The victim was transported to Pristina hospital, listed in serious condition.
PEC Region
ILLEGAL POSSESSION OF WEAPONS
Cerovik, Klina - 28/11 - 0600 hrs. A search of two residences conducted by UNMIK Police resulted in the arrest of four K-Albanian males, including a serving KPS Officer and also an active TMK member. Two AK-47 assault rifles, one sniper rifle, two hunting rifles, six hand grenades, nine fuses, one M70 anti-tank grenade, one demolition charge, twelve fully loaded magazines, eight kilograms of ammunition components and photographs of UCK soldiers were confiscated in the operation.
CRIMINAL DAMAGE
Gorazdevac Village, Pec - 27/11 - 1110 hrs. A K-Albanian male reported that while driving through a Serbian village his vehicle was damaged by children throwing rocks.
MITROVICA Region
ASSAULT
Vucitrn Town - 28/11 - 1430 hrs. Two K-Albanian males assaulted an UNMIK Police officer during a traffic stop. Both suspects were arrested.
THREATS/INTIMIDATION
Srbica Town - 28/11 - 1325 hrs. During the Flag Day celebration, an UNMIK Police officer was intimidated by the crowd after taking a weapon and a weapons permit card from a person that was firing into the air.

Wednesday, 29 November, 2000

I got up at 1000. "Triple Sierra" and oatmeal. I went down to station #2 to get a vehicle to go to Prizren for a hearing test. There were no vehicles free to take so I came back home. I watched the BBC news and ate some noodles and cabbage for lunch. I went to work at 1500. I found out that there had been a shooting in the station #1 AOR in the "thieves" market area. It was some kind of family feud. One guy had an AK-47 and the other had a 9mm pistol. The AK-47 won. The 9mm guy was killed. There was another death threat on an LDK party member. Our station is guarding about twenty VIP locations. There are several static posts (not that it will do any good if someone really wants to make a hit). Not much for my team tonight. We just patrolled our AOR and checked VIP houses. I got off at 2300.

UNMIK POLICE PRESS UPDATE
30 NOVEMBER, 2000
PRISTINA Region
MURDER
Pristina - 29/11 - 1240 hrs. A K-Albanian male was shot dead and four others sustained injuries following an exchange of gunfire during a family dispute. An AK-47 assault rifle was recovered from the scene. A K-Albanian male suspect fled the scene in a vehicle after the incident.
ILLEGAL POSSESSION OF WEAPON
Lapushnik Village, Glogovac - 29/11 - 1410 hrs. Three K-Albanian males were arrested after a search of their van revealed twenty-one mines, twelve mortars, one rifle, two boxes of ammunition, 20 black berets, 162 combat boots, five boxes of thermal underwear and 100 blankets. The suspects were traveling to Pristina from Pec when the vehicle was stopped.
PRIZREN Region
EXPLOSION
Zur Village, Dragash - 29/11 - 1640 hrs. KFOR notified UNMIK Police of a mine explosion that injured three persons. EOD responded to the scene to assist.

Thursday, 30 November, 2000

I got up after 1000. I took a shower (Kosovo style) and got into uniform. I went down to station #2 to get a car to go to Prizren for a hearing test. Still no vehicles available! It was no surprise. I hung around the station for a while and then went to the internet café to check my e-mail. I had none from Carnita but one from John Graham. He said that CNN had called *The Western News* to find out what Libby cop had been killed in Kosovo. I went to the phone café and called Carnita. I woke her up at 0530 her time. She sounded sick with a cold or flu but was glad I called. I told her that I had not been killed if she heard any rumors. I told her about my flight plans and stuff. I went to work at 1500. I ate supper at the KFOR restaurant. Not much happening at work except another shooting in station #3 AOR. I got off work at 2300.

P.S. The weather is still mild. We have had warm, sunny days and chilly nights.

UNMIK POLICE PRESS UPDATE
01 DECEMBER, 2000
PRISTINA Region
ATTEMPTED MURDER
Luzane Village, Podujevo - 30/11 - 2115 hrs. A K-Albanian member of the LDK party was injured when his vehicle was fired upon by unknown suspects in another vehicle.
UXO FOUND
Pristina - 30/11 - 1130 hrs. A UXO was located in the market place. KFOR EOD was notified and disposed of the ordnance by a controlled explosion.
GNJILANE Region
PROSTITUTION
Urosevac Town - 30/11 - 2330 hrs. KFOR arrested five persons for prostitution. One K-Albanian male and four unidentified females were taken to UNMIK Police for detention.
DEMONSTRATION
Kamenica Town - 30/11 - 1055 hrs. Approximately two hundred K-Albanians gathered at checkpoint 75 to protest against not being allowed to cross from Recane into Serbia. UNMIK Police assisted KFOR.
PEC Region
UXO FOUND
Istok - 30/11 - 0715 hrs. A K-Albanian male reported that he found what was believed to be grenade in a hotel parking lot. KFOR EOD responded and disposed of the ordnance.
MITROVICA Region
THREATS/INTIMDATION
Mitrovica North - 29/11 - 1400 hrs. A "bridge watcher" was arrested on 9/11 for possession of illegal weapons by KFOR. Serbians have now threatened that if the suspect isn't released they will "make it impossible for KFOR and UNMIK Police to operate" and control the Mitrovica North area.

Friday, 1 December, 2000

Up at 1000 today. I ate oatmeal for breakfast. I hung my laundry up to dry. I went down to the company building to get my plane tickets. They were not ready yet. They said to come back this afternoon. I walked back to the house (up the hill again!) and ate some noodles for lunch. I caught up some entries in my diary and got some stuff ready for CTO. I went in to work at 1500. I went back to the company building and was told to pick up my tickets at the desk in Skopje airport. I am supposed to meet a company representative there at 0600. He better be there! I got involved in a couple of house searches with Barry Greene (RUC) and the British KFOR. We recovered a couple of rifles and some machine gun ammunition drums. It took half the shift to finish all the paper work. I got involved with KFOR when a fight broke out at our station between two Royal Marines. Station #2 is the HQ and barracks of the KFOR British Royal Marines. The Marines had been allowed to go to a movie and have a ration of two beers. A couple of Marines apparently snuck away to a local watering hole. When they got back to station #2 they got into a fight and started punching each other. I picked up their rifles which they had dropped and told the other CivPol officers to stay back and watch. I told them that the other Marines would take care of it, and they did. The others got the fight broke up and separated the brawlers. One of them was apparently more intoxicated than the other and started mouthing off to the Sergeant who had shown up to find out what was going on. He lipped off a little too much and got an additional pummeling from a few other Marines. I had to give them both a breath test at the request of the unit's Commanding Officer. Both had had more than their two beer ration. One guy was a .099 BAC and the other was a .199 BAC. I got home at about 2330. Craig and I listened to a county music tape one of his Serbian L.A.s made for him. I got to bed about 0100.

UNMIK POLICE PRESS UPDATE
02 DECEMBER, 2000
PRISTINA Region
ARMED ROBBERY
Pristina- 01/12 - 0015 hrs. Four masked gunmen broke into the offices of NGO "Al-Haramain Humanitarian Foundation", bound the guard, and took unspecified items.
ILLEGAL POSSESSION OF WEAPONS
Poklek Village, Glogovac- 01/12 - 1145 hrs. In a joint operation of KFOR and UNMIK Police, assorted weapons were recovered and two K-Albanian males were arrested.

GNJILANE Region
PROSTITUTION
Strpce Town - 30/11 - 1800 hrs. A K-Serbian male was found with two Romanian females who had false passports. One suspect was arrested.
DEMONSTRATION
Dajkovce Village, Strpce - 01/12 - 1740 hrs. UNMIK Police reported a gathering of Serbian people protesting the alleged stabbing of a K-Serbian male by a K-Albanian male earlier in the day. Approximately 60 people eventually gathered and the only serious incident that occurred was a stone thrown through an Albanian's car window. The stabbing was not reported, nor could it be substantiated.
MITROVICA Region
ATTEMPTED MURDER
Srbica Town - 01/12 - 1830 hrs. A K-Albanian female was shot once in the back by a K-Albanian neighbor who fired on her vehicle. The victim was taken to the hospital for treatment and the suspect was arrested.
ROADBLOCK
Mitrovica North - 01/12 - 1720 hrs. A group of K-Serbians blocked the roadway in the "Coca-Cola Hill" area and would not let K-Albanians drive through the area. The demonstration is the result of an ongoing dispute and ended when UNMIK Police units responded to deal with it.

Saturday, 2 December, 2000

Up at 0900. I ate some oatmeal and had coffee with Craig. Ken is going to drive me to the airport about 0400 in the morning. I got my backpack all ready to go. I hope there will be no problems with my tickets. I went in to work at 1500. Not much going on until the traffic unit got into a pursuit. I was monitoring the pursuit on the radio and realized that they were headed toward station #2. I drove down to an intersection just a couple of blocks from the station and intercepted the suspect vehicle. The suspect stopped and we made our approach with guns drawn. The traffic unit officers were behind the vehicle and I was approaching from the front. The driver started to take off and drive toward me. I thought that I was going to have to shoot him but the traffic unit officer got to him and got the vehicle shut off. We pulled the driver out of the vehicle and he started to fight. We kicked his ass. I handcuffed the suspect and walked him back up to station #2 to book him. The British Marine sentry on duty at the front of the station must have been the same one from when I brought in a prisoner after a fight in September or he had at least had been told about the incident. As I walked the bloodied prisoner into the station the sentry said "I see someone else got an American Arse Kicking". On a more serious note, when I re-holstered my weapon as we pulled the driver out of the vehicle I noticed that I could not get the thumb break to re-snap. After the prisoner was secured I check and found that the reason my holster would not snap was that the hammer on my Beretta was at the half cocked position. This means that I was in the process of pulling the trigger but stopped before the hammer fell, catching it at the half cocked position. The suspect came very close to getting shot. I got off at 2300, went home and ate, and finished getting ready for the trip home. I watched a movie while waiting for Ken to pick me up at 0430. Ken picked me up and drove me to Skopje. I got to the airport at 0600 to meet the company guy who had my tickets. He was a half hour late and I almost missed my plane.

P.S. We had another shooting today at about 1300. A KPS officer got shot in the chest in front of the Grand Hotel. The shooting was in retaliation for the officer's brother stabbing a girl yesterday. Another "blood feud".

Sunday, 3 December, 2000- Skopje, Macedonia/JFK

I took off from Skopje at about 0730. The flight to Zurich took about three hours. I slept most of the flight. Zurich to JFK took eight hours. I arrived at JFK a half hour early only to find that my flight to Salt Lake City was cancelled because of no flight crew. Delta rescheduled everyone for a 0650 flight in the morning. I was given a voucher for the Best Western Hotel and a $12.00 meal voucher. I called home but Carnita had already left for Kalispell. I called Carnita's sister, Peggy, to have her try and get a message to Carnita. My flight won't be into Kalispell until 1250 on 4 December. I checked into the Best Western and went to the restaurant to eat. I had a $25.00 steak. I tried to call Carnita again but could not get through from the motel room. The room was pretty nice. I had a queen size bed. There was a coffee maker in the room so I had a cup of coffee, watched some T.V. and went to bed.

P.S. The weather in NYC was cool (35 degrees) but dry. Hopefully it is going to be a mild winter.

UNMIK POLICE PRESS UPDATE
04 DECEMBER, 2000
PRISTINA Region
ATTEMPTED MURDER
Pristina - 02/12 - 1320 hrs. A K-Albanian male, an off-duty KPS officer, was shot once in the chest. The victim was transported to a local hospital where he is listed in stable condition. Three K-Albanian male suspects were arrested in connection with the shooting.
GNJILANE Region
ILLEGAL POSSESSION OF WEAPON
Strpce Town - 03/12 - 1245 hrs. During a Serbian demonstration in protest of an earlier fire, UNMIK Police and KFOR heard automatic weapon gunfire coming from the hills. Several suspects in the shooting were pursued, however none were located. A subsequent search of the area revealed an automatic rifle, two magazines, a bag full of ammunition and a bayonet near a haystack. The K-Albanian male owner of the haystack was located at his home and a search of his home produced more ammunition. UNMIK Police arrested the K-Albanian male suspect.
EXPLOSION
Zitnje Village, Vitina - 03/12 - 1610 hrs. KFOR informed UNMIK police that there was an explosion in the village. An abandoned K-Serb home was damaged.
ARSON
Cernice Village, Gnjilane - 02/12 - 2100 hrs. A K-Serb female reported that her house was on fire. Witnesses stated that they had earlier seen three unidentified K-Albanian males near the house.
UXO FOUND
Urosevac Town - 03/12 - 1530 hrs. A K-Albanian male reported that his children had found an UXO. KFOR EOD was called and the ordnance was removed.
MITROVICA Region
ASSAULT

Mitrovica North - 02/12 - 1510 hrs. A K-Albanian male was arrested by UNMIK Police after assaulting a KFOR soldier.
PEC Region
GRENADE ATTACK
Istok Town - 02/12 - 2100 hrs. A K-Roma home sustained major roof damage after an unknown person threw a grenade inside.
PRIZREN Region
GRIEVOUS ASSAULT
Prizren - 03/12 - 0100 hrs. A Dutch citizen reported that three unknown male suspects forcibly entered his home and demanded money. When the victim stated that he had none he was stabbed once with a knife in the stomach. The suspects then fled. The victim was transported to the hospital for treatment.

Monday, 4 December, 2000- JFK/SLC/Kalispell/Libby

I got up early and took a shower. I could not sleep any longer. I caught the 0430 shuttle to the Delta terminal. I had to wait until after 0500 for the terminal to open. I got checked in and sat and watched CNN until time to board the plane. I got to Salt lake City about a half hour early. I had about an hour and a half layover. I ate and sat around. I left SLC for Kalispell. The flight was on time. Carnita met me at the airport. We went to Costco and had lunch. We gassed up and headed home. We arrived about 1600. The kids were glad to see me. Courtni had made bow tie salad for me. I ate until I was stuffed. I was planning to go to the city council meeting but jet lag set in. I got to bed early. I could not stay awake. It is very good to be home again.

UNMIK POLICE PRESS UPDATE
05 DECEMBER, 2000
PRISTINA Region
GRENADE ATTACK
Lipljan Town - 04/12 - 0040 hrs. Unknown person(s) fired a grenade apparently from a launching device at a house. The ethnicity/nationality of the occupant was not reported. No damage or injuries were reported.
Kosovo Polje Town - 04/12 - 1820 hrs. A K-Albanian male reported that a known K-Serbian male threw a hand grenade inside his home causing damage to the windows and furniture inside the home.

GNJILANE Region
ASSAULT
Ranilug Village, Kamenica - 04/12 - 2200 hrs. A K-Albanian male reported that five unknown males (all wearing black military type uniforms) forced him to stop while he was driving near the village of Ranilug. One offender fired several shots from an automatic weapon without injuring anyone.
ILLEGAL POSSESSION OF WEAPONS
Kamenica Town - 04/12 - 1639 hrs. An employee at Kamenica Hospital found a sub-machine gun with magazines in the hospital's drainage system. UNMIK Police confiscated the items.
Urosevac Town - 04/12 - 1400 hrs. The K-Albanian male manager of Bankkos Bank reported that two handguns and four magazines were found in one of the bank's lockers. UNMIK Police confiscated the items.
UXO
Vitina Town - 04/12 - 1600 hrs. Two K-Albanian boys found an unexploded mine. UNMIK Police and KFOR responded and sealed off the area. KFOR EOD disposed of the ordnance.
PRIZREN Region
GRENADE ATTACK
Prizren Town - 02/12 - 0830 hrs. A K-Bosnian male reported that unknown suspect(s) threw a hand grenade into his shop through a hole in a wire cage. The security pin was found intact and the device did not explode. KFOR EOD disposed of the device.
PEC Region
ROCKET ATTACK
Dakovica Town - 03/12 - 2230 hrs. A K-Albanian male reported that unknown person(s) launched a rocket into his home resulting in damage to a second floor room.

Thursday, 7 December, 2000

Pearl Harbor Day. I got up at 0500 again. I could hear Josiah upstairs rooting around and turning on the furnace. I got up and made us some toast. I had some coffee while watching *M*A*S*H* with Jo. I called Mom and Dad today. Everything is fine in Texas. I got my brother Chris's e-mail address for Ardian (L.A. in Kosovo). He wants to correspond with Chris to better his English. Chris is an English teacher. Mom and Dad said that they saw me and my bombing story on the front page of *The Western News*.

That was fast. I got a couple of calls from people who have sons over in Kosovo in the military. They wanted to know about the place. I had a great meal of roasted chicken, mashed potatoes, gravy, peas and onions. I got stuffed. I watched T.V. and relaxed with the family. I still get sleepy very early in the evening. I went to bed and fell asleep reading the *Reader's Digest*.

Wednesday, December 13th, 2000

I got up about 0730. Josiah and the furnace again. I had tuna fish for breakfast. Today is Courtni's 15th birthday. We got on the road to Kalispell about 1300. We dropped Josiah and Jesse at Cliff and Steph's house in Kila. We bought two pizzas and took them to Carnita's grandmother's house (Isabelle Everett, age 82). We are going to stay with her to save the motel bill. I called Mom and Dad to say goodbye again. I watched Gore finally concede and Bush accept appointment as President Elect. We went to bed early. I have to be at the airport by 0530.

P.S. There is bad winter weather all across the country. The temperature was 5 degrees below zero last night. I hope none of my flights are delayed.

Thursday, 14 December, 2000- Kalispell/JFK/Zurich

We got up at 0415. I started the Suburban to warm it up. We ate leftover pizza for breakfast. I kissed the kids goodbye and Carnita and I left for the airport at 0530. There were no delays so far on my flights. I left at 0630 for Salt Lake City. The flight for JFK was on time. I had a two hour layover at JFK. The flight to Zurich was on time. We had a tail wind and the flight only took six hours to cross the Atlantic. I had good food but no sleep. I landed in Zurich at 0800 local time.

UNMIK POLICE PRESS UPDATE
15 DECEMBER, 2000
PRISTINA Region
WAR MEMORIAL CEREMONY
Glogovac Town - 14/12 - 1200 hrs. Approximately 2,000 people attended a ceremony to commemorate those UCK members who

lost their lives during the war. The event started at 1200 hrs. and ended at about 1400 hrs.

GNJILANE Region

ATTEMPTED MURDER

Pasjane Village, Gnjilane - 14/12 - 1730 hrs. When a K-Albanian male stopped his car to remove an obstacle on the roadway several unidentified suspects stepped into the road and began firing at the victims vehicle several times. The driver was injured by flying glass fragments. Victim was treated at the hospital.

EXPLOSION

Klokot Village, Vitina - 14/12 - 2300 hrs. An explosion completely destroyed an unoccupied K-Serbian house.

Novo Selo Village, Vitina - 15/12 - 0040 hrs. An explosion believed to be a hand grenade caused minor property damage to an occupied K-Albanian owned home.

PRIZREN Region

EXPLOSION

Sredska Village, Prizren - 14/12 - 1410 hrs. Two simultaneous bomb explosions took place in two abandoned homes owned by K-Serbs and caused extensively property damage. No injuries were reported.

MITROVICA Region

ARSON

Zubin Potok Town - 13/12 - 2345 hrs. A K-Serbian male reported that his vehicle was set ablaze by unknown persons while it was parked in front of a café. There were also words etched on the vehicle that could not be read due to the damage.

Friday, 15 December, 2000- Zurich/Skopje/Kosovo

I had a scheduled two hour layover in Zurich. I found my gate for a 1000 departure to Skopje. At 0900 the gate was changed to another terminal. I went to the new gate. At 1000 the flight got delayed because of fog in Skopje. The gate changed again! I went to the next gate and had to wait for news about our departure time. I visited with two Americans and one German girl married to an American in Kosovo. We finally left Zurich around noon. I arrived two hours late in Skopje. I started looking for my ride. I found some Americans waiting for a new U.S. contingent to arrive. I hung out with them and got a ride back. We stopped at McDonald's first before leaving Skopje. I got back to Pristina and to the house about 2100. I was too tired to go into work. I went straight to bed.

UNMIK POLICE PRESS UPDATE
16 DECEMBER, 2000
GNJILANE Region
DEMONSTRATION
Partesh Village, Gnjilane - 15/12 - 1930 hrs. An unknown number of K-Serbs held a peaceful demonstration against the shooting of a K-Serb male.
PRIZREN Region
ATTEMPTED MURDER
Orlat Village, Malishevo - 15/12 - 1430 hrs. A K-Albanian male, who is a member of the LDK party, was shot and wounded in the left shoulder as he drove in his car by an unknown person, who shot at him from a vehicle. The victim was hospitalized. The condition was reported to be serious but stable.
PEC Region
GUNFIRE / GRENADE EXPLOSION
Pec - 15/12 - 1300 hrs. During a dispute between two groups of K-Albanians at the bus station several shots were fired into the air. Also a hand grenade exploded. Five persons sustained minor injuries. UNMIK Police arrested 9 K-Albanians and seized a pistol and a hand grenade.
ATTEMPTED MURDER
Qitak Village, Pec - 14/12 - 2245 hrs. KPS Officers on patrol located a stolen vehicle that was occupied. When the KPS officers stopped and approached the car, an unknown male occupant of the vehicle exited and fired several shots at the officers without hitting or injuring them. As the KPS officers returned fire the suspect fled on foot.
MITROVICA Region
ASSAULT
Zvecan Town - 15/12 - 1430 hrs. A Bosnian male reported that he had been attacked by a group of 30 K-Serbs who wanted to take the fish he was carrying which was meant for the Red Cross. UNMIK Police responded and the situation was brought under control.

Saturday, 16 December, 2000

I did not go into work on night shift last night. I got to bed about 2200. I slept for seventeen hours until 1500. I got up and ate oatmeal and coffee. I got shaved (de-bearded) and had a long shower (Kosovo style). I got unpacked and my gear ready for work. Everyone is gone on CTO except me, Craig, and Brent. I went back into work for one night shift. Things at work seem surprisingly more organized. We now have five vehicles assigned to the FTU (Field Training Unit). This allows the team leader (me on "C" shift) to take the car home after work. That means that I won't have to walk up that hill! Nothing outstanding happened at work. I cut everyone loose an hour early because we have a quick turn around and have to be back in at 1500. I got off at 0700. I drove home!

P.S. The weather is cool and rainy. We had strong wind and rain for about an hour. It is a lot warmer here than in Montana, though.

Sunday, 17 December, 2000

Today is shift change day. I got off this morning at 0700. I got to bed at 0800 and slept in until 1300. I went in to work at 1430 for briefing by the station commander (Pete Anderson, U.K.) to the whole shift. After the briefing he asked me to come to his office. I went in to his office and found the U.S. Contingent Commander (Pete Palmer) and his deputy there. The station commander gave me a certificate and an appreciation letter for my actions at the bombing. The U.S. Contingent Commander gave me a letter also. Not much else happened on shift. Everyone is tired from shift change. The lingering jet lag makes it worse. I got off at 2300. I went home and went to bed.

Letter from Station #2 Commander

To: Clayton L. Coker
P.O. CP04415
From: Pete Anderson
Station #2 Commander

Subj: Letter of Appreciation

At approximately 0440 hours on Wednesday 22nd November 2000 there was a large explosion at the residence of the Serbian Ambassador, an incident with which you were personally involved. Initial reports suggest that the explosion was a result of a bomb being placed at the rear of the Ambassador's residence, some 5-10kg in size, which caused massive structural damage not only to the Ambassador's residence, but to surrounding buildings as well. After being knocked to the ground by the force of the explosion, you conducted yourself with professionalism that was truly exemplary. Your immediate reaction was to get to your feet and detail Officers under your control to secure a potential crime scene. Even with the knowledge that a secondary explosive device may be present, you went into the Ambassador's residence to look for and evacuate casualties. You, along with other International Officers, rendered immediate first aid and helped in the rapid transfer of casualties to the hospital.

I would personally like to thank you for the most professional and courageous efforts you made that morning in which you proved yourself to be a most able and competent Police Officer. I was extremely impressed by your actions and am very proud to have you as a member of this Station. You are a credit to both the United Nations Police Force in Kosovo and your country. I will personally contact your Contingent Commander and congratulate him on your actions. I will also recommend that the U.N. Mission in Kosovo be advised or your truly commendable actions.

Pete Anderson (UK)
Station #2 Commander, Pristina

Letter from Office of the United States Contingent Commander

13 December 2000
Clayton Coker, Police Officer
United Nations Mission in Kosovo
Pristina, Kosovo

The members of the United States Contingent Command wish to express our sincere appreciation for your heroic actions at the scene of a terrorist bombing in Pristina. We completely agree with

the sentiments expressed by your station commander in his letter to you, and we are proud of you as our colleague and countryman. We spoke in my office late in the morning of the explosion. I remember quite vividly your appearance and demeanor. Covered with dirt and dust, clothes in disarray, you were nevertheless calm and composed as you related the events of just a few hours before. On foot in the back of the target residence, you were doing the duty of a police officer helping to search for suspicious persons seen nearby. Although violently shaken by the blast, you got to your feet immediately and began rescue operations. You continued with these, concerned more for the victims of the blast than with your own safety, until relieved hours later. As you told me of your experience, I was struck by your courage and keen sense of duty that came through clearly in your narrative.
All of us come to this mission in Kosovo aware of the dangers and risks. We are prepared to deal with the routine hazards we knew back home: armed aggressors, violent reactions to arrest, and all the rest. The kind of incident you faced however, one can never be completely prepared for. When it happens, we can only hope that our reactions will be as professional, as courageous, and as honorable as yours.

W. Pete Palmer, Commander
United States Contingent
UNMIK Police

Monday, 18 December, 2000

Same morning routine this morning. Oatmeal and coffee. I had water today so I got a hot shower and a shave. The house has been cool inside. I need to buy an electric heater for my room. All the other rooms have one. We are down to our last bottle of propane for the main furnace. It probably won't last another 24 hours. I went to work at 1400. I am working on paperwork to catch up KPS class #7 records. They are scheduled to be released on Sunday the 24th. I looked for a propane store. I need to get our bottles filled or we will freeze. Not much is happening at work. I got off at 2300. I went home, visited with Brent and Craig, and then went to bed.

E-mail home

Hi Hun.
This is the first chance I've had at the internet tonight. The flight was good. I only was delayed from Zurich to Skopje for two hours. Work has been going well. Only three more shifts until I start my straight day job. I will be able to have some time off every weekend since all the trainees have the weekends off. The weather here is cool and rainy but OK. I tried you on the chat just now but no answer. The power is off right now and we are on generator power here at the cafe. I don't know if the house is out too. I just got off work and came here. I will try to call you in the next few days. I've got to go home and eat now and catch up on my diary. Oh, I almost forgot. I got a certificate and appreciation letters from the Station Commander and the American Contingent Commander for the bombing incident and they put me in for some U.N. award also. My next CTO is from 8 Jan to 14 Jan. I am going to send some extra money home to be included in your next check. Talk to you soon. Love and miss you so much. Your hubby, Clay

UNMIK POLICE PRESS UPDATE
19 DECEMBER, 2000
PRISTINA Region
GRENADE ATTACK
Obilic, Kosovo Polje - 18/12 -1335 hrs. Unknown person(s) threw a hand grenade into the rear of a K-Serb owned house. The explosion caused only property damage. No injuries were reported.
PRIZREN Region
ARSON
Decani Town - 17/12 - 1355 hrs. A K-Albanian female was arrested by UNMIK Police after trying to set the municipal building on fire. No major damage or injuries were reported.

Tuesday, 19 December, 2000

I slept in until noon. I got up to no water or power. I had to heat some water in a small propane burner to have coffee and oatmeal. It is to cold to wash with cold water so I went to work at 1400 with greasy hair (covered with a ball cap) and no shave. The temperature dropped off some tonight. We have thick fog in the city. There were several accidents and we assisted with one. We had a bomb threat at the R.T.K. (Radio-Television-Kosova) T.V.

station. We had to search the building and grounds. There was a good view from the rooftop. It turned out to be a prank call. I patrolled until I got off at 2300. I checked my e-mail at the internet café. I bought some noodles at the 24 hour market. I went home and ate and then went to bed early. I am going to town tomorrow to get propane and food. I took the vehicle home.

E-mail from Carnita

Hi my honey.
Glad to finally hear from you. I had e-mailed Marie yesterday to ask if Craig had mentioned you making it back and she said yes that you made it back. I'm so proud of you and your awards and everything you do. You are definitely my hero. You sounded in good spirits in your e-mail. I'm glad you will be doing a day job with weekends off. I was on the CivPol site yesterday reading the messages and it sounds like people are having a harder time getting a mission. There are so many people wanting to go on this mission but now they are being pickier. Love you so much and please be careful. I saw on the BBC news the other night that there was a bombing and a takeover in Mitrovica around the 17th. The Serbs were mad because of someone that got arrested. Love you,
Carnita

UNMIK POLICE PRESS UPDATE
20 DECEMBER, 2000
PRISTINA Region
ARSON
Gracanica Village, Pristina - 18/12 - 2230 hrs. Unknown person(s) broke into the house of a K-Serb male KPS Officer and set it on fire after stealing parts of his duty gear. A substantial amount of property was destroyed. KFOR and the local fire brigade attended the scene and brought the fire under control. The house owner and his family were not at home at the time of the incident.
MITROVICA Region
GUNFIRE /EXPLOSION
Zubin Potok Town - 19/12 - 2230 hrs. A UNMIK van parked in front of the police station exploded, several rounds of automatic rifle fire were fired in the direction of other UNMIK vehicles parked in front of the station and a rocket propelled grenade was fired in a window of the second floor of the building which is

shared with the Municipality. Four UNMIK vehicles were damaged by the gunfire in addition to the van. The front of the building was sprayed with automatic gunfire. First reports indicate that the explosion of the van came from inside the vehicle. No injuries were reported.

Wednesday, 20 December, 2000

Up at 0830. I had oatmeal for breakfast. The power and water is on. Craig and I took my "coke" to town to get our propane bottles filled. I found a place to exchange bottles for 25DM each. I got four full bottles and I bought an electric heater for my room (70DM). We then went to Ardi's and bought some food. I found some Arabic chicken franks to have with sour kraut. I spent 70DM on food. We stopped by Main HQ to pick up our U.N. mission medals and check on Craig's re-deployment to Main HQ. I got home and showered and shaved before the water went out again. I finally got a load of laundry in the washer. I went in to work at 1400. I made a DUI arrest at 1700. An older man was very drunk. It took most of the shift to finish the paperwork. Tonight was my last shift on patrol.

P.S. We had a little skiff on snow when we left this morning but it did not last long. It was a nice, sunny, cool day. I am going to drive Andy Margiota to Skopje airport tomorrow for his CTO. I am then going to drop Craig at K.P. (Kosovo Polje) for work.

UNMIK POLICE PRESS UPDATE
21 DECEMBER, 2000
PRISTINA Region
GRENADE ATTACK
Pristina - 20/12 - 0330 hrs. Unknown person(s) threw a hand grenade in the schoolyard during the early morning hours causing minor damage to the windows and door of the school. The school was closed at the time of the incident.
THEFT
Pristina - 19/12 - 2350 hrs. Unknown person(s) broke into the home of a KPS Officer and took his service weapon and other police equipment.
GNJILANE Region
ATTEMPTED MURDER

Urosevac Town - 20/12 - 0645 hrs. A K-Albanian male reported finding his father lying outside with a gunshot wound to the head. The victim was transported to the hospital for treatment.

ASSAULT

Gnjilane - 20/12 - 1710 hrs. A K-Albanian male was arrested by UNMIK Police for assaulting an off duty KPS Officer.

PRIZREN Region

SHOOTING

Vlasnje Village, Prizren - 19/12 - 2110 hrs. Unknown person(s) shot at the vehicle of a K-Albanian male while he was driving home from work. One bullet was recovered from the victim's car.

MITROVICA Region

ASSAULT

Mitrovica North - 20/12 - 1800 hrs. A K-Bosnian male reported being assaulted by five or six unknown K-Serbian males. The victim was able to escape but received minor injuries.

ASSAULT

Mitrovica North - 20/12 - Daytime hrs. Two K-Serbian males were arrested for throwing rocks at KFOR vehicles.

ASSAULT / THEFT

Mitrovica North - 20/12 - Daytime hrs. Five unknown males assaulted a K-Bosnian male and his son and took their vehicle.

AIDING AND ABETTING AN ESCAPEE

Srbica Town - 20/12 - 1830 hrs. A KPS Officer reported that he had tried to apprehend a K-Albanian prisoner at a local concert who had escaped from prison on murder charges. The officer was unable to complete the arrest as a crowd of persons assisted this individual in escaping.

Thursday, 21 December, 2000

I got up at 0900. I washed my hair, dressed, and ate cream of wheat I had brought from home. I am down to the “plain” flavor now. Andy picked us up at 0945. We went to get MSA. Andy got his but Craig and I had too long a line to wait in so we left without it. Craig and I can get it when we get back tomorrow. We drove to Skopje airport and dropped Andy off. Craig and I drove back into Skopje and picked up some burgers to go from McDonald’s. We drove back to the house and Craig got dressed for work. I took Craig out to Obilic. Craig showed me some of the worst war damaged villages I’ve seen yet. We also went to a Serb village and a Gypsy camp in his area. I went back home and ate leftover burgers and then went to bed and read.

UNMIK POLICE PRESS UPDATE
22 DECEMBER, 2000
PRIZREN Region
ASSAULT ON KPS OFFICER
Malishevo Town - 21/12 - 0900 hrs. Four K-Albanian males assaulted a K-Albanian KPS officer while he was on duty at the wood market. UNMIK Police arrested the four suspects.
UXO FOUND
Pecane Village, Suva Reka - 21/12 - 0930 hrs. A K-Albanian male found an unexploded ordinance. The Civilian British EOD was tasked and disposed of the device.
PEC Region
ILLEGAL POSSESSION OF WEAPONS
Krusevo Village, Klina - 20/12 - 2335 hrs. A K-Albanian male was arrested by UNMIK Police after a joint search of his residence conducted by UNMIK Police and KFOR resulted in the recovery of large cache of weapons and explosives.
MITROVICA Region
ARMED ASSAULT
Mitrovica South - 21/12 - 2215 hrs. Unknown person(s) shot at the vehicle of a Croatian male while he was driving.

Friday, 22 December, 2000

I got up at 0600. It is cold in the house this morning. I had some tuna with noodles for breakfast. "Triple Sierra" and then in to work about 0745. I returned the deputy commander's vehicle to the station. (we used it to drive Andy to Skopje). I hope he didn't mind. I went to the station commander's meeting at 0830 (Every Monday and Friday). I worked on lesson plans for Monday. I am now the Station #2 KPS Training Coordinator. I went down town with Thommy. We went to KFOR hill to get some things at the German PX. I had coffee in the German KFOR canteen. I went and got my MSA at the bank. 5,226DM this month. I am going to send 3,500DM in my next check home. The weather turned off very cold. We had some snow flurries. There was a very cold wind today. The house is very cold. The heaters can't keep up. We are going to have to figure something out for more heat or we will freeze. I went to bed at 2130.

UNMIK POLICE PRESS UPDATE
23 DECEMBER, 2000
PRISTINA Region
GRENADE EXPLOSION
Pristina - 22/12 - 2048 hrs. Unknown person(s) threw an explosive device (apparently a hand grenade) over a protective wall at the Serbian Church. The explosion caused no injuries or damage.
PEC Region
EXPLOSION
Pec Town - 21/12 - 2100 hrs. An explosion of unknown origin occurred in the shop of a business selling paint and caused extensively damage.
MITROVICA Region
ILLEGAL POSSESSION OF WEAPONS
Mitrovica North - 22/12 - Day Time. A KFOR search of several houses resulted in the recovery of five assault rifles, several hand grenades and one communication radio.
ASSAULT
Mitrovica South - 22/12 1630 hrs. Unknown person(s) speaking in the Serbian language attacked a K-Albanian male. He sustained minor injuries and was treated at the KFOR hospital.

Saturday, 23 December, 2000

Up at 0600 again. "Triple Sierra" and a breakfast of coffee and oatmeal. I went in to work at 0730. I worked on lesson plans all day for training week. I am trying to get at least one week of lessons planned. I am going to teach KPS class #11 this month. I am all alone for training this week. I am supposed to get another American officer in a few days. I finished work at 1600. Thommy wanted to play "Delta Force 2" on the computer after work. We played until after 2300. I got a ride home with Thommy. I went to bed and read for a while.

P.S. The weather turned really cold tonight. I hope our heating can keep up. The house is very cold.

UNMIK POLICE PRESS UPDATE

24 DECEMBER, 2000
PRISTINA Region
PROTEST
Pristina - 23/12 -1200 hrs. A protest was organized by the "Liberal Center Party" near the Municipal building in protest of the Serbian elections. The event lasted approximately one hour.
GNJILANE Region
ARSON
Paralovo Village, Gnjilane - 23/12 - 1515hrs. A K-Albanian male was arrested by UNMIK Police after he set fire to a barn belonging to a K-Serb male.
CRIMINAL DAMAGE
Koretin Village, Kamenica - 23/12 - 1020 hrs. A K-Roma female reported that unknown person(s) had destroyed the burial markers/monuments of five graves.
PRIZREN Region
MURDER
Radoste Village, Orahovac - 23/12 - 1345 hrs. A K-Albanian male died instantly after being shot in the head during a shootout with another K-Albanian male. UNMIK Police arrested the suspect. The victim's weapon, a semi-automatic pistol and the weapon of the suspect, an assault rifle with three magazines were seized.
PEC Region
FRY ELECTIONS
Gorazdevac and Crkolez Villages, Pec - 23/12. FRY Elections were peacefully held in these Serbian dominated areas. A low voter turnout was reported with no major incidents.
MITROVICA Region
ARSON
Banja Village, Srbica - 23/12 - 2045 hrs. Unknown persons set two large haystacks and a storage area on fire. Automatic gunfire was heard shortly after the fire, which seemed to have been ignited by some type of detonation device. A KFOR search using night vision equipment revealed two unknown male subjects running from the scene. The area was secured pending a thorough search early in the morning. The fire brigade was notified and they responded to the location.

Sunday, 24 December, 2000

I got up today at 0900. Thommy is going to pick me up at 1030. I had noodles and tuna for breakfast. "Triple Sierra" and then coffee with Craig. Thommy arrived at 1030 and stayed for coffee for a while. He told us about the German Police Service. I made it in to the office by 1100. I started working on this week's lesson plans. I have three days worth finished. At quitting time, Thommy and I played "Delta Force 2" again. Colter and Josiah would have loved it. We played until 1800 and then Thommy drove me home. I worked on lesson plans for a couple of hours, watched the BBC news and then went to bed. I read for a while and then lights out.

P.S. The weather turned colder today with a cold wind. It must be down in the teens.

UNMIK POLICE PRESS UPDATE
25 DECEMBER, 2000
GNJILANE Region
UXO FOUND
Gnjilane - 24/12 - 0800 hrs. A K-Serb female reported that she found an unexploded hand grenade near her home. KFOR EOD was tasked and disposed of the device.
PRIZREN Region
EXPLOSION
Prizren - 24/12 - 0015 hrs. Unknown persons detonated an unknown type of explosive device in the street directly in front of a K-Albanian owned grocery causing extensive damage to property. No injuries were reported as the owner had just closed her business for the day.
PROSTITUTION
Prizren - 23/12 - 1240 hrs. Two K-Albanian males and two Bulgarian females were arrested by UNMIK Police after a search at a coffee bar revealed that the females were engaged in prostitution.
PEC Region
GRENADE ATTACK
Dakovica Town - 24/12 - 0155 hrs. Unknown person(s) threw a hand grenade at the home of a K-Albanian female causing damage to the front door and windows.
MITROVICA Region
ATTEMPTED MURDER

Vucitrn Town - 24/12 - 0210 hrs. Two K-Albanian males shot a K-Serbian male in the back while stealing his cows. The victim was transported by KFOR to the Mitrovica North Hospital. His condition was reported as not life threatening but the precise extents of his injuries were not reported

Monday, 25 December, 2000

I went in to work at 0800. I feel terrible today. I have a sinus headache and feel dizzy. I gave classes until 1100 and then went home. I feel really awful. I went right to bed and slept until 1800. I got up and ate some stew (my first meal today). I went back to bed and slept (restlessly) until morning. There is some kind of bug going around.

P.S. The weather is still cold.

UNMIK POLICE PRESS UPDATE
26 DECEMBER, 2000
GNJILANE Region
GRENADE ATTACK
Gnjilane - 25/12 - 1930 hrs. A grenade exploded outside the home of a K-Serb male. No injuries or damage were reported.
PRIZREN Region
Prizren - 25/12 - 1700 hrs. A K-Goran female reported that a K-Albanian male has been threatening to kill her because of her ethnicity.
MITROVICA Region
ARMED ROBBERY
Zubin Potok Town - 25/12 - 1520 hrs. Two unknown Serb-speaking males, who were armed with a pistol, robbed a Bosnian male truck driver of cash and his mobile phone. The suspects fled in a white motor vehicle.
THEFT
Mitrovica South 21/12 - 1400 hrs. A K-Albanian female reported that unknown persons stole 24 liters of cooking oil, 50kg of beans and 250kg of flour from the offices of the "Mother Theresa Humanitarian Organization."

Tuesday, 26 December, 2000

Up at 0600. The water pressure is low but I got shaved and showered anyway. I had oatmeal for breakfast. Thommy picked me up for work at 0745. I started classes at 0800. I had a pretty good day of teaching. I covered what I didn't get to yesterday and a lot more today. I still feel sick but not as bad. I am going to bed early again tonight. I went to the internet café after work and checked my e-mail. I went home and ate noodles and canned chicken spread. I went up to bed at 1830. I read for a while and then lights out.

P.S. The weather turned off warm and sunny today. It was in the mid 40s. It started to drizzle at nightfall.

E-mails home

Hi Hun,
Sorry about the chat. It has been bitter cold here for a couple of days and hard to get to the café. I have been sick in bed for two days. I feel awful. My new job is good but I have been sick and it has been a pain. I went home early Monday (1100) and slept until 1800. I got up to eat for the first time that day and then went back to bed until 0600 this morning. I am going to go back to bed when I get done here. I still feel dizzy and I have a headache. I will try and check my e-mail again in the morning if I can. Love you so much. Your hubby, Clay

UNMIK POLICE PRESS UPDATE
27 DECEMBER, 2000
GNJILANE Region
GRENADE ATTACK
Cernice Village, Gnjilane - 25/12 - 1925 hrs. Unknown person(s) threw a grenade in front of a K-Serbian male's house. The explosion caused damage to the garage and the windows.
PRIZREN Region
ASSAULT ON OFFICER
Malishevo Town - 26/12 - 1330 hrs. A K-Albanian male was arrested by UNMIK Police for assaulting an UNMIK Police Officer who started to direct traffic to resolve a traffic jam.
MITROVICA Region
ASSAULT ON KPS OFFICER / ARREST OF ESCAPED HOMICIDE SUSPECT

Srbica Town - 26/12 - Day Time hrs. An off duty KPS Officer arrested a K-Albanian male escapee. A crowd of about 30 persons tried to prevent the arrest but was held off by a warning shot. Three to four of the escapee's friends tried to pull him away from the officer, but other KPS Officers arrived on the scene and helped to take the escapee into custody. During the arrest the escapee received a minor injury and was given medical treatment.

DEAD BODY FOUND

Vucitrn Town - 26/12 - 0345 hrs. A K-Albanian male found a dead body of a male person lying on the roadside. The scene was attended by a Doctor who pronounced the victim dead of a heart attack.

Wednesday, 27 December, 2000

Up at 0600 again. I feel much better today. I had oatmeal, coffee, and toast (made in the oven) for breakfast. I visited with Craig during the meal. The water pressure is low again but usable. “Triple Sierra” and then dressed for work. The weather turned off warmer today (about 45 degrees). I went in to work at 0800. I had classes until lunch and then let the KPS go for the day. Today is a Muslim holiday, the last day of Ramadan (fast month). I worked in the office for the rest of the day. I had use of a vehicle (Kia) and got mail at the company building. I put 3,500DM in my next check home. I went to Ardi’s market and bought 100DM worth of food. It should last for at least two weeks or more. I got home at 1600. Craig got home at the same time. I was going to go to the internet café but it was closed for the holiday today. I made supper (wieners and sour kraut), and then went to bed early to read.

UNMIK POLICE PRESS UPDATE

28 DECEMBER, 2000

PRISTINA Region

GRIEVOUS ASSAULT

Pristina - 27/12 - 2300 hrs. Two K-Albanian males were apparently stabbed during a fight with other unknown persons in a coffee bar. Both victims were transported to a local hospital for treatment of their injuries and are listed in good condition.

GRENADE ATTACK

Lipljan Town - 27/12 - 1945 hrs. Unknown suspect(s) attacked a K-Serb bar with a hand grenade. A K-Serb male, who was just

leaving the bar, received serious injuries from flying shrapnel. Two vehicles parked outside the bar were also damaged. The occupants of the bar were not injured.
PRIZREN Region
EXPLOSION
Ljubizhda Village, Prizren - 27/12 - 2330 hrs. Unknown person(s) detonated an explosive device causing extensive damage to a small K-Albanian owned bakery. Several windows of a nearby house shattered. A female occupant sustained a small cut from the flying glass.
PEC Region
CRIMINAL DAMAGE
Pec Town - 26/12 - 2200 -2300 hrs. Unknown suspect(s) broke a rear window out of an UNMIK vehicle and put some burning object inside causing a small fire on the seat.
FOUND UXO
Klina Town - 27/12 - 1700 hrs. Three K-Albanian boys found an unexploded grenade in an abandoned home. UNMIK Police secured the area. KFOR EOD responded to secure the grenade.
ACCIDENTAL DEATH
Vrela Village, Istok - 27/12 - 1155 hrs. A 31-year-old K-Albanian male was apparently electrocuted while taking a shower.
MITROVICA Region
ASSAULT
Mitrovica North - 27/12 - 0230 hrs. Six unknown male persons assaulted a Gypsy male

Thursday, 28 December, 2000

Up at 0630 after a restless sleep. I had bad dreams all night it seemed. I felt tired when I got up. I had oatmeal for breakfast and same morning routine. I went to work at 0800. KPS class #11 is with the FTU today and tomorrow. I have to work on more lesson plans for next week. I wrote five or six pages of notes then typed them up. I got off at 1600 and went with Language Assistant Alban Fataj to his house to meet his family. Having an American guest is a big honor to them. I ate supper with them. It was some kind of rice stuffed chili peppers. It was not bad. I also had homemade dill pickles (just like the U.S.A) and some bread. I had Turkish coffee after supper. I left at about 1730. I went home stuffed and went to bed.

P.S. Alban's father offered me some homemade "Rakia" (Kosovo moonshine). I got out of it by telling him it was against the rules to drink in uniform. It probably would have killed me.

UNMIK POLICE PRESS UPDATE
29 DECEMBER, 2000
PRISTINA Region
ARMED ROBBERY
Besia Village, Podujevo - 28/12 - 0005 hrs. Five unknown suspects armed with knives, axes and guns attacked and robbed two guards employed by OSCE. The suspects took a safe containing currency. The guards sustained minor injuries and were treated at the hospital.
PRIZREN Region
ILLEGAL POSSESSION OF WEAPONS
Mushtiste Village, Suva Reka - 28/12 - 1600 hrs. A K-Albanian male was arrested by UNMIK Police after a search of his motor vehicle revealed a rocket propelled grenade and ammunition.
PEC Region
THREATS / INTIMIDATION
Dakovica Town - 27/12 - 1150 hrs. A K-Albanian male was arrested after he made threats towards an UNMIK Police officer and a group of KPS officers.
MITROVICA Region
HOUSE OCCUPATION
Mitrovica North - 28/12 - Time not reported. A K-Albanian female reported that a K-Serb female had occupied her apartment in her absence.

Friday, 29 December, 2000

Up at 0630. I ate a chicken spread sandwich for breakfast. I showered and shaved. Brent is off for CTO in California today. I went in to work at 0800. Randy Stensaas joined me today in the training program. I worked on lesson plans all day long. I am preparing for next week's classroom period. I played a mission on "Delta Force 2" after work and then went down to the internet café to chat with Carnita. We chatted for an hour. I discussed coming home every CTO. It will make the year go by faster (only seven and a half months now). I went back to the house (up the hill!) and ate some noodles with small chicken franks. I went to bed before

2000 and read for a while. Two more days of Y2K and we are still here.

P.S. The weather is still exceptionally warm. We had partly cloudy skies and it was about 50-55 degrees.

UNMIK POLICE PRESS UPDATE
30 DECEMBER, 2000
PRISTINA Region
MURDER / ATTEMPTED MURDER
Obilic Village, Pristina - 29/12 - 0715 hrs. Three unknown K-Albanian male suspects broke into the home of an elderly K-Serb couple. A K-Serb male was killed and his wife severely injured.
GNJILANE Region
EXPLOSION / GRENADE ATTACK
Gnjilane - 29/12 - 1730 hrs. Unknown person(s) fired an RPG at a K-Albanian house causing extensive property damage.
PRIZREN Region
GRENADE ATTACK
Lubizda Village, Prizren - 28/12 - 1145 hrs. An explosion occurred at a K-Albanian residence causing damage to windows of a bakery on the ground floor. The residence was already the target of a similar attack the previous night. KFOR EOD found two grenade pins at the scene.
RECOVERY OF HAND GRENADE
Prizren - 28/12 - 1530 hrs. A K-Albanian male reported that he had located a person who makes hand grenades and as evidence he had decided to buy one, which he took to the residence of an UNMIK Police Officer to whom he made a prior report. KFOR EOD disposed of the ordnance.
MITROVICA Region
THREAT/INTIMIDATION
Srbica Town - 29/12 - Day Time hrs. Two K-Albanian male employees of the U.N. Civil Administrator's Office reported that they received an anonymous letter stating that they would be killed if they did not leave their jobs immediately.

Saturday, 30 December, 2000

I got up at 0630, washed up, and ate noodles for breakfast. I went in to work at 0800. I worked on lesson plans and my CTO schedule for the rest of the mission. I had to plan CTOs with Randy as to cover our shifts. I spent most of the day tracking down KPS officers for interviews at P.S.U. (Professional Standards Unit- AKA Internal Affairs). P.S.U. is investigating a couple of KPS officers who tried to tip off a suspect to hide a machine gun before KFOR could search his house. The P.S.U. are French UNMK officers. The French officers are required to have office jobs and are not allowed to be out "on the streets." What pussies! I made several trips taking KPS officers from station #2 to P.S.U. Two KPS officers have already been suspended. I got off at 1600. I went home and ate boiled cabbage and franks. I watched some movies that John brought home from CTO. We stayed up until after midnight. I went to bed and read a while.

P.S. The weather is still mild. It was cloudy with intermittent rain today. I am still bothered by bad dreams at night (combat type stuff). Craig had a murder in Obilic today. An older Serbian couple got their throats cut in their home. The old woman survived. Craig had to guard the crime scene. The investigation is really screwed up according to Craig. The crime scene unit came to process the scene. They poured a plaster casting of a foot print outside in the courtyard. Because it was raining they covered it with a tarp to let it dry. Craig was guarding the crime scene and noticed that the other officers (not American) had left several animals (cats and dogs) at the crime scene that apparently belonged to the victims. Craig said that the animals were disturbing evidence, licking up blood, etc. Later in the day an African (Nigerian) CivPol officer showed up and told Craig he was there to pick up the cast (of the footprint). The officer's English was so bad that Craig thought he said that he was there to pick up the "cats." Craig told him to "take the damn dogs with you too." The Nigerian officer looked at Craig like he was crazy.

UNMIK POLICE PRESS UPDATE
31 DECEMBER, 2000
PRISTINA Region
ATTEMPTED MURDER
Slatina Village, Pristina - 30/12 - 2050 hrs. Three suspects attacked an off-duty KPS officer after he had an earlier altercation during the day with one of the individuals. One suspect fired a shot with a handgun at the officer but missed him. After the officer

fired a warning shot in the air the offenders stopped the attack. A KPS Patrol Unit arrested the three suspects.

ARMED ROBBERY

Pristina Town - 30/12 - 2130 hrs. Three unknown suspects, two of them masked, robbed a K-Albanian male at gunpoint of cash and a mobile phone.

GNJILANE Region

ATTEMPTED MURDER

Urosevac Town - 30/12 - 1150 hrs. A K-Albanian male pointed an automatic rifle at Greek KFOR soldiers. The suspect pulled the trigger numerous times while aiming at the soldiers but the magazine was missing and the weapon was not loaded. The soldiers fired two warning shots in the air and one in the ground. The last round ricocheted off the ground and struck the suspect in the leg. The KFOR soldiers arrested the suspect. He was treated at Ferizaj hospital and afterwards was handed over to UNMIK Police.

PRIZREN Region

GRENADE ATTACK

Prizren - 30/12 - 2345 hrs. Unknown person(s) threw a hand grenade at a K-Albanian owned bakery causing extensive damage to property. KFOR EOD attended the scene.

MITROVICA Region

MURDER

Vucitrn - 30/12 - 0325 hrs. A K-Albanian male killed two K-Albanian males with an assault rifle at a coffee bar near the bus station. The suspect, who had walked to Vucitrn Police Station and admitted the offense, stated that he asked the victims if they were Gypsies. A fight broke out, the suspect went out of the bar and came back with an assault rifle with which he shot the victims. The suspect was arrested. The weapon was seized.

Sunday, 31 December, 2000- New Year's Eve

I didn't get up until 0930. I don't have to go in today until 1100. We have short days now on Sundays. I woke up with a headache. It is either from sinus or a stiff neck. I had fruit cocktail for breakfast. I went in to work at 1100. I worked on admin stuff with Randy and then went home at 1430. I ate noodles and spinach and watched a movie. I got invited to the German officers' house for a New Year's Eve party but I decided not to go. I want to get to bed early. There was a lot of fireworks and gunfire this evening for New Years. I just heard several burst from an AK-47 nearby. It is easy to tell the difference. At least it is what they call "happy fire." I went out on my balcony at midnight to watch the show for a while. The fireworks and automatic gunfire went crazy. It was awesome! There were red and green tracers going everywhere. I even saw a neighbor come out of his house and fire a pistol into the air several times. I was having a good time until a ricocheting bullet went whizzing close by and hit the house by my head. I had had enough and went back inside. This was another good reason to stay home tonight. I do not want to get hit by any stray "happy fire." That would definitely not make me happy. I went to bed and read for a while. I slept on the floor with my body armor on top on me tonight. I hope the shooting doesn't keep me up (or hit me)!

UNMIK POLICE PRESS UPDATE
01 JANUARY, 2001
PRISTINA Region
MURDER
Pristina - 31/12 - 0330 hrs. A K-Albanian male died of injuries that he sustained after a shooting. UNMIK Police arrested two K-Albanian male and three female suspects. A pistol together with ammunition was recovered from the suspects. No further information given.
DEMONSTRATION
Plementina Village, Obilic - 31/12 - 1220 hrs. A group of approximately 100 K-Serbs gathered at the train station in protest against the insecure environment and threats on their lives and property following the murder of a K-Serb on 29/12. The demonstration ended peacefully after an assurance of more security from the authorities.
PRIZREN Region
FATAL TRAFFIC ACCIDENT
Orahovac Road, Prizren - 31/12 - 1300 hrs. Two passenger cars driven and occupied by K-Albanians collided. Five persons were injured in the accident. A 5-year-old girl died on the way to Pristina hospital. Three other injured persons were hospitalized and reported to be in satisfactory condition. UNMIK Police arrested one of the drivers, a K-Albanian male.
PEC Region
GRENADE ATTACK

Dakovica Town - 30/12- 2135 hrs. Unknown suspect(s) threw a hand grenade into the yard of a K-Albanian male causing damage to the victim's car. No injuries were reported.
MITROVICA Region
EXPLOSION
Mitrovica North - 01/01/01 - 0030 hrs. An explosion occurred at a residence in "Little Bosnia" (Confidence Zone Area), causing damages to windows. No injuries were reported.

Monday, 1 January, 2001- New Year's Day

I got up at 0600. I showered and then ate a breakfast of oatmeal. It is colder this morning and about a quarter inch of snow fell overnight. Craig got in from work about 0730 and said that the roads were very slick. We were able to find a turkey and I got it in the oven before I left for work. I got to the office at 0800. The German officers didn't make it in until 1000. Both Thommy and Joe had bad hangovers from the New Year's Eve party. I'm glad I didn't go. Randy and I had a full day of classroom teaching and we covered a lot of material. I got off work at 1600 and went to the internet café. I checked e-mails and was able to chat with Carnita for about an hour. I walked back up the hill to the house. We had turkey, cabbage and sweet potatoes for supper. Craig and I watched a movie and then I boned out the rest of the turkey and boiled the bones for some soup broth. I will make some soup tomorrow. I got to bed at 2030 and read for awhile.

P.S. One of the German officers that works in investigations showed me a bullet that was found lodged in the headrest of a UNMIK vehicle today. It was apparently some stray "happy fire" from last night. I'm glad I stayed at the house.

UNMIK POLICE PRESS UPDATE
02 JANUARY, 2001
PRISTINA Region
ILLEGAL POSSESSION OF WEAPON
Kosovo Polje Town - 01/01 - 0200 hrs. A K-Albanian male was arrested by UNMIK Police after he was caught shooting into the air with an assault rifle. The weapon was confiscated.
Kosovo Polje Town - 01/01 - 0045 hrs. A K-Albanian male, who was stopped and searched after a traffic violation, was arrested by

UNMIK Police when he was found in possession of a hand grenade and a bayonet.

PRIZREN Region

GRENADE ATTACK

Zhur Village, Prizren - 01/01 - 0020 hrs. An explosion occurred causing property damage (mostly broken windows) to thirteen shops. Two hand grenade pins and fragments of a mine were recovered from the scene by KFOR EOD. No injuries were reported.

ILLEGAL POSSESSION OF WEAPON

Prizren - 01/01 - 0140 hrs. A K-Albanian male was arrested by UNMIK Police after a search of his car resulted in the recovery of a machine gun and ammunition.

PEC Region

EXPLOSION

Decani Town - 01/01 - 0200 hrs. An explosion occurred which caused the windows of nearby local shops to shatter. No injuries were reported.

GRENADE ATTACK

Pec Town - 01/-01 - 2320 hrs. Unknown suspect(s) threw a hand grenade into a K-Albanian owned shop, causing damage to the door and windows. No injuries were reported.

MITROVICA Region

ASSAULT ON PEACEKEEPING FORCES

Srbica Town - 01/01 - 0005 hrs. During a New Year's Eve celebration at the Municipal Building a crowd of approximately 1,500 persons became unruly and violent towards UNMIK Police officers and KFOR personnel attempting to make an arrest. Some members of the crowd were shooting into the air and throwing firecrackers indiscriminately into the crowd. While attempting to make the arrest, members of the crowd attacked the UNMIK Police officers and KFOR personnel. Warning shots were fired and during the struggle both UNMIK Police officers and KFOR personnel were beaten to the ground and kicked. During this assault one officer had his weapon and two magazines stolen. KFOR and TMK command staff members safely extracted the UNMIK Police officers and KFOR personnel from the crowd. After approximately thirty minutes the crowd dispersed with no further incident. Two UNMIK Police officers and three KPS officers did receive minor injuries during the incident.

Tuesday, 2 January, 2001

Up at 0630 to no water. I shaved with bottled water and had leftover turkey for breakfast. I was in to work by 0800 and taught classes again. I showed the class some pursuit videos that I brought back from the states. They really liked it and were impressed by the massive size of a large freeway. I got off work at 1630 and went to the internet café to chat with Carnita. I only had enough small change for a half hour. I only had large bills that the café attendant could not break. I need to get to the bank and get some smaller bills. I went home and ate more turkey and watched a movie with John and Ken. I went up to bed at 2200 and read for a while.

P.S. Carnita said that a Paris, Texas police officer shot and killed someone yesterday. The Paris Police Department was the first agency I worked for after I got out of the Marines Corps. She had no information yet on who the involved officer was. There was more military action in the Presevo valley again. The U.S. KFOR troops had to rescue some Serbian hostages from the Albania insurgents (UCPMB).

UNMIK POLICE PRESS UPDATE
03 JANUARY, 2001
PRISTINA Region
ILLEGAL POSSESSION OF WEAPON
Sedllare Village, Lipljan - 01/01 - 0001 hrs. An UNMIK Police search of a K-Albanian residence resulted in the recovery of ammunition for an assault rifle. The suspect was arrested.
GNJILANE Region
ILLEGAL POSSESSION OF A WEAPON
Drobesh Village, Vitina - 02/01 - 1150 hrs. UNMIK Police searched a gas station and recovered a machine pistol and ammunition. Two K-Albanian males were arrested.
PEC Region
ATTEMPTED MURDER
Decani Town - 02/01 - 0230 hrs. Two known K-Albanian males shot a K-Albanian male. The victim was brought to Pec Hospital for treatment of chest injuries and later transported to Pristina Hospital due to his serious injuries. UNMIK Police arrested the two suspects and seized a machine gun and a pistol. The exact

extents of injuries are unknown yet but the victim is in stable condition.

ATTEMPTED MURDER

Decani Town - 02/01 - 1330 hrs. Two groups of unidentified K-Albanian males approached the home of a K-Albanian male. The first group forcibly entered the victim's home and began shooting an unknown type of weapon at him. As the victim ran to the upper level of the home to escape he exited onto his balcony where a second group of K-Albanian males were waiting outside. The second group then began to fire weapons at the victim who managed to jump from his balcony and flee without injury. The circumstances of the incident, especially the motive, are under investigation.

Wednesday, 3 January, 2001

Up at 0630 and same morning routine. I ate soup and made a turkey sandwich for my lunch. I got in to the office at 0800 and taught classes all day. I got out of the office about 1500 and went to eat at Alban Fetaj's home again. They really like having me over. We had traditional Albanian food: burek, fli and more homemade pickles. I got stuffed again. We had coffee and looked at their family album. I was able to avoid the "moonshine Rakia" again because I had to go back to the office for awhile. I got back to the office at 1700 to finish some administrative work and visit with Thommy and Joe. We had a murder near our house about 1900. The suspect was still at large when I got back to the house.

UNMIK POLICE PRESS UPDATE

04 JANUARY, 2001

PRISTINA Region

MURDER

Pristina - 03/01 - 1900 hrs. A K-Albanian male was shot once in the lower abdomen by his neighbor, a K-Albanian male. The victim was admitted to Pristina Hospital for treatment but died of his injuries. The suspect apparently fled the scene and is currently being sought by police.

DISTURBANCE

Pristina - 03/01 - 2205 hrs. Security guards reported a fight between students at the local university. During the incident, it was alleged that a weapon was involved. UNMIK Police responded. The situation was diffused and no weapons were found.

GNJILANE Region

SHOOTING/GUNFIRE

Kamenica Town - 03/01 - 1100 hrs. Unknown suspect(s) shot one round through the first floor window of a K-Albanian owned grocery. No injuries were reported.

PRIZREN Region

ROBBERY

Luzhnica Village, Suva Reka - 03/01 - 1730 hrs. Two unknown male passengers of a bus, which was on the way from Prizren to Istanbul, produced a pistol and a hand grenade. They forced the driver to leave the main road and to stop a few kilometers later. The offenders were joined by two other unknown males, masked and armed with rifles. The suspects collected jewelry and miscellaneous items from the passengers. Three passengers were injured.

PEC Region

BURGLARY

Klina Town - 03/01 - 0845 hrs. Unknown person(s) broke into a K-Albanian owned jewelry shop and stole jewels worth 10,000 Deutsch-Marks.

MITROVICA Region

ROBBERY

Banje Village, Zubin Potok - 02/01 - 0350 hrs. A Serbian male reported that four unknown males forced open the door of his truck as he was taking a rest by the road side, hit him on the head with a stick, and then took several items and cash. The victim was taken to hospital for treatment of a head wound.

ASSAULT

Mitrovica North - 03/01 - 1040 hrs. A K-Albanian male reported that he was walking home when a vehicle stopped and three K-Serb males got out and attacked him with an iron bar. The victim was taken to hospital for an unknown type of injury.

Mitrovica South - 03/01 - 1600 hrs. A K-Albanian male was arrested by UNMIK Police for assaulting a K-Albanian female. No injuries were reported.

Thursday, 4 January, 2001

Up at 0630. "Triple Sierra" and then instant soup for breakfast. I had coffee with Craig when he got off work and waited for Thommy and Joe to pick me up. They were supposed to arrive at 0745. At 0815 I decided to walk to work and found Thommy and Joe already there. They had forgotten about giving me a ride. They owe me now. No classes today. The KPS officers are in their FTU shifts on Thursday and Friday. We are moving to a new office space today. New metal buildings have been placed out in front of the station. We spent most of the day moving the office furniture and equipment to the new building. We have no power hooked up yet and it was very cold. Randy and I covertly moved our phone line to the new building. We will beg forgiveness later. We are supposed to get our power and internet access within a day or so. I got back to the house about 1700. Ken got back about 1900.

P.S. Two more days until CTO. My last one "in country". 39 days until my next trip home.

UNMIK POLICE PRESS UPDATE
05 JANUARY, 2001
PRISTINA Region
BURGLARY
Pristina - 03/01 - 0131 hrs. The accommodation of an employee of the "International Rescue Committee" was burglarized. A cellular telephone and 100 U.S. dollars was taken. The employee is currently on leave and was not home at the time of the occurrence.
DEAD BODY FOUND
Podujevo Town - 04/01 - 1030 hrs. The dead body of an infant was found at a garbage dumpsite. The victim's age was estimated at three to four months. The body was apparently placed in a garbage container that was emptied at the site. The cause of death is unknown at this time.
GNJILANE Region
FALSE IMPRISONMENT/DOMESTIC ABUSE
Gnjilane Town - 04/01 - 1600 hrs. A K-Albanian male reported that his sister was being held against her will by a K-Albanian male she had been living with since August. The suspect had threatened the victim with an AK-47 rifle. UNMIK police responded and rescued the victim, who bore signs of a recent beating. The victim returned to her family and the suspect was arrested.

LAND MINE EXPLOSION
Drenusha Village, Kacanik - 03/01 - 1340 hrs. A K-Albanian male apparently stepped on a land mine while tending his cows. The victim lost his left foot and received injuries to his right leg in the blast.
PRIZREN Region
THEFT
Prizren - 04/01 - 0800 hrs. Two Goran male residents of Belgrade that ran taxi services between Belgrade and Dragash reported that uniformed TMK soldiers stopped their mini vans and took their motor vehicle registration plates without giving any explanation. One suspect was arrested.
PEC Region
ILLEGAL POSSESSION OF WEAPONS
Jossanica Village, Klina - 04/01 - 0545 hrs. A K-Albanian male was arrested after a house search by KFOR revealed that he was in possession of one "Scorpion" sub machine gun, two silencers, and four rounds of ammunition.
MITROVICA Region
ASSAULT
Mitrovica North - 04/01 - 1030 hrs. Three K-Serbian males reported that a group of about fifteen K-Albanian males threw rocks at them in "Little Bosnia." One KFOR soldier who tried to intervene was struck in the hand. Three persons were detained but later released.

Friday, 5 January, 2001

Up at 0630. “Triple Sierra” and a breakfast of noodles. I had a bath instead of a Kosovo shower this morning. I had coffee with Craig until Thommy and Joe showed up. They stayed for a cup of coffee and then off to work. We attended the Friday staff meeting in the stations commander’s office. I gave the training report. We are still working on getting power to our new office. We have to stay on the lazy logistics officer from India to make sure it gets done. I went to town with Randy and Alban to find hardware to put our desk together. Our “new” desk was missing several parts and pieces. Still no power by the end of the day. I got off at 1600 and went to the house and had a supper of noodles and beans.

P.S. I got an e-mail from Dale Wood (Paris P.D.). He wanted me to e-mail him with details about the mission. He is considering it. I also found out from him that it was officer Billy Hill (Paris P.D.) that had shot and killed a suspect and the end of a pursuit. It sounds like it was accidental and the local Texas Ranger is investigating the shooting.

UNMIK POLICE PRESS UPDATE
06 JANUARY, 2001
PRISTINA Region
ARMED ROBBERY
Pristina - 04/01 - 2115 hrs. Three unknown suspects robbed a K-Turkish male at gunpoint while he was seated in his parked truck. The suspects demanded the victim's money and passport. The victim handed over money and the suspects fled in a vehicle where they were apprehended by UNMIK Police approximately 30 minutes later. No injuries were reported.
Bernica Village, Pristina - 05/01 - 1940 hrs. A K-Albanian male and female were robbed at gunpoint of cash and jewelry by four unknown male suspects. The suspects also demanded another 500DM by the end of next week or the victims would be killed.
RAPE
Pristina - 05/01 - 1405 hrs. A K-Albanian female reported that she was raped by a known K-Albanian male who forced her into his car at gunpoint.
Kosovo Polje - 05/01 - 0305 hrs. A female KPS Officer (ethnicity unknown) reported that unknown person(s) fired a single gunshot at her home. A bullet was later located in her garage wall. No injuries were reported.
GNJILANE Region
HARBORING A FUGITIVE
Vrbestica Village, Strpce - 05/01 - 0515 hrs. A K-Serbian male was arrested for hiding a male subject who was wanted via an arrest warrant.
PRIZREN Region
MISSING PERSON
Orcusa Village, Dragash - 04/01 - 0830 hrs. A 71-year-old mentally ill K-Albanian female is reported missing in the area of the minefields. A search using a helicopter was carried out but she could not be located.
PEC Region

ATTEMPTED MURDER

Klina Town - 05/01 - 1830 hrs. A K-Albanian male was apparently shot in the back by unknown person(s) while standing in the doorway of his residence. Two unknown persons were seen running away near the railroad tracks. The victim was transported for medical treatment and is reportedly responding to treatment.

ASSAULT

Klina Town - 03/01 - 1100 hrs. TMK members allegedly assaulted four K-Albanian family members. Reportedly the assault occurred over a traffic dispute.

Saturday, 6 January, 2001

Same morning routine this morning. I had a vitamin shake for breakfast. I went in to work at 0800. Still no power at the new office. We can't work today without power so Randy, Thommy, Joe and I went to KFOR hill. We shopped at the German PX and had coffee at the German coffee shop. It is easier when you have German speakers with you. We had lunch at a pizza place downtown. There was not much happening today. We heard more rumors about Depleted Uranium (D.U.) munitions causing leukemia in some of the KFOR soldiers. They are calling it "Balkan Syndrome". I chatted with Carnita at 1700. She also had heard on the news about the D.U. munitions and "Balkan Syndrome". She was very concerned and wanted me to come home if we were at risk. I will check it out more during my CTO. I ate rice for supper, watched a movie, and then went to bed.

UNMIK POLICE PRESS UPDATE

07 JANUARY, 2001

PRISTINA Region

THEFT

Pristina - 06/01 - 1845 hrs. A female German National reported the theft of her handbag from a local restaurant. The handbag contained her diplomatic passport, driver's license, credit card and cash. Investigation continuing.

HUMAN REMAINS FOUND

Maticane Village, Pristina - 05/01- 0015 hrs. A group of children located a human skull and notified UNMIK police. The scene was secured for further investigation.

GNJILANE Region

MISSING PERSON
Gnjilane Town - 28/12 - Unknown Time. A K-Albanian male reported that his cousin has been missing since 28/12/00 when he left Macedonia for Gnjilane.
PRIZREN Region
ASSAULT
Prizren - 06/01 - 1300 hrs. A K-Albanian male taxi driver was arrested when he attacked a fellow taxi driver with a knife during a dispute over customers.
PEC Region
GRENADE ATTACK
Dakovica Town - 07/01 - 0200 hrs. Three shops and two vehicles were damaged when a grenade exploded on the street. No injuries were reported.
MITROVICA Region
ILLEGAL POSSESSION OF WEAPON
Zvecan Town - 06/01 - 1200 hrs. KFOR reported that they had seized one AK-47 assault rifle from a K-Serbian male. The suspect was handed over to UNMIK Police.
Srbica Town - 06/01 - 0500 hrs. Two K-Albanian males were arrested after a joint KFOR and UNMIK Police search of their residence revealed one AK-47 assault rifle and two fragmentation grenades.

Sunday, 7 January, 2001

I slept in today. There is still no power at the office so I am not going in. I'll use this as my "travel day" since I have to go in on the 15th to cover for Randy. Craig got off work at 0800. We visited for a while and planned what we are going to do on CTO. I stayed around the house all day watching movies and doing laundry. I went to the internet café to chat with Carnita at 1700. She is still concerned about the D.U. risk. I will try and get the facts about the issue and let her know. The weather is cool and sunny today. It feels like spring in Montana. Thommy went to the Skopje airport to pick up Brent. He got back to the house about 1800.

UNMIK POLICE PRESS UPDATE
08 JANUARY, 2001
PRISTINA Region
SHOOTING

Alisha Village, Podujevo - 07/01 - 2315 hrs. A K-Albanian male using an illegal pistol fired two rounds at KFOR soldiers. The subject denied knowing they were soldiers and surrendered himself and his weapon.

FOUND BODY

Gracanica Village, Pristina - 07/01 - 1330 hrs. A Serbian male reported finding a body in a field. Investigators responded to the scene.

GNJILANE Region

RAPE

Kacanik Town - 06/01. K-Albanian female alleged that her brother has raped her three times over a six months period. The suspect was arrested.

ASSAULT

Gnjilane - 06/01- 1600 hrs. A K-Albanian male was struck in the face and assaulted with tear gas by another K- Albanian male during a dispute. One suspect arrested.

UXO FOUND

Cernica Village, Gnjilane - 07/01 - 1030 hrs. A K-Albanian KPS officer found a rocket launcher across the street from a Serbian store. EOD arrived and they determined the launcher was previously fired. The launcher was taken as evidence.

PRIZREN Region

RECOVERY OF DEAD BODY

Orcusa Village, Dragash - 07/01 - Time not reported. A mentally ill K-Goran female, who was reported missing since 04/01, was found dead in a ravine near the village. No foul play has been suspected.

UXO FOUND

Pecane Village, Suva Reka - 06/01 - 1400 hrs. A K-Albanian male reported that he found a hand grenade in his yard. EOD disposed of the device.

PEC Region

GRENADE ATTACKS

Banja Village, Istok - 06/01 - 2145 hrs. UNMIK Police investigated a report of an explosion in the field of a K-Serbian family. The officers located evidence of a recent explosion, an unexploded grenade, and damage to two vehicles parked nearby. EOD disposed of the remaining grenade. Suspects are unknown at this time.

Dakovica Town - 07/01 - 0200 hrs. An unknown suspect detonated a grenade in front of an unoccupied K-Albanian shop. The front door of the shop was damaged as were two vehicles parked in the street. There were no injuries reported.
MITROVICA Region
BURGLARY
Zubin Potok Town - 06/01 - 0230 hrs. A K-Serbian female reported that someone had broken into her residence and the suspect had been apprehended by her neighbors. A patrol unit later traced the suspect to the hospital where he was taken for treatment of injuries he sustained while being apprehended by the neighbors. The suspect was arrested.

Monday, 8 January, 2001

I got up at 0800. I ate tuna and noodles for breakfast. I had coffee with Craig. John and Ken got to the house about 0900 so we had use of a vehicle. Ken drove us to the company building and got this week's water supply. Craig and I walked from the company building to a barber shop. We both got haircuts and then walked to the market to buy some food. We took a taxi back to the house. I spent the rest of the day finishing laundry, writing e-mails and watching movies. I had beans and noodles for supper. The power went off two or three times today. We all ended the day by visiting in the kitchen by candlelight.

P.S. The weather was great today. It was clear, sunny and about 62 degrees. I can't believe it's winter.

UNMIK POLICE PRESS UPDATE
09 JANUARY, 2001
PRISTINA Region
STOLEN VEHICLE
Pristina - 08/01 - 0600 hrs. A white Mitsubishi Pajero that belongs to OSCE was stolen by unknown suspects from a parking lot in the Sunny Hill area. Investigation continuing.
GNJILANE Region
ILLEGAL POSSESSION WEAPONS
Gnjilane - 08/01 - 0900 hrs. A K-Albanian male was arrested for illegal possession of a weapon after UNMIK Police and KFOR searched his house.

PRIZREN Region

REPORTED SUICIDE

Prizren - 08/01 - 2150 hrs. A KPS officer reported that his girlfriend had committed suicide by shooting herself. The exact nature of the incident has not yet been determined.

ASSAULT

Siroko Village, Suva Reka - 06/01 - 1315 hrs. A K-Albanian male assaulted a KPS officer after he had received a traffic ticket. No injuries were reported.

PEC Region

ARMED ASSAULT

Pec - 08/01 - 0915 hrs. During the arrest of a K-Albanian male for armed assault, the suspect resisted and one round was fired by the officer causing minor injuries to both persons. No other information reported.

ILLEGAL POSSESSION OF A WEAPON

Boksic Village, Klina - 07/01 - 2130 hrs. A K-Albanian male was arrested after he was found in possession of one AK-47 rifle, pistol magazine and ammunition. The weapon was seized.

Boksic Village, Klina - 07/01 - 2130 hrs. During a search of his residence by KFOR, a K-Albanian male was found to be in possession of one AK-47 rifle, two magazines and two gas masks. The suspect was arrested and the items seized.

MITROVICA Region

GRENADE ATTACK

Srbica Town - 08/01 - 1236 hrs. Unknown suspects driving a red mini bus, marked "Taxi" dropped a hand grenade at the KFOR checkpoint. Although the pin had been pulled from the grenade it did not explode. EOD responded to disarm the device.

THREATS/INTIMIDATION

Mitrovica North - 07/01 - 2115 hrs. Two K-Albanian males threatened to shoot KFOR soldiers for not allowing them to cross the bridge.

Tuesday, 9 January, 2001

I got up at 0830 and had oatmeal and coffee. I took a shower but I am not shaving during CTO. I finished my laundry. Our washing machine is acting up and I hand wrung my cloths and hung them out on my balcony to dry. Craig and I had the use of Ken's vehicle. We went to the travel agency and made reservations for our next CTO. We got flights from Skopje to Amsterdam then Seattle to Kalispell. We went to the company building to see if we could get better rates. We should hear something in a couple of days. We saw a segment on the D.U. issue on the BBC at the company building. It is not supposed to be a problem where we are. We drove out to K.P. to get a letter that was left there for Craig. We went to the Maxi PX and then the Supreme PX. I went to the internet café at 1700 and chatted with Carn. We discussed the D.U. issue and decided that I would get tested when I come home on my next CTO. I went home and ate noodles for supper and then went to bed to read for awhile.

P.S. The weather is still mild and sunny. CTO going good. I'm getting a lot of sleep.

UNMIK POLICE PRESS UPDATE
10 JANUARY, 2001
GNJILANE Region
GRENADE ATTACK
Urosevac Town - 09/01 - 1030 hrs. A K-Albanian male reported that his home, which was under construction, was completely destroyed by a hand grenade. No injuries reported.
DEMONSTRATION
Urosevac Town - 09/01 - 1645 hrs. A group of K-Albanians gathered to demonstrate in reference to the earlier grenade attack. There were approximately 200 persons in attendance and the crowd dispersed peacefully.
PRIZREN Region
THREATS/INTIMIDATION
Prizren - 05/01 - 1200 hrs. A K-Albanian male doctor reported receiving death threats over his telephone. The threats are in relation to him being married to a K-Serbian female.
PEC Region
DOUBLE SHOOTING
Pec - 09/01 - 1945 hrs. Two K-Albanian males were wounded in a shooting incident at the Café-bar "Art". Witnesses described the suspect as being male, about 185cm in height, slim build, with shoulder-length brown hair, wearing a T-shirt and blue jeans, and armed with a pistol. The suspect fled in the company of two other males, both about 160 cm in height, one with short blond hair who was wearing a dark-gray pullover & blue jeans, and the other with

short black hair who was wearing a black leather jacket & blue jeans. The motive has not been determined.

THREATS/INTIMIDATION

Istok Town - 08/01 - 0730 hrs. A K-Albanian male was arrested for threatening KFOR soldiers after he was refused permission to pass a checkpoint. The suspect threatened to put a land mine in the roadway.

MITROVICA Region

ASSAULT

Mitrovica North - 9/01 - 1845 hrs. Three K-Albanian males reported that they were assaulted by a group of approximately six K-Serbian males.

Wednesday, 10 January, 2001

Woke up at 0700. I had oatmeal this morning. I got cleaned up and sat around visiting with Craig. Not much going on today. Craig and I walked to Main HQ about noon to check on his redeployment orders to DPU. We stayed downtown until 1700 to make our chat dates with the wives. We did not want to walk up the hill twice today. We chatted for an hour and then went to the house. I ate rice for supper. I went to bed about 2100 and read for a couple of hours before lights out. I woke up about 0300 and could not sleep. I read until about 0400 until the power went out. I finally got back to sleep.

P.S. Reggie delivered a donation we took up for the orphans at the Pristina hospital. We gave money to buy diapers and supplies. It sounds like there are a lot of abandoned kids at the hospital. Many are just infants that get left at the door or at a military base. Some are just found abandoned in various locations.

UNMIK POLICE PRESS UPDATE

11 JANUARY, 2001

PRISTINA Region

UXO FOUND

Kacikoli Village, Pristina - 10/01 - 0930 hrs. A local woodcutter located a land mine and informed UNMIK Police. EOD responded to the scene where the device was disposed of.

Kacikoli Village, Pristina - 10/01 - 0820 hrs. UNMIK Police observed a container hanging from a tree limb that was later identified as an unexploded cluster bomblet. EOD responded to the scene where the device was disposed of.

GNJILANE Region

EXPLOSION

Ferizaj Town - 10/01- 0143 hrs. There was a large explosion along the downtown roadway. Investigation revealed that the explosion damaged a 130-meter area and caused damage to twenty-five buildings including shops and a supermarket. Three K-Albanian males sustained minor injuries. Motive and suspects are unknown.

CIVIL DISPUTE

Strpce Town - 10/01 - 2100 hrs. A Serbian male reported to the station that he had been evicted from the local Refugee Center after making too much money by working for KFOR. The Red Cross runs the refugee center.

PRIZREN Region

UXO FOUND

Pecani Village, Prizren - 09/01 - 1530 hrs. A K-Albanian male reported finding a hand grenade. EOD responded and disposed of the device.

Thursday, 11 January, 2001

I got up at 0800 to the power still being off. I ate oatmeal heated on our small propane backup stove. I lay around all day and wrote e-mails on the laptop (battery power). Craig and I took Ken's vehicle down to the company building to return some movies and pick up a few more. We picked up some time cards and were given a letter from President Clinton. We went back home and noticed that there was power back on around our house but we were still out. I worked with the breaker box and finally got the power back on. The power goes off and on so often that it is now causing problems with our breakers tripping. I had a supper of noodles and tuna. Craig and I watched a movie and then I went up to bed, read for an hour and then lights out.

P.S. The weather is still mild but the KFOR forecast calls for snow by Saturday. We got a price quote back from the company on our flights. It will be $1,043 round trip to Kalispell. Reggie is moving out. He found a Serbian apartment downtown closer to his office.

Letter from President Clinton

THE WHITE HOUSE
Washington
December 22, 2000

At this holiday season, I want to thank all U.S. civilian police serving abroad for helping to bring peace, stability, and a renewed sense of hope to those rebuilding their lives after devastating conflicts around the world.

America values the work you do and the sacrifices you make as international civilian police officers. Our nation stands for freedom and democracy, and your sacrifices embody those values in places like Bosnia, East Timor, Kosovo, and eastern Slavonia. Your contributions as law enforcement officers, mentors to local police, and symbols of America help to promote the rule of law in places struggling to recover from violence.

I am proud that the United States has supported a dramatic increase in the use of civilian police from just 50 officers in Haiti in 1994 to an elite group of more than 850 officers overseas today. In recognition of the importance of civilian police to our foreign policy, I signed a directive earlier this year to enhance the civilian police capacities of the United States Government and to improve the capacities of international institutions and other contributing states.

I know that you are far from your homes and loved ones during this holiday season, and, on behalf of a grateful nation, I thank you for your dedication. Hillary joins me in extending best wishes for the future.

Bill Clinton

UNMIK POLICE PRESS UPDATE
12 JANUARY, 2001
GNJILANE Region
ASSAULT
Vitina Town - 11/01 - 0400 hrs. A K-Albanian male was arrested for assaulting a KFOR soldier.

DISORDERLY CONDUCT
Strpce Town - 11/01 - 1115 hrs. A group of K-Serbians encountered a group of K-Albanians in front of the registration center. A dispute between the two groups escalated into violence and three K-Albanians received minor injuries. No arrests were made.
ARSON
Gnjilane - 10/01 - 1730 hrs. A house belonging to a K-Serbian male was set afire. The owner lives in Serbia. The perpetrators are unknown.
PEC Region
THREATS/INTIMIDATION
Klina Town - 10/01 - 1745 hrs. A K-Albanian male threatened an Italian employee of the NGO "Muvimundo". The suspect was arrested.
MITROVICA Region
ATTEMPTED MURDER
Mitrovica South - 11/01 - 0400 hrs. A K-Albanian male shop owner was attacked and stabbed in the back by two unknown suspects. The victim was transported to the hospital for treatment. The suspects fled the scene.

Friday, 12 January, 2001

I got up at 0730. I couldn't stay in bed any longer. I had coffee with Craig and ate leftover noodles for breakfast. We need to go to the company building and turn in our time cards. I went to station #2 to get my lesson materials for Monday morning. On my way back up the hill I stopped at the war memorial in the park across from the house. The park was big and must have been very nice at one time. The memorial has been defaced and all the bronze plaques have been stolen. There are twenty fresh war graves in the park. The dead are buried in any open space around the city. The park was also full of trash. I went to the house and had a lunch of beans and spinach. Craig and I went down to the company building and turned in our time cards and then went to the internet café. After an hour at the café we went back up to the house and watched movies. I ate and then went to bed.

P.S. Reggie is going to Skopje tomorrow to try and find a real bed for his new apartment. I plan to ride along for the trip to McDonald's.

UNMIK POLICE PRESS UPDATE
13 JANUARY, 2001
PRISTINA Region
SHOOTING
Llpashtica Village, Podujevo - 12/01 - 2000 hrs. A K-Bosnian male truck driver reported that unknown person(s) fired at his vehicle while he was enroute to Pristina. No injuries were reported but the truck was damaged by the gunfire.
GNJILANE Region
ASSAULT
Binac Village, Vitina - 12/01- 1915 hrs. Two K-Serbian males reported they were surrounded by approximately thirty K-Albanians that tried to beat them and damage their vehicle. They only knew one person in the crowd.
THEFT
Vitina Town - 12/01 - 1230 hrs. K-Albanian male reported that Macedonian soldiers took his livestock.
PRIZREN Region
ILLEGAL POSSESSION OF WEAPONS
Korisa Village, Prizren - 12/01 - 1104 hrs. A joint UNMIK Police /KFOR operation resulted in an undisclosed amount of weapons seized.
PEC Region
FOUND UXO
Hulaj Village, Decani - 11/01 - 1715 hrs. A K-Albanian male reported finding a hand grenade. KFOR responded and disposed of the device.
Zamberj Village, Klina - 12/01 - 0900 hrs. A K-Albanian male reported finding a hand grenade. EOD disposed of the ordnance.

Saturday, 14 January, 2001

I got up at 0530. The power is still out and was out most of the night. The house is cold. I had to get dressed by flashlight. I ate some oatmeal and got Reggie up at 0600. There is about two inches of snow on the ground this morning. Reggie and I left for Skopje at about 0730. We took an L.A. named Bennie and drove a white U.N. van. The roads were slick but not too bad. They were clear and dry after we crossed the Macedonian border. We shopped all day in Skopje and Reggie bought a bed frame. He could not find a mattress the right size. We walked over a 400 year old bridge to the old part of the city to check out the gold shops. I bought a gold "Balkan's Mission ring" at one of the shops. I was going to buy a ring for Carnita but I did not know her ring size. I will return another time and get one for her. We went to McDonald's and ate. I bought some burgers to take back to Craig. We started back to Kosovo at about 1700 with a bed frame strapped to the top of the van. It started snowing in Macedonia by the time we left. The roads are still not too bad for an experienced winter driver. We got back across the border and then stopped in Ferizaj for Reggie to order a mattress. A large bomb exploded downtown there three days ago at about 0200. Only three people were injured because of the time of the explosion. There were twenty-five buildings damaged downtown by the blast. It was about the same size bomb as the one on 22 November. We got into Prishtina about 2000 but it took another hour to get back to the house because of the slick roads and our steep hill to the house. I had to get out and push the van but we could not make it all the way up the hill. We finally had to park it and walk the last hundred yards to the house. We are still having power problems with the breaker box.

P.S. We finally figured out that it was Brent's new refrigerator he bought a few days ago that has been tripping out the breaker. Something is wrong with it. As soon as we unplugged it the breaker stopped tripping out. That is only half the problem. The power still keeps going off. It went off at about 2200 and stayed off all night. It got really cold in my room without my electric heater. Blowing snow is still coming down. I guess winter is finally here.

UNMIK POLICE PRESS UPDATE
14 JANUARY, 2001
PRISTINA Region
GRENADE ATTACK
Obilic Village, Kosovo Polje - 13/01 - 2125 hrs. An unidentified suspect threw a hand grenade into a local shop. The explosion caused property damage to the shop and to a neighboring shop and

minor injuries to a K-Albanian female. The victim was taken to the hospital for treatment.
EXPLOSION
Obilic Village, Kosovo Polje - 13/01 - 2335 hrs. Unidentified suspects threw an incendiary device at a local bar. A K-Albanian female occupant of the bar sustained injuries of unknown extent. The victim was taken to the hospital for treatment.
GNJILANE Region
DEAD BODY FOUND
Urosevac Town - 13/01 - 2000 hrs. A K-Albanian male was found lying outside his residence unclothed, not breathing and unresponsive to UNMIK Police officers. He was pronounced dead at the scene. The cause of death is under investigation.
PEC Region
ARSON
Loxhe Village, Pec - 10/01 - 0130 hrs. Unknown suspect(s) burned down a rebuilt K-Bosnian house.
THREATS/INTIMIDATION
Zillapek Village, Pec - 12/01 - 1225 hrs. A K-Bosnian male was threatened by unknown masked and armed suspects to quit speaking the Serbian language.

Sunday, 14 January, 2001

I got up at 0800 and ate pancakes and hash browns that Ken and John had leftover from their breakfast. It is about 28 degrees with blowing snow. I shined my new winter boots and wore them to get them broke in. I prepared my lesson plans for tomorrow's class. The power came on briefly but went off again at 1000. This is really a pain. The power was off until 1500. I cleaned my room and started getting stuff together to take home on my next CTO. I walked down the hill to the internet café with Craig. We had to wait for a while for a free computer. The power kept going off and on and we got disconnected a few times. I was able to chat with Carnita for about an hour and asked her ring size for my next trip to Skopje. We walked back to the house in the snow and ice. I watched a movie and then went to bed.

P.S. I used my ice cleats for the first time today. They worked great. I am starting to feel like I am getting sick. My left ear is starting to hurt and my sinuses are acting up.

UNMIK POLICE PRESS UPDATE
15 JANUARY, 2001
PRISTINA Region
ARSON
Obilic Village, Kosovo Polje - 14/01 - 1500 hrs. Unknown suspect(s) set fire to an unoccupied K-Serbian home.
PRIZREN Region
ABDUCTION
Prizren - 14/01 - 1815 hrs. As two Moldavian females were walking to a nightclub, where they are employed, three unknown male suspects grabbed one of the females and forced her into a car. The suspects drove away at high speed. The remaining Moldavian female sustained no injuries.
PEC Region
GRENADE ATTACK
Klina Town - 13/01- 1830 hrs. A K-Albanian male reported that an unidentified person threw a hand grenade at his home. KFOR EOD responded to the scene and found that the pin was missing but the grenade did not detonate. The ordnance was disposed of.

Monday, 15 January, 2001

I got up at 0630. I feel awful. I have sinus congestion today. I skipped breakfast and had only coffee. CTO is over and I went in to work at 0800. This is my last week with KPS class #11. I taught classes for half the day and then released the class. I went with Joe Massing to Main HQ. On the way we were flagged down by a man with what appeared to be serious burns. Something apparently had exploded in his face. His face and hands were totally black from flash burns. We took him to the Emergency Room at Prishtina hospital. We continued to Main HQ where I helped Joe pick up body armor for the KPS. I went home early at about 1400. I ate some sauerkraut and then went to bed early. I had trouble getting to sleep. I am still feeling bad and have terrible pain in my left ear and it seems to be leaking fluid. I am not sure if it has anything to do with the bombing. I have had constant ringing and noticeable hearing loss.

P.S. The weather is still cold and snowy. The electric heater is barely keeping up in the room. It is very cold.

UNMIK POLICE PRESS UPDATE
16 JANUARY, 2001
PRISTINA Region
GRIEVOUS ASSAULT
Pristina - 15/01 - 1555 hrs. Two unknown male suspects stabbed an 18-years-old K-Albanian male student in the back. The victim was transported to Pristina hospital. His condition was reported to be stable.
GNJILANE Region
ARSON
Vitina Town - 15/01 - 1925 hrs. Unidentified suspect(s) set fire to an unoccupied K-Serbian home.
PRIZREN Region
EXPLOSIONS
Istok Town - 16/01 - 0230 hrs. Four explosions rocked the town of Istok. Two explosions destroyed two unoccupied houses near the bus station. Two other explosions occurred near the market place and damaged approximately twenty-five businesses. No injuries were reported.

Tuesday, 16 January, 2001

Up at 0630. "Triple Sierra" and a breakfast of instant soup brought from home. I walked down the hill in the ice and snow. It is a good thing I brought my ice cleats. I was in to work at 0800. I taught KPS class #11 for the last time today. I had a guest instructor (Kevin Trimbath, USA) teach the morning session on first responder crime scene preservation. Kevin is an evidence technician back in the states. I went to lunch at Napoli Pizza with Joe and had a veggie pizza. After lunch I taught classes on blood borne pathogens and basic first aid. I got off work at 1600 and went home. I skipped supper but drank a lot of water. Keeping hydrated seems to help with the sinuses but keeps you making trips to the head. I hate to get up in the cold and go downstairs to the head so I use an empty water bottle and empty it the following morning.

UNMIK POLICE PRESS UPDATE
17 JANUARY, 2001
GNJILANE Region
REPORTED ABDUCTION

Urosevac Town - 16/01 - 1215 hrs. A K-Serb female reported being abducted by two known K-Serb males. The victim said that the suspects promised to transport her to Kosovo Polje to visit relatives but instead brought her to Dubrava village. The suspects assaulted her inside the car and afterwards threw her out of the car. She was later found by a KFOR unit. The circumstances of the incident are under investigation.

PEC Region

ARMED ROBBERY

Dobrusha Village, Istok - 10/01 - 1830 hrs. Two unknown male suspects armed with a machine gun forcibly entered the residence of a K-Albanian male and robbed him of an undetermined amount of cash.

MITROVICA Region

THREATS / INTIMIDATION

Mitrovica North - 16/01 - 1530 hrs. Three unknown K-Serbs threatened to kill a K-Albanian and burn down his house. The suspects beat on the door of the residence with metal bars causing damage to its frame.

ARSON

Zubin Potok Town - 16/01 - 1145 hrs. A K-Serb male reported that unknown person(s) burned his haystack, which was located near a K-Albanian village.

Wednesday, 17 January, 2001

Up at 0630 again and more instant soup for breakfast. I got a ride to work with Ken and John. I worked on lesson plans and records. I helped Joe write memos and get caught up with work. I went to Main HQ with Joe to pick up the daily paperwork and check out some counterfeit money from the Intelligence Officer to use for tomorrow's class at Station #3. Joe is going to teach the KPS about false documents and counterfeit money. We went to lunch at Edi's pizza place on Police Blvd. It was the first time I ever went there. It was pretty good food. Joe and I went to Prishtina airport to pick up Thommy returning from CTO in Germany. This is the first time I have been back to the airport since arriving in mission. The airport is still under Russian KFOR control. It still seems unusual to me to see armed Russian troops that are not the enemy. Thommy brought me a traditional German "Bier Krug" as a gift.

The Germans dropped me at the house. I tested the krug and then went to bed.

P.S. Ken and John came home late (about 2100) and told me that they found a new place closer to Main HQ and would be moving out at the end of the month. That leaves only Brent, Craig and I in the house. We need to find at least two or three more roommates or we may be forced to move. The three of us don't want to pay the 2,500DM rent.

UNMIK POLICE PRESS UPDATE
18 JANUARY, 2001
GNJILANE Region
GRENADE ATTACK
Binac Village, Vitina - 17/01 - 1530 hrs. Unknown suspect(s) threw a hand grenade at a K-Albanian residence. The explosion caused only property damage to a gate. No injuries were reported.
PEC Region
GRENADE ATTACKS
Dakovica Town - 17/01 - 0200 hrs. Unknown suspect(s) threw a hand grenade at a K-Albanian male's residence. The explosion caused only property damage to a gate. No injuries were reported.
Dakovica Town - 17/01 - 0200 hrs. Unknown suspect(s) threw a hand grenade at a K-Albanian female's residence. The explosion caused only property damage to a garage door.
MITROVICA Region
THEFTS
Vucitrn Town - 17/01 - 0001 hrs. Unknown suspect(s) stole forty chickens and nine turkeys from a K-Albanian male's henhouse.
EVICTION
Mitrovica North - 17/01 - 2330 hrs. A K-Albanian male reported that unknown K-Serbs had illegally occupied his apartment. The suspects were later evicted by UNMIK Police officers from Mitrovica North station and KFOR soldiers. No arrests were reported.

Thursday, 18 January, 2001

Up at 0630. I skipped breakfast again and got a ride to work with Ken and John. I went with Joe and Thommy to Station #3. Joe gave a class to Station #3 KPS on forged documents and counterfeit money. Classes lasted until noon. I met up with Brent at the company building to pick up our water supply. We dropped the water at the house and then went to get more propane. I got back to Station #2 about 1400. I worked on lesson plans and the training schedule. I got off at 1600 and went to the internet café for an hour. I walked back to the house and ate noodles for supper and went to bed and watched the BBC for a while.

P.S. The weather started warming up and most of the snow is gone. There is a lot of mud in its place. Most of the predicted snow hasn't gotten here yet.

UNMIK POLICE PRESS UPDATE
19 JANUARY, 2001
GNJILANE Region
GRENADE ATTACK
Urosevac Town - 18/01 - 0030 hrs. Unknown suspects(s) threw a hand grenade at a K-Albanian owned electrical shop. The explosion caused only property damage; no injuries were reported.
PRIZREN Region
ILLEGAL POSSESSION OF WEAPONS
Sopi Village, Suva Reka - 18/01 - 1430 hrs. UNMIK Police arrested three K-Albanian males after a search of a grain store revealed 7 rockets with chargers, one RPG rocket launcher, one disposable rocket launcher, two machine guns (one light/one heavy), two hand grenades, two magazines for an assault rifle and ammunition.
PEC Region
EXPLOSIONS
Gurakoc Village, Istok - 14/01 - 2345 hrs. A former K-Serbian residence was damaged by an explosion, which also caused minor damage to nearby buildings. No injuries were reported.
Istok Town - 14/01 - 2345 hrs. A kiosk was totally destroyed by an explosion, which also caused minor damage to nearby buildings. No injuries were reported.
Pec - 19/01 - 0115 hrs. A K-Albanian house was heavily damaged by an explosion. No injuries were reported.
ILLEGAL POSSESSION OF WEAPONS
Dakovica Town - 18/01 - 1200 hrs. During a joint search operation performed by UNMIK and KFOR, a K-Albanian male was found

to be in possession of six hand grenades. UNMIK Police arrested the suspect and seized the items.
Krstove Village, Pec - 18/01 - 1400 hrs. During a search operation a K-Albanian male was found to be in possession of war items and ammunition. UNMIK Police arrested the suspect and seized the items.
MITROVICA Region
ILLEGAL POSSESSION OF WEAPON
Mitrovica South - 18/01 - 1000 hrs. A K-Serb male was arrested by UNMIK Police after he was found to be in possession of a pistol with three magazines, two grenades and four loaded machine gun magazines.

Friday, 19 January, 2001

Same routine this morning as usual. I skipped breakfast and went in to work at 0800. I worked on lesson plans and arranged my teaching materials. I helped Thommy and Joe with their paperwork. Joe is leaving for CTO today. I left the office early to take Joe to the airport. We stopped off at their house so Joe could pick up his luggage. Another German CivPol roommate (Stephan) of theirs is also going on CTO. I had coffee with Thommy and another German CivPol (Gabriel) while Joe and Stephan finished getting ready. I drove them to Prishtina airport and dropped them off. I ran some errands at Main HQ with Thommy and then he dropped me off at the internet café. I chatted with Carnita for an hour and then went to the house. I had a can of tuna for supper and went to bed. I watched the BBC news for awhile before lights out.

P.S. Ken and John moved out today instead of waiting for the end of the month. We are going to have to decide soon about staying or moving. Craig and I are going to stay together but we are unsure if Brent wants to stay with us. We haven't had a chance to discuss it with him yet.

UNMIK POLICE PRESS UPDATE
20 JANUARY, 2001
PRISTINA Region
ARSON

Stimlje Village, Lipljan - 19/01 - 0300 hrs. Unknown person(s) set an unoccupied Ashkali residence on fire. KFOR and UNMIK Police brought the fire under control. No injuries were reported.
SHOOTINGS
Podujevo - 19/01 - 2000 hrs. Unidentified gunmen fired four shots at a factory after they were refused entry onto the premises.
PRIZREN Region
ASSAULT / THREATS
Gronje Selo Village, Prizren - 19/01 - 1030 hrs. Three K-Albanian males were arrested by UNMIK Police for threatening and assaulting a handicapped K-Bosnian male.
PEC Region
EXPLOSION
Pec Town - 19/01 - 0115 hrs. An explosion occurred in a K-Albanian owned shop. The explosion caused only property damage. No injuries were reported.
MITROVICA Region
ARMED ROBBERY
Mitrovica North - 19/1 - 1830 hrs. Unknown armed K-Serb males robbed a K-Albanian male of his tractor. No injuries were reported.

Saturday, 20 January, 2001

Up at 0630. I had coffee and canned chicken franks for breakfast. Thommy was supposed to pick me up at 0800 but had not shown up by 0815 so Craig and I started walking down the hill. A KPS officer from Station #1 stopped and picked us up. Not much going on at work today. All my lesson plans are about done. I worked on making copies of handouts for next week's class. Randy should be back tomorrow. I got off at 1600 and went home. I watched President Bush's inauguration on the BBC. Lots of good coverage of it. Brent and Craig got home and we talked about moving. Brent is going to try to find a place in K.P. Craig is going to ask Reggie if he wants any roommates at his new apartment. I had rice and carrots for supper and off to bed by 2000. I watched the BBC and then read until lights out at 2200.

UNMIK POLICE PRESS UPDATE
21 JANUARY, 2001
PRISTINA Region

ARMED ROBBERY

Pristina - 20/01 - 0300 hrs. Unknown armed persons broke into the offices of "Kuwait Joint Relief Committee" and stole an empty safe box, video camera, and a video cassette recorder after threatening a security guard. No injuries were reported.

GNJILANE Region

GRENADE ATTACK

Gnjilane - 20/01 – 1630 hrs. Unknown subject(s) threw a concussion grenade in the yard of a K-Serb female. The victim sustained minor injuries to her face and legs.

ILLEGAL POSSESSION OF WEAPONS

Urosevac Town - 20/01 - 0125hrs. During a joint operation between KFOR and KPS Officers a vehicle with four K-Albanian males was stopped and searched. The search resulted in the seizure of a live hand grenade. The four suspects were arrested.

PEC Region

ARMED ROBBERY

Sicevo Village, Klina - 20/01 - 0005 hrs. A group of unknown male subjects armed with rifles, entered a local K-Albanian owned shop and began looting several items from the store. When the storeowner attempted to stop them, the group opened fire on the victim and also threw a hand grenade in the direction of the victim. The grenade did not explode and the group of subjects fled. Numerous empty shell casings were located at the scene. KFOR EOD disposed of the hand grenade.

Sunday, 21 January, 2001

Up at 0630. "Triple Sierra" and coffee only this morning. I visited with Craig until Thommy picked me up for work. In to work at 0800 but today is an administrative day. Randy got back from CTO today. I brought him up to date on what's planned for the coming week. One of the KPS officers heard I was looking for a new house and took me to see a third floor studio apartment near Station #2. It had two very small bedrooms for 1200DM per month. Craig stopped by and said we could move in to Reggie's place but that we would need to paint the rooms and buy a few things. Craig and I went to meet with Reggie but we could not find him. We went to Ardi's market and got a few days worth of food. I am completely out of food. We went back to the house and I was up to bed by 2000. I plan to go have breakfast at the British KFOR chow hall with Craig in the morning.

UNMIK POLICE PRESS UPDATE
22 JANUARY, 2001
PRISTINA Region
ABONDONED INFANT
Stanovc Village, Pristina - 21/01 - 2010 hrs. Two K-Albanian males reported that they had found an abandoned newly born baby at the bus stop. The infant was taken to hospital where his condition was reported as serious due to exposure but that he was expected to recover.

Monday, 22 January, 2001

I got up at 0600 and got ready. We went to the British KFOR chow hall at the BBC compound. Craig has a vehicle and it is only a ten minute drive at this time of the morning. Craig discovered a few days ago that UNMIK personnel can eat for free by just signing in with our CivPol I.D. number. We got there at 0700 and had a good British military breakfast of scrambled eggs, potatoes and beans, all covered with Tabasco sauce. They did not have any coffee. Only tea! We were done and gone by 0715. Craig dropped me off at work by 0730. I have no classes until tomorrow so I helped Thommy with some of his work. I got a ride down to where Craig works and went back to the British KFOR chow hall with him for lunch. This is the best food we have had yet in mission. I got off work at 1700 and Craig and I looked at another house. It was way too small. Craig and I talked to our landlord, through one of his English speaking family members, and he agreed to let us stay next month for 500DM each until we can find more roommates. Brent moved out today to a house in K.P. I moved from the third floor down to the second floor where the head is. It took me a couple of hours to make the move. The power went out and the house is very cold.

UNMIK POLICE PRESS UPDATE
23 JANUARY, 2001
GNJILANE Region
BOMB THREAT

Gnjilane - 22/01 - 1250 hrs. A language assistant at the UNMIK Police station received a phone call from a K-Serbian male who stated that a bomb would detonate in five minutes. The building was evacuated. KFOR and bomb dogs from the Ukrainian SPU K-9 unit searched the building with no results.

DEAD BODY FOUND

Urosevac Town - 22/01 - 0930 hrs. The dead body of a baby was found at the dumping site along Lleiza village. The body was brought to Urosevac Hospital for autopsy and was declared to be a male baby possibly Albanian ethnicity.

PRIZREN Region

GRENADE ATTACK

Prizren - 21/01 - 2300 hrs. A K-Albanian male was arrested by UNMIK Police after throwing a hand grenade at the home of another K-Albanian.

ILLEGAL POSSESSION OF A WEAPON

Suva Reka Town - 22/01 - 1800 hrs. A K-Albanian male was arrested by UNMIK Police after he was found in possession of a hand grenade at a checkpoint.

PEC Region

GRENADE ATTACK

Dakovica Town, Pec - 22/01 - 0015 hrs. An unknown person threw a hand grenade at a K-Albanian house. The explosion caused only minor property damage.

ILLEGAL POSSESSION OF A WEAPON

Diec Village, Klina - 20/01 - 2030 hrs. A K-Albanian male was arrested by UNMIK Police after being found in possession of three hand grenades and two gas masks.

Tuesday, 23 January, 2001

Up at 0630. Craig does not have a vehicle today so no British chow. I had a can of tuna for breakfast. We had no coffee because Brent took his coffee maker with him to K.P. I walked to work by 0800. I started a three day in service training cycle with KPS class #8. I started the day with my Police Ethics class. It went pretty well. One of my Station #2 KPS officers from class #1 brought us some homemade fli for lunch. It was pretty good. My afternoon class was Use of Force. I lectured for a couple of hours and then showed some shooting videos. I finished work at 1600 but stayed around using the office computer with Thommy until about 2000.

I went to the house and had tuna with noodles for supper. The power went out again after supper. We had no movies to watch anyway as Brent also took his VCR. I got to bed about 2200 and read by candlelight until about 2245. The power came back on from 0300 to 0500. I know this because I woke up when my electric heater came on. It has been pretty cold in the house at night because the power has been out a lot. You can see your breath in the bedroom.

UNMIK POLICE PRESS UPDATE
24 JANUARY, 2001
PRISTINA Region
ATTEMPTED MURDER
Pristina - 23/01 - 1930 hrs. Two unknown male suspects attacked an international employee of "OSCE" (nationality not reported), striking the victim in the head with an iron pipe as he attempted to enter his accommodation after work. The suspects then fled. The victim was treated for his injuries.
GNJILANE Region
GRENADE ATTACK
Vitina Town - 23/01 - 0010 hrs. Unknown suspect(s) threw hand grenades at two occupied K-Serb houses. The explosions caused only minor property damage.
Vitina Town - 23/01 - 1920 hrs. Unidentified suspects threw two hand grenades at an occupied K-Serb house. A K-Serb female was injured and transported in stable condition to Gnjilane Hospital.
UXO FOUND
Vitina Town - 23/01 - 1440 hrs. A K-Albanian male reported to UNMIK Police that school children found four hand grenades in a K-Serbian field. KFOR EOD was tasked and secured the scene.
PEC Region
ASSAULT
Klina Town - 23/01 - 2010 hrs. Three K-Albanian males were arrested after assaulting KPS Officers who were on duty at Klina Police Station. A female KPS Officer was slightly injured by one of the suspects.
ILLEGAL POSSESSION OF WEAPONS
Pec - 23/01 - 0830 hrs. A search of seven K-Albanian homes by UNMIK Police (Spanish SPU) revealed a large cache of weapons including a grenade launcher, grenades, pistols, rifles, ammunition and magazines. Two K-Albanian males were arrested.

MITROVICA Region
ATTEMPTED MURDER
Srbica Town - 23/01 - 1930 hrs. Two unknown male suspects, who were armed with pistols and an iron pipe, accosted two K-Albanian males as they walked a roadway. The suspects began to strike one of the victims with the pipe and as the victims ran, the suspects began to shoot at them with pistols. The victim who was beaten with the iron pipe sustained minor injuries.

Wednesday, 24 January, 2001

I got up at 0600. The power is still off and the house is very cold. I lit candles and got the propane heater going. I woke Craig and we got our "Triple Sierra" routines done. Craig had a vehicle today so we drove to the BBC compound for breakfast at the British KFOR chow hall again. We got to the chow hall at 0655. I had scrambled eggs, potatoes, beans and mushrooms. It was a great breakfast except for the lack of coffee. We were done with chow by 0710. Craig had me to work by 0730. I worked on my CTO schedule until Randy arrived. I got today's class started by 0800. I discussed Officer Safety all morning. I had a banana for lunch. Randy had Kevin Trimbath come back and teach his Crime Scene Preservation class and fingerprinting. We let the class go at 1500 and we all went to Main HQ and then to KFOR hill. I bought a case of "Schwarzbier" at the German PX and had coffee at the German KFOR coffee bar. While there, I spoke with a U.S. KFOR major for a while. I also bought a new coffee maker. I got back to the house and had noodles for supper and tested my new bier krug with the schwarzbier.

UNMIK POLICE PRESS UPDATE
25 JANUARY, 2001
PRISTINA Region
KIDNAPPING
Stimlje Village, Lipljan - 24/01 - 1530 hrs. A 7-year-old K-Albanian boy was abducted by a group of unknown suspects while walking on the street. The suspects demanded a cash ransom from the parents of the victim. The boy was brought to a house but later managed to escape unharmed. While he was fleeing he recognized a house of a KPS officer and asked for help. The KPS officer

brought him to Lipljan Station. UNMIK Police raided the hide-out and arrested three suspects (ethnicity not reported).

GNJILANE Region

EXPLOSION

Uglare Village, Gnjilane - 24/01 - 1745 hrs. An unknown person threw a homemade bomb at a K-Albanian house. The explosion caused only minor property damage. No injuries were reported.

PRIZREN Region

EXPLOSIONS

Velika Hodja Village, Orahovac - 24/01 - 2200 hrs. Explosive devices damaged six K-Serb owned houses, two of which were occupied. No injuries were reported. UNMIK Police is investigating the case together with KFOR EOD

MURDER/SUICIDE

Prizren - 24/01 - 0430 hrs. A K-Albanian female shot her K-Albanian husband with a firearm in the head and then used the same weapon to kill herself. The husband victim was rushed to hospital in Pristina but died shortly thereafter. The wife died at the scene.

MITROVICA Region

THREATS/INTIMIDATION

Mitrovica North - 24/01 - 1000 hrs. A K-Albanian female reported that four unknown K-Serbs in a motor vehicle threatened to kill her for living on the northern side.

Vucitrn Town - 24/01 - 2200 hrs. A K-Albanian male reported that his brother was threatening to kill his family. UNMIK Police arrested the suspect and confiscated a machine gun.

Thursday, 25 January, 2001

I got up at 0630 and found that I had power and water. I made coffee in our new coffee maker. I got ready and Craig and I went to the British KFOR chow hall again. I had scrambled eggs, potatoes, beans and Tabasco on all. Craig got me to work at 0730. The KPS coordinators gave most of the instruction today on KPS policy and procedures. I worked on finalizing my CTO schedule after a new U.N. policy change. I called Carnita during my lunch break to set up a chat time. It was 0400 in Montana. After work I went to the internet café and chatted with Carnita from 1700 to 1800. I went back to the office and hung out with Thommy and Andy. Thommy bought us chicken burgers. I stayed at the office until about 2200. Thommy dropped me at the house and I went straight to bed.

P.S. We found out that the power trouble is intentional. The power plant can only put out three hours of power at a time. Three on and three off.

UNMIK POLICE PRESS UPDATE
26 JANUARY, 2001
PRISTINA Region
RAPE
Obilic Village, Kosovo Polje - 24/01 - 0100 hrs. A K-Roma male raped a K-Roma female at a refugee camp. UNMIK Police arrested the suspect.
PEC Region
UXO FOUND
Upper Luka, Decani - 25/01 - 0645 hrs. A K-Albanian male located five unexploded rockets near a roadway. KFOR EOD disposed of the items.

Ground Zero- 22 November, 2000 bombing of Serbian Ambassador's residence

Clay Coker's position at time of explosion

Damage area at rear of house

Clay after the bombing

Large demonstration (November, 2000)

Demonstration photo

Demonstration photo

Burning trash

War damaged homes- Pristina

Destroyed Serbian Tank- Klina

Destroyed Serbian Tank- Klina

Destroyed Serbian Armored Vehicle- Klina

KFOR Signpost

Destroyed Roma homes- Mitrovica

German KFOR- Prizren

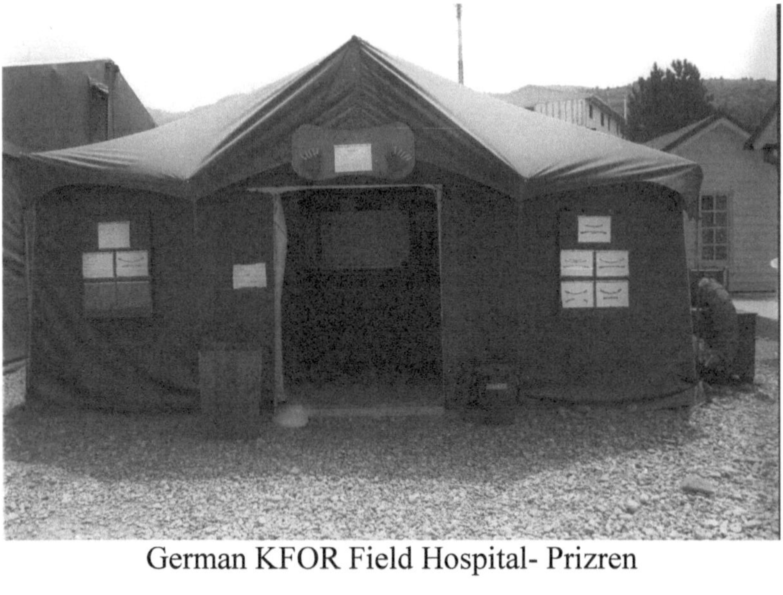
German KFOR Field Hospital- Prizren

Prizren

Seized weapons

More seized weapons

Entrance to discovered weapons cache

Recovered weapons from cache

British Royal Marine with recovered explosives

Recovered crates of military TNT

Rrustem Mustafa (left) AKA “Commander Remi”

Craig Martin before U.N. Medal parade

British Navy Corpsman Andy McCrum with Clay Coker

Streoc Village, Decani - 25/01 - 0300 hrs. A K-Albanian male found two unexploded hand grenades in his garden. KFOR EOD disposed of the items.

MITROVICA Region

GRENADE ATTACK/SHOOTING

Zvecan Town - 25/01 - 2345 hrs. A known K-Serb male entered a K-Serb owned coffee bar and started shooting in the air with an assault rifle. After exhausting his ammunition he threw a grenade. The explosion caused only minor property damage. No injuries were reported. The occupants of the café managed to overcome the offender. During the struggle the suspect sustained minor injuries. UNMIK Police arrested the suspect and transported him to hospital for treatment. The motive for the attack was not reported yet.

Friday, 26 January, 2001

Up at 0600 and another trip to the British KFOR chow hall. In to work at 0730. Randy and I gave a fingerprinting class to the KPS who are assigned to investigations. Not much else going on. Our MSA is not going to be dispersed today for some reason. They say not until Monday. This is the first time that it has been delayed from the last Friday of the month. I wonder what the problem is. I had a leftover chicken burger for lunch that was in the office refrigerator. I got to the house at 1700. I skipped supper and visited with Craig for awhile.

UNMIK POLICE PRESS UPDATE

27 JANUARY, 2001

GNJILANE Region

GRENADE ATTACK

Vitina Town - 26/01 - 1750 hrs. Four K-Serbian males sustained minor injuries after an unknown male suspect threw two hand grenades into a K-Serb shop occupied by the victims. Two victims were transported to the hospital and released after treatment. The two others refused to go for medical treatment. The shop was moderately damaged.

EXPLOSION

Cernice Village, Gnjilane - 26/01 - 2015 hrs. An abandoned K-Serb house was completely destroyed and two others sustained minor damages by an unknown type of explosion. No injuries were reported.

PRIZREN Region

Prizren - 26/01 - 2310 hrs. A KPS Officer reported that unknown suspect(s) broke into his apartment and stole his service weapon, ammunition and a pair of handcuffs.

Saturday, 27 January, 2001

I slept in until 0800 this morning. Craig went to chow without me. I got a hot bath and had coffee. I got to work at 0900. Not much going on today. Randy was finishing up with the fingerprinitng class. I worked on putting my Use of Force class on a PowerPoint presentation. I went to Main HQ with Thommy to pick up some new computers for our station. We got four new computers for our KPS units. I spent the rest of the day setting up the new computers. Randy and I got one of them. We should have our internet connection in a week or so. I went to the house at 1500 and ate some tuna and noodles. It was my first meal today. I lay down in the living room to watch the BBC world news and fell asleep. I think I may be coming down with another case of the "Kosovo Krud." It has been going around again.

P.S. The weather was really mild today. The sun even came out for a while. It feels like Spring in Montana. Hopefully we have made it through most of the cold weather.

UNMIK POLICE PRESS UPDATE

28 JANUARY, 2001

PRISTINA Region

MURDER

Pristina - 27/01 - 2000 hrs. The dead body of an unidentified male was found near a local school. The victim had been stabbed multiple times.

ASSAULT

Plementina Village, Kosovo Polje - 27/01 - 0900 hrs. A K-Serb male assaulted the Danish driver of a UNHCR bus when he was told he could not ride the bus because all seats were already occupied. When a nearby KFOR unit intervened the suspect fled and could not be apprehended. The driver received minor injuries.

THREATS / INTIMIDATION

Obilic Village, Kosovo Polje - 27/01 - 1455 hrs. An OSCE official was chased in his vehicle and intimidated by TMK members after he photographed their installation while carrying out his duties.
GNJILANE Region
ILLEGAL POSSESSION OF WEAPONS
Kamenica - 27/01 – 1730 hrs. UNMIK Police and KFOR searched two houses and found the owners in possession of several illegal weapons, which were confiscated. Two suspects, a K-Roma male and a K-Serb male, were arrested.
PEC Region
UXO FOUND
Drenovac Village, Decani - 26/01 - 1300 hrs. A K-Albanian male reported that he saw a grenade on the side of the road. KFOR EOD disposed of the device.
Ljubusa Village, Decani - 26/01 - 1630 hrs. A K-Albanian male reported that he found a grenade in a field near the village. KFOR EOD confirmed that it was an active AF17 Yugoslavian grenade. The device was disposed of.
MITROVICA Region
ATTEMPTED MURDER
Mitrovica South - 27/01 - 1720 hrs. When a K-Albanian male purchased items from a store, a car with two unknown occupants stopped next to him. One suspect fired one round at the victim with a pistol, hitting him in the upper arm. The suspects fled the scene. The victim was transported to the Moroccan hospital where his wound was described as not critical.
ASSAULT
Mitrovica North - 27/01 - 1436 hrs. A K-Albanian male was assaulted by five unknown K-Serb males. As the suspects left the scene they fired two shots into the air. The victim sustained minor injuries.

Sunday, 28 January, 2001

Up at 0600, started the coffee and woke up Craig. Water was off this morning so no hot shower. We left for the British KFOR chow hall and arrived there at 0700 to find that it does not open on Sundays until 0830. We drove to Craig's office to wait and use the computers. We were back at the chow hall at 0830. We ate another good British military breakfast and then left for work. Craig dropped me off at my office. Not much going on today. I worked on my Use of Force PowerPoint and went to the house early at 1400. I made some beans and spinach for supper. I went down to the internet café to make my chat date. I had to walk in a cold rain. After an hour chat I went back up the hill and straight to bed.

P.S. The weather is still spring like with the temperature getting up to 48 degrees today. The rain made it feel colder.

E-mail Home

Hi Hun,
Sorry about the chat. I got home at 1500 and ate. I wasn't feeling good so I lay down on the couch in the TV room and watched the BBC until time for chat. I fell asleep and didn't wake up till after 1800. Sorry. Nothing new here. I got a new computer for my office yesterday. The internet should be connected in about a week. That should make it easier to communicate with you. I can just go to the office instead of the café. I'm sending this from Craig's office. They have the internet now. We are about to go to the British KFOR Chow hall again for breakfast. Talk to you soon.

UNMIK POLICE PRESS UPDATE
29 JANUARY, 2001
PRISTINA Region
ROAD BLOCK
Gotovusa Village, Strpce - 28/01 - 1225 hrs. A group of approximately 150 K-Serbs blocked the road in protest of another K-Serb male being taken to the station for questioning. The matter was resolved peacefully when the subject was returned after questioning.
PEC Region
MURDER
Dakovica Town - 28/01 - 0030 hrs. Unknown persons armed with handguns and assault rifles entered a local club and open fire at three K-Albanian males, two of them alleged active members of TMK. A 19-year-old K-Albanian male died at the scene. Two others sustained non-life-threatening injuries. They were transported to hospital for medical treatment.
MITROVICA Region
CIVIL UNREST

Mitrovica North - 28/01 - 1300 hrs. A UNMIK Police foot patrol detected a fight between a group of 50 to 100 K-Albanians and K-Serbs in "Little Bosnia" (confidence zone). Together with the backup of 15 other UNMIK Police officers and KFOR soldiers they tried to ease the situation and break up the crowd. During the incident an unknown person fired one shot in the air. A K-Albanian male was slightly injured during a fist-fight with his opponents and was transported to the Moroccan hospital. A small group of K-Serbs prepared petrol bombs but were stopped by UNMIK Police officers before being able to use them. Finally the civil unrest calmed down. No injuries of UNMIK Police officers or KFOR soldiers were reported.
ASSAULT
Mitrovica North - 28/01 - 0500 hrs. A K-Albanian male panicked and ran away after observing a group of K-Serbs outside his home. The group chased and assaulted him. UNMIK Police responded to the area and extracted the victim from the group. The victim sustained minor injuries.

Monday, 29 January, 2001

Both Craig and I woke up at 0500 today. We had water and power. We completed our “Triple Sierra” routine and had our coffee. We made the trip to breakfast again. Same routine at work today. I got a ride downtown with Joe to draw our MSA. We got 4,887DM. Craig showed up at the bank while we were there. We went to the company building to pay for our plane tickets. Later in the afternoon we went to the Green Market area to find the “black market” money changers. I exchanged 2,000DM for $938.00 US; an excellent rate.

UNMIK POLICE PRESS UPDATE
30 JANUARY, 2001
PRISTINA Region
AUTO THEFT
Pristina - 29/01 - 0700 hrs. Unknown person(s) stole a white 4WD motor vehicle belonging to the NGO "Global Development".
Pristina - 29/01 - 0600 hrs. Unknown person(s) stole a white 4WD motor vehicle belonging to the "European Agency for Reconstruction".
GNJILANE Region

EXPLOSION

Mogila Village, Vitina - 30/01 - 0130 hrs. An unoccupied residence belonging to a K-Serb male living in Serbia was totally destroyed by an unknown type of explosion.

GRENADE ATTACK

Don Budriga Village, Gnjilane - 29/01 - 0400 hrs. A grenade explosion occurred in front of an empty kiosk causing only property damage.

MITROVICA Region

MURDER/ATTEMPTED MURDER

Mitrovica North - 29/01 - 1330 hrs. Unknown person(s) opened fire with pistols and automatic rifles at a group of K-Albanians as they watched a K-Albanian house burning down. They also threw two hand grenades into the group. Four injured K-Albanians were transported to the Moroccan hospital, where one K-Albanian male was pronounced dead upon arrival. Two others are in serious condition.

GRENADE ATTACK

Mitrovica North - 29/01 - 2220 hrs. Unknown person(s) threw a hand grenade into an abandoned home causing minor property damages. No injuries were reported.

ASSAULT / CRIMINAL DAMAGE

Mitrovica North/South - 29/01 - 1415 hrs. A group of K-Albanians gathered on the East Bridge after a grenade attack in Mitrovica North. During the gathering a train passed and the crowd began to throw stones and rocks at it. UNMIK Police intervened to disperse the crowd and four UNMIK Police Officers sustained minor injuries while executing their duties. Three UNMIK Police vehicles were reported damaged and one OSCE vehicle was set ablaze. Danish KFOR responded to the scene and after firing tear gas shells the situation was brought under control. No occupants of the train were injured.

CRIMINAL DAMAGE

Srbica Town - 29/01 - 1530 hrs. The Cultural Center sustained moderate damages after a group of approximately 2,500 people attempted to force their way into a concert. UNMIK Police managed to control the crowd.

Tuesday, 30 January, 2001

We did the same morning routine once again. We went for our British breakfast of scramble eggs, potatoes, white beans in tomato sauce and English tea. There is often a pan of cooked mushrooms to add to the mix. I got to work at 0730 and planned to teach Ethics and Use of Force but most of the KPS officers did not show up for some reason. We had a Q and A session instead for those that showed up. The KPS officer that showed me the small apartment last week found me and said that he had another house available. The German CivPol officers that were living there moved out at their EOM. I went and looked at the house. It was a two story, two bedroom house about a hundred yards from Station #2. It was a little more run down than our current house but it was the perfect size for Craig and I and very close to my office. I got Craig to look at it and we decided we would take it. We need to get out of our current house by tomorrow to avoid paying next month's rent. I packed up my stuff for the move. The rent will be 600DM each but it will only be the two of us and we will not need to find any roommates. I will also be able to use the office computer instead of the internet café. The best thing is that we will not have to deal with the hill.

UNMIK POLICE PRESS UPDATE
31 JANUARY, 2001
PRISTINA Region
SHOOTING
Lebane Village, Pristina - 30/01 - 0955 hrs. Unknown person(s) shot at a motor vehicle occupied by two K-Serbian males, one female, and three children, which was in a convoy of 30 other vehicles driving along Pristina Highway towards Podujevo/Gate 3 escorted by Ukrainian KFOR. The vehicle was slightly damaged; the occupants were not injured.
PRIZREN Region
CIVIL DISTURBANCE
Prizren - 30/01 - 1150 hrs. A crowd of approximately 500 persons gathered outside the Municipal building to protest against the verdict of a war crimes trial. After a delegation of the demonstrators negotiated with UNMIK officials the demonstration ended at approximately 1445 hrs. without further incidents. No injuries were reported.
MITROVICA Region
RIOTS

Mitrovica South - 30/01 - 1520 - 2100 hrs. A group of approximately 1,500 K-Albanians surrounded the Municipality Building and the nearby KFOR checkpoint. The crowd then began charging towards the main bridge where French KFOR used teargas to disperse them. Later groups of K-Albanians tried to attack the Serb-Orthodox Church in South Mitrovica. French and Danish KFOR brought the situation under control. Two KFOR vehicles were set on fire during the civil unrest.

Wednesday, 31 January, 2001

Craig and I got up at 0530, did our "Triple Sierra" routine and had our coffee. We made the trip to the British chow hall. We arrived at 0655 and were out by 0705. Craig dropped me off at Station #2 and I taught Police Ethics until 1100. During lunch I moved our heaters to the new house and got them all turned on to warm the house up. Craig came to Station #2 at 1300 and we moved the rest of our gear to the new house. The weather was rainy and colder today. I hope winter will be over soon.

UNMIK POLICE PRESS UPDATE
01 FEBRUARY, 2001
PRISTINA Region
UXO FOUND
Kamenica Town - 31/01 -1430 hrs. Three K-Albanian children found a hand grenade in the back of a refugee building. KFOR EOD responded and disposed of the ordnance.
PRIZREN Region
DEMONSTRATION
Prizren Town- 31/01 - 1305/1430 hrs. A peaceful but unauthorized demonstration by approximately 60-70 persons concerning the war crimes verdict rendered 29/01 has taken place in front of Prizren District Court. Later the crowd proceeded to the UNMIK administration building. The demonstration ended around 1430 hrs.
MITROVICA Region
RIOT
Mitrovica South - 31/01 - 1500 to 0700 hrs. A group of approximately 400 persons approached the Main Bridge and UNMIK headquarters and prepared to throw petrol bombs. When KFOR intervened the rioters threw hand grenades at the soldiers.

21 KFOR personnel were reported to be injured during the riot, one of them seriously but not life-threatening. KFOR brought the situation under control.

ATTEMPTED MURDER

Mitrovica South - 31/01 - 2130 hrs. Two unknown male suspects driving a motor vehicle shot a Montenegro male who was driving his truck. The victim sustained serious injuries and was taken to a local hospital where his condition is presently listed as unstable.

Thursday, 1 February, 2001

I got up at 0600. My new bed sleeps pretty good. This is the first morning in our new house. It is not as good as our old house but is OK. We were off to the British chow hall at 0645 and had another good, and free, British breakfast. Craig dropped me off at work at 0730. There has been bad rioting for the past two days in Mitrovica. The Serbs killed a 15 year old Albanian boy on Monday. The French KFOR did nothing. Worthless bastards! Now the Albanians are rioting. They are throwing rocks and Molotov cocktails. The German KFOR had to go up and assist the French KFOR (Funny!) The standing joke here is that when the German forces entered the French controlled area of Mitrovica that the French raised a white flag and the Germans said "Hey, we're not here for that this time."

P.S. One of our Pakistani CivPol officers was trying to pay for some Law Enforcement training course out of Florida but was having trouble with the transaction. I e-mailed Carnita to pay for the course on her end and the Pakistani officer paid me in DM. I will send the money home in my next check. I am planning to go to Skopje with Reggie at 0400 in the morning.

UNMIK POLICE PRESS UPDATE

02 FEBRUARY, 2001

PRISTINA Region

ATTEMPTED ABDUCTION

Pristina - 01/02 - 0830 hrs. A K-Albanian female became the victim of an attempted abduction when an unknown male subject attempted to subdue her while she walked to her office. The victim managed to escape uninjured.

GNJILANE Region

EXPLOSION

Vitina Town - 01/02 – 2040 hrs. An explosion destroyed an abandoned K-Serb house. The explosion also damaged a neighboring house where flying glass slightly injured the members of a K-Albanian family: 2 adults and 2 children. UNMIK Police and KFOR EOD responded and sealed off the scene.

THREATS

Gnjilane - 01/02 – 1000 hrs. A K-Serb female states that an unknown K-Albanian male threatened to kill her.

PRIZREN Region

DEMONSTRATION

Orahovac Town - 01/02- 1200 – 1315 hrs. A crowd of approximately 2,000 persons protested peacefully against the War Crimes conviction recently handed down.

PEC Region

HUMAN REMAINS FOUND

Nec Village, Dakovica - 31/01 – 1000 hrs. Acting on information from a K-Albanian male, UNMIK Police located skeletal remains of an unknown person killed in 1999.

MITROVICA Region

EVICTIONS

Mitrovica North - 30/01 - Nighttime hrs. A K-Albanian female reported that K-Serbs had evicted her and her husband from their residence.

Mitrovica North - 30/01 - Nighttime hrs. A K-Albanian female reported that K-Serbs had evicted her from her residence.

Mitrovica North - 30/01 - Nighttime hrs. A K-Albanian male reported that a large group of K-Serbs had evicted his mother from her residence.

DEMONSTRATION

Mitrovica South - 01/02- 1850 hrs. Several crowds gathered at various locations throughout the day with the largest being 350-400 people in front of the Maison de France. At this particular location two K-Albanian KPS officers were slightly injured when trying to de-escalate the situation. KFOR used tear gas grenades to disperse the crowds.

ILLEGAL POSSESSION OF A WEAPON

Mitrovica North - 01/02 – 1850 hrs. One K-Albanian adult male and two K-Albanian male juveniles were arrested for possessing three gas bombs.

Friday, 2 February, 2001

I got up at 0300 and did my "Triple Sierra." I had tuna and fruit for breakfast and made a half pot of coffee for myself. Reggie was supposed to pick me up at 0400. I was ready and waiting and went to check the temperature on the outside thermometer that Craig had bought for the house. I found a note on the door from Reggie saying the trip was cancelled. Oh well. I changed into a uniform and went in to the office. There was nothing else to do. It is colder today with a north wind and blowing snow. We got about four inches overnight. I taught KPS class #8 fingerprinting. I am supposed to get thirteen KPS officers on Monday from the academy. Class #12. Supposedly it is going to be an all female class. I went to lunch at the KFOR café near Station #2 and had "Chicken American" and a Sprite. Thommy paid for lunch. After lunch I worked on paperwork and got off work at 1700. I walked down to the internet café and checked my e-mail. I chatted with Carnita for an hour and then walked back to the house. I stopped at the corner store, called Goldie's, and got a few things. I did some laundry and watched the BBC World News before going to bed.

UNMIK POLICE PRESS UPDATE
03 FEBRUARY, 2001
PRISTINA Region
SHOOTING
Obilic Village, Kosovo Polje - 02/02 - 1000 hrs. A K-Serb male reported that unknown persons fired five rounds towards his vehicle, which had broken down and was parked along the roadside. The victim, who was sitting in the vehicle at the time of shooting, was not injured.
GNJILANE Region
UXO FOUND
Urosevac - 02/02 - 1630 hrs. Two K-Albanian children were playing in an abandoned house when they found a fragmentation grenade. UNMIK Police and KFOR EOD responded to the scene and disposed of the ordnance.
PRIZREN Region
THREATS
Prizren - 01/02 – 2030 hrs. A K-Roma male prosecutor reported that an unknown male called by phone and demanded that he acts

favorably on a murder case currently before the courts or else he would be killed.

PEC Region

GRENADE ATTACK

Dakovica Town - 03/02 - 2130 hrs. Unknown persons threw a hand grenade on the roof of a K-Albanian house. The explosion caused minor damage. No injuries were reported.

DEAD BODY FOUND

Dakovica Town - 02/02 - 1515 hrs. A K-Albanian male found a partially decomposed female body in a wooded area. The corpse was transported to the morgue in Pec. Preliminary investigation revealed no signs of violence or foul play at this time.

Saturday, 3 February, 2001

I woke up at 0600 because I heard Craig in the head. He got up at 0530 and was the first in the shower. We had coffee before heading out to the British chow hall. The temperature this morning is 18 degrees, the coldest day so far. We arrived at the British KFOR chow hall at 0645 and had a good British breakfast. Scrambled eggs, potatoes over white beans in tomato sauce, cooked mushrooms and Tabasco sauce over all. I was in to work at 0730 and worked out the following week's schedule. I went to lunch with Randy at the KFOR "fish restaurant". I was not in the mood for fish and had the Chicken Cordon Bleu for 15DM. I went to the house at 1600 and did some laundry. I skipped supper and I went to bed at 2200.

UNMIK POLICE PRESS UPDATE

04 FEBRUARY, 2001

GNJILANE Region

EXPLOSION

Vitina - 03/02 - 2030 hrs. There was a powerful explosion directed at a K-Serbian house. A K-Serbian female was injured.

PRIZREN Region

BOMB THREAT

Prizren - 03/02 – 0230 hrs. A K-Albanian female nurse reported that she had received a phone call stating that a bomb was to explode at 1515 hrs. in the hospital. UNMIK Police and KFOR responded but no bomb was located.

PEC Region

GRENADE ATTACK
Dakovica - 03/02 - 2130 hrs. Unknown persons threw a hand grenade on the roof of a K-Albanian house. The explosion caused minor damage.

Sunday, 4 February, 2001

I slept in today until about 0700. I got up and did the same morning routine. Craig and I watched the BBC news while having our morning coffee. There were two interesting stories on the news. President Bush is withholding $100 million in aid to Serbia until they turn over Milosevic for war crimes. The deadline is 31 March. The other was that Secretary of State Colin Powell said that U.S. troops are not going to leave the Balkans anytime soon. We were at the British KFOR chow hall at 0830 for our breakfast and were out the door by 0840. Craig dropped me off at Station #2 at 0900. No one else arrived until 1000. I worked on lesson plans for Monday. KPS class #12 is due in for training on Monday. We went to lunch at Gresia's downtown. It is a German restaurant. Randy, Thommy, Joe and I went to lunch together. I had Chicken Schnitzel. It was very good and there was more food than I could eat. I took a "doggie bag" with me. Randy paid for all of us. I got to the house about 1930. I had a few beers with Craig and watched the BBC until the power went out at 2100. We sat around and told stories by candle light until about 2200. The weather has been warming up. It was clear and sunny today and the snow is beginning to melt.

UNMIK POLICE PRESS UPDATE
05 FEBRUARY, 2001
PRISTINA Region
DOMESTIC VIOLENCE
Pristina - 04/02 – 1600 hrs. A U.S. male citizen was arrested for assaulting his K-Albanian girlfriend with whom he has a seven-months-old child. No injuries were reported. The suspect was brought to Pristina Detention Center and released after processing.
PEC Region
THREATS/INTIMIDATION
Brekovac Village, Dakovica - 03/02 - 2000/2300 hrs. A K-Albanian female reported that her husband has been receiving death threats from unknown individuals for approximately one

week. The suspects have further threatened to burn the victim's home for allegedly collaborating with Serbians.

Monday, 5 February, 2001

I got up at 0600. Craig had been up for about half an hour and already had the coffee made. We did the same morning routine today. Breakfast at 0645 and in to work at 0730. KPS class #12 reported for training today. They had thirteen females in the class. I gave the orientation and introductions and then turned the class over to the KPS coordinators. I scanned the class's I.D. cards into our program and made their shift assignments to the FTU. After lunch I had Besnik (L.A.) give a computer orientation class. We cut the class loose at 1400. At 1430 there was a bomb threat near the station. Someone left a television set by the side of the road and called and said that there was a bomb inside of it. I helped evacuate the area and called The British KFOR EOD unit. It turned out to be a false alarm. I got off at 1600 and went to the house. I cleaned the house and put away laundry. Craig got to the house at 1800. We ate and watched the BBC. I got to bed at 2100.

UNMIK POLICE PRESS UPDATE
06 FEBRUARY, 2001
PRISTINA Region
BOMB THREAT
Pristina - 05/02 – 0700 hrs. A K-Albanian male shop owner reported that two unknown male suspects placed a television set in front of his business and stated it contained a bomb. KFOR EOD responded to the scene where the device was found to be a hoax.
ILLEGAL POSSESSION OF WEAPONS
Muzicane Village, Lipljan - 05/02 – 2200 hrs. Two K-Albanian males were arrested after they were found in possession of a Thompson submachine gun, 5 magazines, ammunition and two bayonets. The weapons were seized.
SUDDEN DEATH
Kuzmin Village, Pristina - 05/02 – 0700 hrs. A 50-year-old male Estonian citizen was found dead in his bedroom from apparent asphyxiation due to an extremely high alcohol intake.
GNJILANE Region
POSSESSION OF ILLEGAL WEAPONS

Vitina Town - 04/02 – 2230 hrs. UNMIK Police and KFOR responded to a local wedding where gunfire was heard. A search of a K-Albanian male's house resulted in the seizure of an assault rifle and two magazines. A second K-Albanian male was found in possession of a shotgun and ammunition. The weapons were confiscated and both suspects were arrested by UNMIK Police.

PRIZREN Region

ARSON

Orahovac Town - 05/02 - 1630 hrs. Unknown persons set an unoccupied K-Serb house on fire. A female (ethnicity not reported) at the scene protested against both the fire brigade and the UNMIK Police carrying out their duties.

PEC Region

FOUND UXO

Dakovica Town - 05/02 - 1015 hrs. During a search of a restaurant conducted by UNMIK Police two mines and ammunition were located. The ammunition was seized and KFOR EOD disposed of the mines. No arrests were reported.

Tuesday, 6 February, 2001

Same morning routine. Started classes at 0800. I gave more orientation about Station #2 and our AOR. I got off work at 1600 and had the same evening routine before bed.

UNMIK POLICE PRESS UPDATE

07 FEBRUARY, 2001

PRIZREN Region

MURDER

Crnovrane Village, Malisevo - 06/02 - 1100 hrs. A K-Albanian male was arrested after he shot dead another K-Albanian male with a pistol. Preliminary investigation indicates that the motive may be to avenge the killing of the suspect's relative 25 years ago, which was allegedly carried out by the victim.

DEAD BODY FOUND

Gorozup Village, Prizren - 05/02 - 1200 hrs. A complete skeleton (gender not known) was located along the banks of the river Vrbnicko Jaz that appeared to have been lying there for more than one year.

PEC Region

MURDER

Istinic Village, Decani - 06/02 - 0930 hrs. A 25-year-old K-Albanian male was found shot to death in his vehicle. The victim was transported to Pec Morgue. Motives and suspect(s) are unknown at the time of report.
ROCKET ATTACK
Novo Selo Village, Pec - 06/02 - 0115 hrs. Unknown person(s) fired a rocket-propelled grenade at the building containing the local ambulance center causing some structural damage. No physical injuries were reported.
MITROVICA Region
EXPLOSION
Mitrovica South - 06/02 - 2345 hrs. Unknown person(s) threw an unknown type explosive device on to the roof of a K-Bosnian female's house. The explosion caused extensive damage. No physical injuries were reported.

Wednesday, 7 February, 2001

Same morning routine. I gave weapons instruction today. I went over safe handling, assembly and disassembly, cleaning, immediate actions for a malfunction, etc. I also showed the Wolf Creek shootout video. I left work early and took Andy Marjiota to Prishtina airport at 1430. I got to the house and watched the BBC. There was a breaking news story about shots being fired near the White House and a gunman being shot.

P.S. The weather today was very mild and warm with sunny skies. Sundown tonight was beautiful. The sky was red with a full moon rising.

UNMIK POLICE PRESS UPDATE
08 FEBRUARY, 2001
GNJILANE Region
EXPLOSION
Gornji Livoc Village, Gnjilane - 07/02 - 2145 hrs. An unknown type of explosion destroyed a K-Serb church. No injuries were reported.
PRIZREN Region
BOMB EXPLOSION
Orahovac Town - 07/02 - 1945 hrs. A K-Serb house was partly destroyed in an explosion that took place in the K-Serb quarters of

the town. One K-Serb was present in the house at the time of the incident but was not injured.

VEHICULAR ASSAULT

Prizren - 07/02 - 2230 hrs. A K-Albanian male was arrested after he deliberately chased and tried to run over a KPS Officer with a motor vehicle. No physical injuries were reported.

PEC Region

SHOOTING

Rznic Village, Decani - 06/02 - 2230 hrs. Unknown suspect(s) shot with an unknown type of firearm several rounds at a local K-Albanian owned shop. Due to the business being closed no injuries were reported. Investigating UNMIK Police officers also located a live anti-tank explosive inside the shop. The device was removed by KFOR EOD.

MITROVICA Region

ARMED ASSAULT

Mitrovica North - 07/02 - 1300 hrs. When a K-Serb male was tending to his cows in a field unknown person(s) began to shoot at him from a wooded area. The victim was struck once in the leg where he sustained a minor injury. The victim then fled to a safe area where he informed KFOR and UNMIK Police of the incident.

DEMONSTRATION

Leposavic Town - 07/02 - 2355 hrs. A group of approximately 10 K-Serbian males demonstrated in front of the police station after UNMIK Police attempted to tow an illegally parked vehicle. Verbal negotiations ensued and the situation ended peacefully without any incident.

Thursday, 8 February, 2001

Got up early at about 0530. Same morning routine as the last few days. I got to work at 0730 and started preparations for today's class. The traffic unit has four KPS officers in training and they want to combine our classes this morning to watch videos of pursuits and shootings. We watched videos for about two hours and then I taught map reading and radio communications. I went to the internet café during my lunch break. About 1400 Randy and I went downtown to see if we can use the ITC facilities and tried to located some overhead projector transparency film. There is none in Prishtina so Randy and I may go to Skopje tomorrow to look for some. I got to the house about 1600, had my tuna and noodles and went to bed.

P.S. I saw a fighter jet over the city today. I am pretty sure it was a MIG. If I had seen a Soviet MIG so close twenty years ago I would probably have been seeking cover.

UNMIK POLICE PRESS UPDATE
09 FEBRUARY, 2001
PRISTINA Region
PROSTITUTION
Pristina - 08/02 - 2326 hrs. One K-Albanian male was arrested after investigators conducted an operation in relation to the possible trafficking of women in prostitution. Eight women (6 Moldovan, 1 Hungarian, and 1 Romanian) were removed from a club in the Sunny Hill area and provided assistance. It should be noted that the status of the women involved has not been confirmed. They will be treated as victims unless the investigation determines they were willingly engaged in prostitution.
DEMONSTRATION
Kujmin Village, Pristina - 08/02 - 1800 hrs. Approximately 60 people gathered, protesting the power being out for seven days. The matter was turned over to municipal authorities and the incident ended peacefully.
GNJILANE Region
EXPLOSION
Budriga Village, Gnjilane - 08/02 - 0045 hrs. A K-Serbian owned home was completely destroyed by an explosion. No injuries were reported.
ARSON
Vitina Town - 08/02 - 1143 hrs. Unknown suspect(s) set three K-Serbian owned houses on fire.
GUNFIRE
Odonovce Village, Kamenica - 08/02 - 0900 hrs. A KFOR patrol reported hearing automatic gunfire near the Serbian border.
UXO FOUND
Kacanik Town - 08/02 - 1310 hrs. A K-Albanian male located an unexploded rocket. EOD disposed of the device.
PRIZREN Region
GRENADE ATTACK

Mushnikovo Village, Prizren - 07/02 - 2245 hrs. The roof of a K-Serbian home was damaged in a grenade attack. No injuries were reported.
EXPLOSION/GUNFIRE
Velika Hoca, Orahovac - 08/02 - 0004 hrs. KFOR patrols heard grenade explosions and gunfire.
GRIEVOUS ASSAULT
Radesa Village, Dragash - 07/02 - 2100 hrs. A K-Goran male was arrested after entering a coffee bar and stabbing two K-Albanian males. The extent of injuries is unknown at this time.
PEC Region
UXO FOUND
Klina Town - 07/02 - 1330 hrs. A hand grenade was found beside the road leading to Pec. EOD disposed of the grenade without incident.

Friday, 9 February, 2001

I got up at 0500, performed my morning routine and made the coffee. Craig got up at 0530 and we were watching the BBC news by 0600. We went to chow and had another good British military breakfast. Same menu as always. I got to work at 0730 and prepared a training report for the KPS Regional Coordinator. I taught Officer Safety today and the KPS are enjoying the instruction. I arranged for a white U.N. vehicle to go to Skopje tomorrow. We are going to look for overhead projector film and other training supplies. I am also going to try and get a ring for Carnita. I got to the house at 1600 and made my "special" tuna and noodles meal with onions and fresh garlic.

P.S. John Hatchell came over for a visit and stayed about an hour. He needed to see where we live now so he can pick us up and give us a ride to the airport for our next CTO.

UNMIK POLICE PRESS UPDATE
10 FEBRUARY, 2001
PRISTINA Region
ILLEGAL POSSESSION OF WEAPONS
Pristina - 09/02 - 2336 hrs. UNMIK Police conducted a search operation and seized five bricks of TNT explosive, two detonators,

one kilo of gunpowder, and 100 meters of detonator cable. No arrest was reported at this time.

UNATTENDED DEATH

Pristina - 09/02 - 2045 hrs. An Italian male was found deceased in his accommodation. Illegal narcotics were located at the scene where preliminary investigation revealed a self-induced drug overdose.

PRIZREN Region

EXPLOSION

Dragash - 09/02 - 2050 hrs. An explosion occurred in an apartment building occupied by K-Albanians and K-Gorans. The area was sealed off by UNMIK Police and searched by Turkish EOD. No physical injuries were reported.

PEC Region

EXPLOSION

Banja Village, Istok - 09/02 - 0030 hrs. Unknown suspect(s) threw an explosive device into the yard of a residence owned by a K-Bosnian male. No injuries were reported although a bus parked nearby received some minor damage.

Saturday, 10 February, 2001

I got up at 0430 and made the coffee. Same morning routine and off to chow with the Brits. Craig dropped me back off at the house and I changed into civilian clothes for the trip to Skopje. I met Randy at the office and then we went and picked up a friend of his from station #3. He was also from Texas and had been a Navy Corpsman. It turns out that he was working at the Naval Hospital at Camp Pendleton when Courtni was born. After exchanging details it appears that he may have been the very Corpsman that helped deliver her. It truly is a small world. It took us about two hours to get to Skopje. There was about an hour delay at the border crossing. When we got to Skopje we found our overhead film and a few supplies. We walked over to the old part of the city where the gold shops were. I tripped on some old stone steps and skinned my knee. I bought Carnita a ring from the same shop where I got mine. We checked out some of the other shops and Randy bought some gold coins. He has been collecting them. There were a lot of shops with old coins; some were very old. I think some were bronze and may have been from the Roman Empire. I should have bought some. We went to McDonald's for lunch and picked up some burgers for the guys back at the office. We also went to a store next to McDonald's and I bought 12 cans of Tuna for the equivalent of 15 cents per can. The tuna was canned in Vietnam. The trip back took about an hour and a half. The traffic was bad but we got across the border pretty quick. We dropped the burgers at the office and then I dropped the guys off. I got back to the house after refueling and turning in the U.N. vehicle at 1600. I watched the BBC until the power went out at 1730. I had to make this entry by candlelight.

P.S. Today is Asa's third birthday. I wish I could have been there. I also saw a dead wolf on the road to Skopje. It was very large and dark colored, almost black.

UNMIK POLICE PRESS UPDATE
11 FEBRUARY, 2001
PRISTINA Region
SHOOTING/GUNFIRE
Lipljan Town - 10/02 - 2400 hrs. An unknown person fired five shots through the front door of a home owned by a K-Serbian female causing only minor property damages.
GNJILANE Region
CRIMINAL DAMAGE
Budriga Village, Gnjilane - 08/02 - 1030 hrs. A vehicle driven by a K-Albanian male was stoned by unknown K-Serb suspects while he drove through the village. A window was broken but no physical injuries were reported.
PRIZREN Region
MURDER
Rogova Village, Orahovac - 10/02 - 1000 hrs. An unidentified male dead body was found approximately 200 meters off the main road by a farmer who was working with his tractor in the field. The body was covered with soil and both hands and feet were tied together. An autopsy will be conducted on Monday.
PROSTITUTION
Prizren - 10/02 - 0345 hrs. A Moldavian female, who was found living in a K-Albanian male's house, was arrested for prostitution. She was also charged for being in the country illegally as she had no passport. The male was arrested and charged with illegal confinement.
PEC Region

EXPLOSIVE ATTACK
Pec - 10/02 - 2340 hrs. Unknown suspect(s) threw an explosive device on the roof of a home causing minor damage to the roof. The ethnicity of the homeowner is unknown at this time. No physical injuries were reported.
UXO FOUND
Berisha Village, Decani - 09/02 - 1120 hrs. A K-Albanian reported finding two cluster bombs in a ditch. KFOR EOD responded to the area where the devices were disposed of.
MITROVICA Region
DEMONSTRATION
Mitrovica North - 09/02 - 1200 hrs. A group of approximately 3,000 K-Serbians attended a peaceful demonstration regarding the "Confidence Zone" extension. The group then walked to the Main Bridge. The group did not display any hostility towards UNMIK Police or KFOR. No incidents were reported and the demonstration ended peacefully.

Sunday, 11 February, 2001

I slept in until 0700. The chow hall doesn't open today until 0830. We had coffee and watched the BBC until chow. We had the same British breakfast as usual except there were no potatoes today. After breakfast we went back to the house. I do not have to be in until 1000 today and Craig does not report until noon. Not much going on at the office since the KPS are off. I went to lunch at a new German restaurant downtown with Joe and Randy. I had Chicken Schnitzel, potatoes, and traditional German noodles called spaetzle. I got back to the house at 1600 and the power was out until 1730. When the power came back on I watched the BBC and then got to bed about 2000.

P.S. The weather cooled back off today. It was cloudy with a stiff north wind. We have one more day to work until CTO.

UNMIK POLICE PRESS UPDATE
12 FEBRUARY, 2001
PRISTINA Region
GRENADE ATTACK / EXPLOSION

Pristina - 11/02 - 0110 hrs. An unknown suspect threw a hand grenade in the yard of a K-Albanian residence. No damage or injuries were reported.

Pristina - 11/02 - 1910 hrs. A grenade explosion occurred on a public street near UNMIK Police Station #4. No damage or injuries were reported.

GNJILANE Region

EXPLOSION

Vitina Town - 11/02 - 2020 hrs. An unknown type explosion occurred at the home of a K-Albanian male resulting in slight injuries to his son who was taken to hospital for treatment. KFOR EOD responded to the scene.

Parallovo Village, Gnjilane - 11/02 - 1830 hrs. A bomb explosion extensively damaged an unoccupied K-Serbian house. No physical injuries were reported.

ARSON

Cernica Village, Gnjilane - 11/02 - 1430 hrs. Unknown suspect(s) set a K-Serbian house on fire. The owner of the house managed to put out the fire before it could cause major damage. No physical injuries were reported.

PRIZREN Region

GRENADE ATTACK

Suva Reka Town - 11/02 - 2215 hrs. Two unknown suspects driving in a passenger car threw two hand grenades at a K-Albanian male's residence. Just one of the grenades exploded causing only minor property damage. KFOR EOD was notified and attended the scene. No physical injuries were reported.

CHILD ABUSE

Prizren - 10/02 - 1750 hrs. A K-Albanian male left his three children at a motel, after saying that he was going to Bosnia to look for his wife. The children were reportedly found in poor condition and were taken to hospital.

PEC Region

GRENADE ATTACK

Dakovica Town - 10/02 - 2300 hrs. An unknown suspect threw a hand grenade on the roof of a K-Albanian male's house. The explosion caused only minor property damage.

Brekovac Village, Dakovica - 11/02 - 0505 hrs. Unknown suspect(s) threw two hand grenades in front of a K-Albanian business. Just one exploded causing damage to the windows of the establishment. No physical injuries were reported.

MITROVICA Region
THEFT
Vucitrn Town - 11/02. UNMIK Police arrested a K-Albanian male after he stole a tractor.
DEAD BODY FOUND
Mitrovica North - 10/02 - 1655 hrs. A K-Serbian male reported that he had found the dead body of another K-Serbian male in an apartment. Preliminary investigation revealed the death to be of natural causes.

Monday, 12 February, 2001

Same morning routine this morning. We left the house at 0600 to visit with Ken McCarty at Main HQ. Ken is going to drive Craig, John and I to the Skopje airport in the morning. Ken filled us in on some of the details of the recent riots in Mitrovica. Some U.S. CivPol had been slightly injured by rocks and bottles. Apparently the U.S. CivPol held the line and really kicked some Serbian butt. A Serbian church in the Gnjilane region was bombed a few days ago and early this morning there were some rocket attacks in the Station #4 area. I got to the office at 0730 and taught traffic law and citation writing. During lunch I went to the barber shop and got a haircut. I took off early from work at 1500 and went to the house to pack.

P.S. I opened a can of my Vietnamese tuna and it was awful. It looked like the scrapings off the canning room floor. I went next door and traded the tuna to our KPS neighbor for some Croatian canned tuna. I kept one can to take home and show Carnita.

UNMIK POLICE PRESS UPDATE
13 FEBRUARY, 2001
PRISTINA Region
GRIEVOUS ASSAULT
Pristina - 12/02 - 1620 hrs. A K-Albanian male attempted to assault a KPS officer with a knife. The suspect was disarmed and arrested.
GNJILANE Region
ILLEGAL POSSESSION OF WEAPONS
Zllatar Village, Urosevac - 12/02 - 0600 hrs. Three K-Albanian males were arrested after a combined KFOR/UNMIK Police

search of several houses in the village revealed two rifles, two pistols, four rifle magazines, three grenades, two rockets, ten U.S. chemical camouflage suites, one U.S. vehicle antenna, one stick with trip wire, and several rounds of ammunition.

CRIMINAL DAMAGE

Koretin Village, Kamenica - 12/02 - 0700 hrs. Two unknown K-Albanian males threw stones at a vehicle driven by a K-Serbian male, which broke the windshield and two side windows. No physical injuries were reported.

Monday, 13 February, 2001

We were up at 0230 to get ready for our trip home. I had a banana and a can of tuna for breakfast. Ken and John picked us up at 0400. The trip to Skopje took about an hour and a half. We had some thick fog on the Kosovo side of the border. We had a 0740 Avioimpex flight from Skopje to Zurich, then Swiss Air to JFK. The flights went OK. We took a Northwest flight from New York to Missoula with an hour layover in Minneapolis. We took a twenty minute Horizon flight from Missoula to Kalispell. The wives met us there at midnight. Carnita and I went to breakfast at Finnegan's and then to her grandmother Isabell's house instead of a motel. It is great to be back home.

UNMIK POLICE PRESS UPDATE

14 FEBRUARY, 2001

PRISTINA Region

BOMB ATTACK

Lipljan Town - 13/02 - 1950 hrs. Unknown suspect(s) bombed the residence of a K-Roma family. The explosion destroyed the contents of a room and the front door. The roof of a neighboring house (ethnicity of owner not reported) was also damaged. No physical injuries were reported.

DEAD BODY FOUND

Glogovac Town - 13/02 - 1315 hrs. Human remains buried in a ravine were found by a K-Albanian male. Preliminary investigation indicated that the victim appeared to had been deceased for a length of time. The cause of death is unknown at this time.

GNJILANE Region

MURDER / PUBLIC UNREST

Brod Village, Strpce Town - 13/02 - 1600 hrs. A KFOR escorted convoy was fired on by an unknown sniper. A K-Serbian male bus driver was shot and killed, one other person was seriously injured and another received minor injuries. Shortly after the incident about 1,500-2,000 K-Serbs gathered in Strpce Town in front of the police station and began to riot. The crowd gained entry to the station house and caused heavy damage both inside and out, destroying the power system. Two UNMIK Police and two KPS vehicles were destroyed by fired, four other UNMIK Police vehicles were heavily damaged and are not operational with one other damaged but drivable. Additionally, one civilian employee's vehicle was heavily damaged and equipment is missing from the station. Several UNMIK Police officers sustained minor injuries.

GRIEVOUS ASSAULT

Klokot Village, Vitina - 13/02 - 1425 hrs. While tending his cattle a K-Serbian male was shot in the leg by a K-Albanian male.

EXPLOSION

Cernica Village, Gnjilane - 13/02 - 1025 hrs. Unknown person(s) detonated an explosive device in an unoccupied building at a K-Serbian property causing only minor property damage.

Cernica Village, Gnjilane - 13/02 - 1740 hrs. An unknown person threw a hand grenade at the home of a K-Serbian male causing only minor property damage. At the time of the attack the house owner was not at home.

CRIMINAL DAMAGE

Budriga Village, Gnjilane - 13/02 - 1445 hrs. A group of K-Serbian males attacked the vehicle of a K-Albanian male as he drove through the village. The front window of the vehicle was damaged. No physical injuries were reported.

PEC Region

GRENADE ATTACK/SHOOTING

Strelleji Village, Decani - 13/02 - 2100 hrs. Unknown persons shot a machine gun at a K-Albanian house and threw hand grenades at it. One of them exploded outside and one inside the house. No physical injuries were reported.

MITROVICA Region

EXPLOSION

Krasta Village, Srbica - 13/02 - 1030 hrs. Three K-Serbian males were injured, two of them seriously, when their tractor drove over a land mine. The injured were transported to Mitrovica North hospital for treatment. Subsequent to the incident, a crowd of about 75 to 100 K-Serbians gathered in front of the Zubin Potok Station where the crowd attacked one UNMIK Police officer and an UNMIK vehicle. After negotiations between the station commander and a local community leader the situation was calmed. No injuries were reported to the UNMIK Officer. The condition of one victim is listed as critical, the other's as serious.

UNMIK POLICE PRESS UPDATE
15 FEBRUARY, 2001
PRISTINA Region
MURDER
Lipljan Town - 14/02 - 0540 hrs. The body of a Bosnian Roma male was found along a roadside with a single bullet wound to the head.
EXPLOSION
Lipljan Town - 14/02 - 2055 hrs. A K-Serbian residence was damaged by a bomb placed near the home. The windows and doors of a neighboring house were also damaged. No physical injuries were reported.
CRIMINAL DAMAGE
Preludze Village, Pristina - 14/02 - 0710 hrs. Unknown suspect(s) damaged the railway track by unscrewing it from its coupling, causing the U.N. train to be delayed. No additional incidents or injuries were reported.

UNMIK POLICE PRESS UPDATE
16 FEBRUARY, 2001
PRIZREN Region
ABANDONED INFANT
Prizren - 14/02 - 1535 hrs. A three-day-old infant (gender not reported) was found by local residents and turned over to UNMIK Police. The infant is reported to be in good condition.

UNMIK POLICE PRESS UPDATE
17 FEBRUARY, 2001
PRISTINA Region
EXPLOSION / MURDER
Podujevo Town - 16/02 - 1130 hrs. Two K-Albanian male suspects are in custody for the bombing of a bus carrying 59 Serbians from the Serbian border. Seven are reported dead and

forty injured. The bus was in a KFOR escorted convoy. The circumstances of the incident are under investigation.

RIOT

Caglavica Village - 16/02 - 1434 hrs. Approximately 1,000 K-Serbians gathered on a roadway after learning of the bus attack. The group then began to throw rocks and burned two vehicles in protest of the incident. A K-Albanian restaurant was also burned and eight K-Albanians were reported with minor injuries.

CRIMINAL DAMAGE

Laplasela Village, Pristina -16/02 - 1345 hrs. A K-Albanian bus carrying 17 passengers was stopped on a road by a group of K-Serbians who were protesting a bombing incident. The passengers were allowed to exit the bus, which was then burned by the group. No physical injuries were reported.

Laplasela Village, Pristina - 16/02 - 1345 hrs. A K-Albanian driving on a road was stopped by a group of K-Serbians, protesting the bombing incident, which threw rocks at his vehicle causing damage to it. The victim managed to avoid injury and fled the area in his vehicle.

GNJILANE Region

MURDER

Kamenica Town - 16/02 - 0830 hrs. The body of a K-Albanian male was discovered in the hills west of town. The incident was determined to be a murder. A K-Serbian male suspect was arrested.

CRIMINAL DAMAGE

Vitina Town - 16/02 - 1415 hrs. A K-Albanian male reported that while he was driving through Gushteric Village, unidentified Serbians stoned his vehicle, damaging the rear window. No physical injuries were reported.

PRIZREN Region

ARSON

Orahovac Town - 16/02 - 1830 hrs. Unknown person(s) set a K-Serbian home ablaze. The home was totally destroyed. No physical injuries were reported.

MITROVICA Region

ATTEMPTED MURDER

Maxhumi Village, Mitrovica South - 16/02 - 0500 hrs. A K-Albanian male shot an UNMIK Police officer during a search of the suspect's residence. The officer received a minor injury to the hand. The suspect was taken into custody.

UNMIK POLICE PRESS UPDATE
19 FEBRUARY, 2001
PRISTINA Region
DEMONSTRATION
Kosovo Polje Town - 18/02 - 1445 hrs. Approximately 100 K-Serbians gathered for a demonstration when approximately 80 K-Albanians also gathered to protest the Serbian demonstration. UNMIK Police began negotiations and the demonstration ended peacefully. No major incidents were reported.
GNJILANE Region
UXO FOUND
Gnjilane - 18/02 - 1730 hrs. Children playing in a shed behind an abandoned K-Serbian residence found a hand grenade. KFOR EOD disposed of the device.
PRIZREN Region
ARMED ASSAULT
Prizren - 18/02 - 1330 hrs. Unidentified person(s) opened fire on German KFOR troops who were conducting foot patrols. Nine shots were directed at the soldiers who were not hit or injured.
ARSON
Orahovac Town - 18/02 - 1850 hrs. Unknown person(s) set a K-Serbian residence ablaze using a petrol bomb. The fire caused extensive damage. No physical injuries were reported.
DEAD BODY FOUND
Orahovac Town - 18/02 - 1210 hrs. The dead body of a Moldavian female was found. No further information given.
UXO FOUND
Orahovac Town - 18/02 - 1045 hrs. A K-Albanian male found six hand grenades in his farm field. KFOR EOD disposed of the devices.
MITROVICA Region
CIVIL UNREST
Zubin Potok Town - 18/02 - 1720 hrs. A group of approximately 30-40 K-Serbians gathered on a roadway, starting fires and throwing rocks at passing vehicles. KFOR responded to the area and the group was dispersed without incident.
DEAD BODY FOUND
Zhabar Village, Mitrovica South - 18/02 - 0930 hrs. The dead body of a newborn female infant was found in front of a garage.

UNMIK POLICE PRESS UPDATE

20 FEBRUARY, 2001
GNJILANE Region
DEMONSTRATION
Partes Village, Gnjilane - 19/02 - 1313 hrs. Approximately 300 K-Serbians blocked the road in protest over the recent attacks on K-Serbians. Members of the crowd caused damage to at least two UNMIK vehicles by throwing rocks. No physical injuries were reported.
Pasjane Village, Gnjilane - 19/02 - 1530 hrs. K-Serbian protesters gathered and threw stones at passing vehicles, damaging a K-Albanian owned vehicle. A grenade explosion was heard and a K-Albanian male was arrested in connection with it.
ARSON
Gnjilane - 19/02 - 1640 hrs. Unknown suspect(s) broke into a K-Serbian female's residence and set it on fire. The fire was extinguished before it caused any damage. No physical injuries were reported.
MITROVICA Region
ATTEMPTED MURDER
Vucitrn Town - 19/02 - 1010 hrs. A hand grenade placed in a vehicle owned by a local TMK Commander exploded when the owner open the door causing extensive damage to the vehicle. No physical injuries were reported.
EXPLOSION
Mitrovica North - 18/02 - 2330 hrs. An unknown suspect detonated an explosive device in a garden of a K-Albanian residence causing minor damage to the home and an adjacent dwelling. No physical injuries were reported.
ASSAULT
Leposavic Town - 19/02 - 1100 hrs. Two Gypsy males were arrested for beating another Gypsy male at the refugee camp.
CIVIL UNREST
Zubin Potok Town - 19/02 - 1150 hrs. A group of approximately 40 K-Serbians gathered on a roadway, blocking the roadway and burning tires.
DEMONSTRATION
Mitrovica North - 19/02 - 1200 hrs. A crowd of approximately 1,500 K-Serbians gathered at the center of Mitrovica North where radical speeches were held.
Leposavic Town -19/02 - 1200 hrs. Approximately 300 K-Serbians gathered for a peaceful demonstration.

UNMIK POLICE PRESS UPDATE
21 FEBRUARY, 2001
GNJILANE Region
ASSAULT/DEMONSTRATION

Pasjane Village, Gnjilane - 20/02 - 1400 hrs. A crowd of approximately 300 K-Serbians gathered to protest, became unruly, and began throwing stones at both UNMIK and KFOR personnel. One UNMIK Police officer was injured. The crowd was eventually brought under control at approximately 1600 hrs. Another protest is scheduled for 21/02.

CRIMINAL DAMAGE

Koretin Village, Kamenica - 20/02 - 1700 hrs. Unknown persons threw rocks at the car of a K-Serbian male while he was driving through the village, causing some damage. No physical injuries were reported.

PRIZREN Region
DEMONSTRATION

Velika Hoca Village, Orahovac - 20/02 - 1345 hrs. Approximately 50 K-Serbians gathered in front of the police station to protest KFOR cancelling the bus convoy to Mitrovica. The crowd was spoken to by UNMIK Police and dispersed peacefully.

MITROVICA Region
DEMONSTRATION

Mitrovica South - 20/02 - 1150 hrs. Approximately 30 K-Albanian staged a peaceful demonstration outside of the offices of NGO "World Vision". The demonstration ended peacefully.

Zubin Potok - 20/02 - 1150 hrs. Approximately 40 K-Serbians blocked a road and staged a demonstration. The demonstration ended peacefully.

Mitrovica North - 20/02 - 1200 hrs. An unknown number of K-Serbians gathered for a demonstration where the streets were blocked. The demonstration ended peacefully.

UNMIK POLICE PRESS UPDATE
22 FEBRUARY, 2001
PRISTINA Region
ASSAULT

Kosovo Polje Town - 21/02 - 1555 hrs. A K-Albanian male was arrested after he assaulted an Albanian male and a pregnant Albanian female. Preliminary investigations indicate that the suspect believed the victims were of Serbian descent. Both victims were transported to a local hospital for treatment of their injuries.

GNJILANE Region

DEMONSTRATION

Pasjane Village, Gnjilane - 21/02 - 1200 hrs. For approximately one hour 500 K-Serbians peacefully blocked the road between Pasjane and Gnjilane. The purpose of the demonstration was to protest the recent bombing deaths of Serbians. The demonstration was conducted without incident. This is the third straight day of such protests.

MITROVICA Region

DEMONSTRATION

Mitrovica North - 21/02 - 1200 hrs. Approximately 600-700 K-Serbians gathered in the town center blocking traffic during a peaceful demonstration, which lasted approximately twenty-five minutes.

Zubin Potok - 20/02 - 1245 hrs. Approximately 80 K-Serbians gathered in a roadway burning tires during a peaceful demonstration. The demonstration dispersed without incident.

UNMIK POLICE PRESS UPDATE

25 FEBRUARY, 2001

PRISTINA Region

ILLEGAL POSSESSION OF WEAPON

Lebane Village, Pristina - 24/02 - 2130 hrs. A K-Albanian male was arrested after he was found with an unknown type of explosive device by KFOR. The device was seized and his residence searched but nothing else was found.

EXPLOSION

Pristina - 24/02 - 1715 hrs. A natural methane explosion in the sewer line, which blew off three sewer caps at different locations, occurred. No injury or damage to property was reported.

GNJILANE Region

EXPLOSION

Vitina Town - 24/02 - 2025 hrs. An explosion of unknown origin occurred at a K-Serbian owned home. No injuries were reported.

DEMONSTRATION

Pasjane Village, Gnjilane - 24/02 - 1700 hrs. A crowd of approximately 40 K-Serbians blocked the road in protest of recent incidents in the village. The crowd began to throw rocks at passing K-Albanian vehicles and was dispersed without further incident.

UXO FOUND
Urosevac Town - 24/02 - 1450 hrs. A K-Albanian male who found a grenade notified UNMIK Police. EOD safely disposed of the device.
PRIZREN Region
ARSON
Orahovac Town - 24/02 - 1930 hrs. Unknown persons set an unoccupied K-Serbian house on fire in the Serbian quarter of the town.
PEC Region
ATTEMPTED ABDUCTION
Pec - 22/02 - 2100 hrs. A Serbian female reported that she had been threatened by two unknown males who attempted to abduct her. The victim was able to flee and spent the night in a church. The victim had no relative in Kosovo and was returned to the Montenegro border.
UXO FOUND
Lumbarda Village, Decani - 24/02 - 1100 hrs. A K-Albanian male reported having found an unexploded rocket in the forest. EOD responded and safely disposed of the device.

Sunday, 25 February, 2001

I got up at 0430 in the Blue and White motel in Kalispell. I had my last U.S.A. shower for a while. We came to Kalispell last night. We got on the road to the airport at 0515 and checked in at 0530. I met Craig at the airport. Our flight to Salt Lake City left on time at 0630. We had a two hour layover in Salt Lake and then on to Dulles in DC. We left the states an hour late but the flight across the Atlantic was uneventful. I had a hard time sleeping this time. We had another two hour layover in Zurich and then on into Skopje.

P.S. I opened the can of Vietnamese tuna I got in Macedonia. Carnita could not believe how awful it was. I tried to feed it to our dog and it refused to eat it. That is really bad!

UNMIK POLICE PRESS UPDATE
26 FEBRUARY, 2001
PRISTINA Region
ASSAULT

Kosovo Polje - 25/02 - 1450 hrs. Two K-Albanian males knocked a K-Serb female to the ground and repeatedly attacked her until she became unconscious. She was taken to the hospital in serious condition and required surgery.
GNJILANE Region
ASSAULT
Vrbovac Village, Vitina - 24/02 – 2200 hrs. A K-Serbian male reported that a K-Albanian male assaulted him. The victim was taken to the hospital for treatment.
MITROVICA Region
SHOOTING/CRIMINAL DAMAGE
Srbica Town - 25/02 - 0230 hrs. Unknown suspects shot two K-Albanian males shortly after they left a teashop. The victims were taken to hospital. One pistol with four rounds of ammunition was recovered from the scene.

Monday, 26 February, 2001

We arrived into Skopje airport about noon but it was about 1230 before we got through the passport check and customs. This was the first and only time anyone looked at our passports during the entire trip. Andy Marjiota and a female KPS officer were waiting for us. This was the first time she has ever been out of Kosovo. She had a new Yugoslavian passport (obviously fake) and this trip got her first stamp in it. We went to McDonald's for a lunch. This was the KPS officers first time ever at a McDonald's so we got her a "happy meal" for a joke. Andy paid for lunch and then we started back for Kosovo. The weather was nice in Macedonia but we hit snow again after we crossed the border. The roads were slushy. Craig and I slept most of the drive back to the house. We got back into Prishtina about 1500 and Andy dropped us off. We walked over to my office and I got my pistol from Randy Stenssas and then we walked down to Craig's unit to get his pistol from Reggie Godwin. Reggie wasn't there so we walked over to the company building. We met Reggie there, got our water supply and then drove to pick up some beer at a local distributor. We went to Reggie's place to get Craig's pistol and dropped Reggie off so we could have the vehicle to go to breakfast in the morning. We got to the house and unpacked. The power went off at 1900 and the house is very cold. I wrote this entry by flashlight.

UNMIK POLICE PRESS UPDATE
27 FEBRUARY, 2001
PRISTINA Region
ATTEMPTED MURDER
Pristina - 25/02 - 1530 hrs. A K-Albanian female, admitted to the hospital after giving birth to a baby, attempted to strangle the infant. Doctors found strangulation marks on the baby's throat.
ARREST OF ESCAPEE
Podujevo Town - 26/02 - 2000 hrs. A K-Albanian male wanted for armed robbery and escape from lawful custody was located and arrested.
GNJILANE Region
DEAD BODY FOUND
Nerodime Village, Urosevac - 26/02 - 1530 hrs. A K-Albanian male reported finding the body of a newborn floating in the river. The body was recovered and the investigation is continuing.
PEC Region
POLICE DISCHARGE OF A FIREARM
DAKOVICA - 24/02 - 1355 hrs. An UNMIK Police officer fired a warning shot when aggressive/threatening behavior occurred among a group of people being searched for weapons. No injuries occurred and the situation was stabilized.
ILLEGAL POSSESSION OF WEAPONS
PEC - 24/02 - 1600 hrs. A K-Albanian male was arrested after a search discovered an AK-47 rifle and 135 rounds of ammunition.
FOUND WEAPONS
Krusheva Village, Klina - 26/02 - 0730 hrs. A K-Albanian female reported finding an AK-47 and a pistol in the ceiling of her residence. The weapons were seized.
DEAD BODY
ZATRA - 25/02 - 1700 hrs. The dead body of an infant was discovered in a well.
MITROVICA Region
ASSAULT
Srbica Town - 26/02 - 1625 hrs. A K-Albanian male reported that another male he believes to have been K-Serbian assaulted him.
DEMONSTRATION
Mitrovica South - 26/02 - 0910 hrs. A group of 50 K-Serbians gathered in a peaceful protest at the engineer's compound. The event lasted about 30 minutes and no incidents were reported.

Mitrovica - 26/02 - 1300 hrs. A group of approximately six hundred K-Albanians gathered in a demonstration near the Regional HQ. The event lasted approximately one and one half hours and no incidents were reported.

Tuesday, 27 February, 2001

I got up at 0600. I had to shave off my CTO beard. It took three razor blades. We had some coffee and then off to the British chow hall for breakfast. Everything there is still the same. I got to work at 0730 and e-mailed Carnita. I'm starting to feel the jet lag again. I showed the video *Surviving Edged Weapons* for class this morning. Randy and I went to Regional HQ to pick up some things for the office. We met Craig there and he went with us to have pizza for lunch. At about 1400 I drove Randy to Prishtina airport. He is going to meet his wife in London for CTO. I also picked up Joe Massing coming back from Germany. I went back to the house about 1600 and watched a movie on our new VCR that Craig picked up today. We tried to stay awake until at least 2100 to help with the jet lag but couldn't. I crashed before 2000 and Craig fell asleep in a chair in the living room.

P.S. We got MSA today. We only get paid for a 28 day month which made it a little short. Only 4,469DM.

E-mail home

Hi Hun,
Just a note to let you know we made it back OK. I have e-mail at the office now. I just got in to work. Jet lag is already kicking my butt. I will write more latter and set up a chat time. I don't know if I can chat tonight because of the jet lag. Contact you soon. Love you lots, Clay

E-mail from Carnita

Don't worry about chatting. Just take a few days to get back on track. I had to call the London office today and have them send me your most recent pay stub. Our loan officer called and said we needed two pay stubs. I got that taken care of. I already miss you allot! I'm going to go for now, and remember to just relax and get back into a routine and over jet lag before trying to chat. Love you, Carn

UNMIK POLICE PRESS UPDATE
28 FEBRUARY, 2001
PRISTINA Region
UXO FOUND
Vranidol Village, Pristina - 26/02 - 0900 hrs. UNMIK Police recovered one hand grenade from a K-Albanian male. EOD disposed of the device.
BORDER INCIDENT
Gate No. 4, Pristina - 26/02 - 2130 hrs. A K-Albanian male reported that, after straying across the Serbian border in the company of his nephew, they were detained by Serbian Police. The police arrested his nephew when they found a pistol on him and he was transferred to a prison in Serbia. The reporting person was released after being held for a period of 24 hours.
DEMONSTRATION
Pristina - 27/02 - 1200 hrs. Approximately 2,000 people took part in a peaceful protest march organized by the Union of Independent Trade Unions of Kosovo. Protesters assembled in front of the OSCE building, marched towards the government building, then gathered outside the National Theatre for speeches.
GNJILANE Region
MURDER
Carakovce Village, Kamenica - 27/02 - 1800 hrs. The bodies of an elderly Serbian couple, ages 70 and 65, were found inside their residence. Both victims appeared to have been beaten to death.
ASSAULT
Gnjilane - 26/02 - 2355 hrs. A K-Albanian male assaulted a Bulgarian female after an argument.
PEC Region
ARMED ROBBERY
Istok Town - 27/02 - 0100 hrs. Nine to twelve masked gunmen entered the local hospital and stole the safe.
MITROVICA Region
ARMED ROBBERY
Leposavic Town - 24/02 - 1830 hrs. A K-Serbian male truck driver reported that, on the road between Pristina and Leposavic, he was attacked by four unknown males who robbed him. The victim

received minor injuries. No information as to the suspects' ethnicity or weapons was reported.
DEMONSTRATION
Mitrovica South - 27/02 - 0945 - 1100 hrs. Approximately twenty-five K-Albanian employees of "SHALA" held a peaceful demonstration in protest of UNMIK's use of certain buildings.

Monday, 28 February, 2001

I was up at 0530. The power and water were on so I got my morning routine taken care of. Craig and I went to the British chow hall again. I got to the office by 0730. KPS officer Shaban taught KPS policy to class #12 the first half of the day. Today is class #12's final day of Stage II classroom training. I taught handcuffing and searching techniques in the afternoon. After work I went to the corner market and picked up a few things: Tuna, noodles and onions. I was back at the house by 1630 and had some canned chicken spread on crackers for supper. The power went off at 1700 and stayed off until after 2100. I went to bed and read by candlelight. It is very cold in the house because of the sporadic power. The temperature is in the mid thirties.

E-mail home

Hi Hun,
Got your e-mail this morning. It will take a couple of days before I figure out a chat schedule. I am still very tired and off track with sleep. Nothing new going on here. Power has been awful and it has been really cold in the house. You can see your breath most of the time. I will contact you again soon. Love forever, Clay

UNMIK POLICE PRESS UPDATE
01 MARCH, 2001
PRISTINA Region
EXPLOSION
Lipljan Town - 28/02 - 2000 hrs. Unknown persons threw a hand grenade at an unoccupied K-Serbian house. No injuries were reported. Two suspects were detained.
GNJILANE Region
ROBBERY

Meganovce Village, Kamenica - 28/02 - 0200 hrs. A K-Serbian male reported that four unknown males broke into his residence and assaulted him and his wife. The suspects then stole a hunting rifle and two cows.
PRIZREN Region
ILLEGAL POSSESSION OF WEAPONS
Prizren - 27/02 - 1400 hrs. A K-Albanian male was arrested after he was found in possession of an AK-47 rifle and 150 rounds of ammunition.
PEC Region
ASSAULT ON A POLICE OFFICER
Pec Town - 28/02 - 2255 hrs. An UNMIK Police officer was assaulted during a traffic stop involving a K-Albanian male. The officer was struck with the suspect's fists, feet and was also struck in the mouth with a flashlight. The officer was treated at the hospital for his injuries. The suspect was arrested.

Thursday, 1 March, 2001

I got up at 0450 to try and beat the power going off. It has been three hours on and three hours off since we got back. I got a pot of coffee made and then the power went off at 0500. The water is off also. It seems worse than when we first arrived in country. I got a small propane burner going to keep the coffee warm. It was thirty-eight degrees and raining this morning. Craig and I went to breakfast again at the British KFOR chow hall. The good breakfast kind of makes up for the power and water hassle. I got in to the office at 0720 and worked on paperwork most of the day. I had to go to the U.S. Contingent Commander's office to get a new U.N. beret for our medal parade on the 16th. Mine is blood stained from the November bombing. I got back to the house at 1645. Craig and I went downtown to a local gym and joined for a month. It cost 130DM. This is the best gym in the city but most of the CivPol are afraid to use it because it is rumored to be associated with the local mafia. So far only the U.S. and Canadian CivPol use it. We worked out for about two hours and then walked back to the house. I got to bed by 2200 just as the power went off again.

E-mail home

Hi Hun,
How are you doing? I haven't been able to get the chat program to work yet on this computer but I will keep trying. Nothing new to report except that I joined the gym and stated working out after work. It is really kicking my butt. I am sore today. I did about three miles on the running machine and five different weight machines plus abs. Let me know how it's
going. Love you, Clay

UNMIK POLICE PRESS UPDATE
02 MARCH, 2001
PRISTINA Region
CRIMINAL DAMAGE
Gracanica Town - 01/03 - 1320 hrs. Four K-Albanian owned vehicles, including one bus, were slightly damaged from stones thrown by K-Serbians during a demonstration. One K-Albanian male sustained slight injuries to his head and was treated at the KFOR hospital.
EXPLOSION
Kosovo Polje Town - 02/03 - 0050 hrs. An explosion resulting from the breakdown of the main power line from Pristina occurred at the power station causing extensive damage.
GNJILANE Region
FOUND DEAD BODY
Urosevac Town - 01/03 - 1354 hrs. A K-Albanian male reported finding a male body in an unoccupied residence. There were no signs of foul play.
FOUND UXO
Cernica Village, Gnjilane - 01/03 - 0830 hrs. A K-Serbian male reported that a child had found a hand grenade in an unoccupied residence. KFOR EOD disposed of the device.
Vitina - 01/03 - 0845 hrs. A K-Serbian male reported finding an unexploded grenade that had been thrown through the window of an unoccupied room. KFOR EOD disposed of the device.
MITROVICA Region
GREVIOUS ASSAULT
Mitrovica North - 01/03 - 2342 hrs. While assisting a KFOR unit with a traffic stop at the intersection of King Peter and Lola Ribera, two UNMIK Police officers and a Language Assistant received moderate injuries when attacked by a K-Serbian crowd. Additionally, two vehicles were damaged.

Friday, 2 March, 2001

I stayed in bed until 0530. There is no power so no coffee this morning. The water was on so I got a cold shower and shave. I am really sore from the gym. We went to breakfast at 0630. We were the first ones in the chow hall this morning. It was the same menu as usual but it is good, safe food. I got to work at 0710. The internet was down so I worked on the training program. I went to the house for lunch at noon and had noodles. The power was on so I put in a load of laundry. I got off work at 1700. Craig did not get back until 1800. He had a late arrest. We watched a video of *Lonesome Dove* until the power went off.

UNMIK POLICE PRESS UPDATE
03 MARCH, 2001
PRISTINA Region
DEAD BODY FOUND
Pristina - 02/03 - 1000 hrs. A K-Albanian female reported that she found the body of her father in his apartment. The body was taken to the hospital for a post mortem examination to establish the cause of death.
GNJILANE Region
CRIMINAL DAMAGE/DEMONSTRATION
Sevce Village, Strpce - 02/03 - 2220 hrs. A group of approximately thirty K-Serbians surrounded an UNMIK Police vehicle in protest of a K-Serbian male being issued a traffic citation. During the incident two tires on the UNMIK vehicle were punctured. No injuries were reported and the crowd finally dispersed.
PRIZREN Region
TRAFFICKING IN HUMANS/ILLEGAL BORDER CROSSING
Prizren - 02/03 - 2340 hrs. A K-Albanian male suspected of involvement in prostitution was arrested following investigation into his illegal purchase of a Moldavian female and her use as a prostitute at his bar. An Albanian female working at the same bar was also arrested after it was proved that she was in the country illegally and was without travel documents.
PEC Region
MURDER

Deic Village, Klina - 02/03 - 1210 hrs. The body of an individual believed to be a K-Albanian male reported missing in February was located in a forest. Due to injuries on the body, the death is believed to be a homicide. Documentation was found on the body but a positive identification has not been completed at the time of report.

Saturday, 3 March, 2001

Up to the same morning routine. Another day in the Balkans. Not much going on at work today. We have a new class coming in on Monday. I went to lunch at the Napoli Pizzeria with Joe and Thommy. It was my turn to buy. I had a pizza they call the "four seasons." It was good. I got off work at 1600 and went to the house to get Craig. We went down to the gym at 1700 and worked out until 1830. We had a good workout. Craig has a DPU party tonight. I stayed at the house and watched some more *Lonesome Dove*. Craig got back about 2200.

P.S. The weather turned warmer today. It got up to 58 degrees.

UNMIK POLICE PRESS UPDATE
04 MARCH, 2001
PRISTINA Region
ASSAULT
Milosobelic Village, Obilic - 03/03 - 1900 hrs. Unknown persons threw a tear gas canister into a Gypsy owned residence. The shell exploded and three people who were in the house at the time of the attack were affected by the gas. One male sustained a minor injury to his right hand.
GNJILANE Region
ASSAULT
Urosevac Town - 03/03 - 1600 hrs. A K-Bosnian female reported that she had briefly left her son in a restaurant and, when she returned, she found that a K-Albanian male had manhandled him and tied him with a rope.
ILLEGAL POSSESSION OF A WEAPON
Novo Selo Village, Kamenica - 03/03 - 1930 hrs. A K-Albanian male was arrested after he was found to be in possession of a submachine gun.
FOUND UXO

Urosevac Town - 03/03 - 0750 hrs. A K-Albanian male reported finding an unexploded grenade in front of his shop. KFOR EOD safely disposed of the device.
PRIZREN Region
UXO FOUND
Orahovac Town - 03//03 - 0830 hrs. An unidentified person reported to a KPS Officer that he had found a hand grenade. KFOR EOD disposed of the device without incident.
MITROVICA Region
BURGLARY
Mitrovica North - 02/03 - No time reported. An UNMIK Police officer reported that unknown suspect(s) had burglarized his residence and taken cash and property valued at 2,500DM.
FOUND UXO
Mitrovica North - 03/03 - 1910 hrs. A K-Serbian male reported locating an unexploded grenade in the street. KFOR EOD safely disposed of the device.

Sunday, 4 March, 2001

I slept in until 0645. Sunday chow schedule today. I got to work at 0900. The Germans didn't make it in until 1000. We didn't do much today but surf the net. About 1400 we heard a transmission from Pristina Control that the border between Kosovo and Macedonia was closed until further notice. There was a battle on the border between UCPMB and Macedonian forces. Three Macedonian police officers were killed and one tank was destroyed. The President of Macedonia closed the border. There are some UNMIK personnel stranded there.

UNMIK POLICE PRESS UPDATE
05 MARCH, 2001
GNJILANE Region
ATTEMPTED MURDER
Kopernica Village, Kamenica - 04/03 - 1730 hrs. A K-Albanian male reported that, while he was driving towards Kamenica, three unknown suspects in a vehicle that was parked beside the roadway began firing at his vehicle. The victim's vehicle was struck five times causing minor injury to the victim from broken glass.
ILLEGAL POSSESSION OF A WEAPON

Letnica Village, Vitina -04/03 - 0530 hrs. Two K-Albanian males were arrested after they were found to be in possession of one 60mm mortar round, two rifle grenades, one hand grenade and ammunition.

EXPLOSION

Nika Village, Kacanik - 03/03 - 1700 hrs. Three K-Albanian children, ages five, seven and twelve, were injured when an apparent mine exploded. All victims were transported to the hospital for treatment.

UXO FOUND

Gaqka Village, Urosevac - 04/03 - 1010 hrs. A K-Albanian male reported finding an unexploded missile. KFOR EOD safely disposed of the device.

PEC Region

UXO FOUND

Dakovica Town - 04/03 - 0950 hrs. An UNMIK patrol located an unexploded grenade near a roadway. KFOR EOD safely disposed of the device.

MITROVICA Region

THREATS/INTIMIDATION

Mitrovica South - 04/03 - 0955 hrs. An off-duty KPS officer was following a vehicle which then stopped and four suspects exited. Two of the suspects were armed with knives and began to approach the KPS officer. Another KPS officer who had arrived on the scene fired a warning shot to prevent the attack. Three suspects were then apprehended while one was able to flee.

UXO FOUND

Samadrexha Village, Vucitrn - 04/03 - 1155 hrs. A group of villagers reported that they had found an unexploded hand grenade. KFOR EOD safely disposed of the device.

Monday, 5 March, 2001

I got up at 0530 and had power for coffee. We left for breakfast at 0645. The free British breakfast is the best meal of the day and we are glad to have it. I got to my office at 0715 and sent an e-mail to Carnita. Class #13 reported for training today. I introduced myself and then turned the class over to KPS officer Xhevat to teach KPS policy. I let the class go at noon because today is a Muslim holiday. I went to the house for lunch. Craig came back for lunch also. We had tuna fish sandwiches. After lunch I taught two

Nigerian CivPol officers from the investigation unit how to dust and lift fingerprints. I got off at 1600 and Craig and I went to work out. The weather was in the sixties today.

P.S. The Macedonian border is still closed. The BBC building in London was bombed a couple of days ago. Not sure if it is related to what is going on here.

E-mail home

Hi Hun,
Glad things are OK at home. Can't wait until next CTO. Still working out after work every night. The border between Kosovo and Macedonia was closed yesterday because of fighting on the border. It may be awhile before it is open again. Some of the guys that had flights scheduled out of Skopje have to take a U.N. helicopter to the airport. Three Macedonian cops got killed and a Macedonian tank was blown up. Albanian guerillas are fighting on the border area. They are called the UCPMB. It's a fringe outfit of the old UCK (Kosovo Liberation Army). Hope the border opens back up before my next CTO or I'll have to fly from Prishtina and it will take and extra day travel. Well, I better go back to class now. Talk to you later. Love you, Clay

E-mail from Carnita

I hope things are okay where you are. If the fighting gets to your area and it gets bad you need to stay out of it and try and get home. Love you, Carn

UNMIK POLICE PRESS UPDATE
06 MARCH, 2001
PEC Region
SHOOTING
Glodane Village, Decani - 05/03 - 0230 hrs. A K-Albanian male reported that an unknown suspect had fired several rounds of automatic weapon fire at his residence. No injuries were reported and the motive for the attack is unknown.
THREATS/INTIMIDATION
Durakovac Village, Istok - 03/03 - 2015 hrs. A K-Albanian male reported that four masked males dressed in black and armed with

automatic weapons had tried to enter his residence by claiming they were the police. The victim refused entry and the suspects left without further incident.
MITROVICA Region
MURDER
Mitrovica South - 06/03 - 0130 hrs. A K-Albanian male security guard of a disco bar died on arrival at the KFOR hospital after he was shot by an unidentified male suspect. The shooting occurred after the suspect was ejected from the bar. He briefly left, came back in the company of two friends and then shot the victim. Five empty cartridges were found at the scene.
BORDER POLICE
The border with Macedonia remains closed.

Tuesday, 6 March, 2001

I got up this morning at 0530 and we had power. I got a shower and made the coffee. I watched the 0600 BBC World News until Craig got ready. The Macedonia border is still closed and there is more fighting today. Macedonia mobilized its reserves and is shelling some town just over the Kosovo border. It looks like this may get worse before it gets better. I wonder if the U.S. or German KFOR will get involved. We went to breakfast at 0645 and in to work at 0715. It was cool and rainy today. Randy got back from CTO today. We taught classes all day that were mostly orientation type information, paperwork requirements and station #2 details. I got off at 1600, changed for the gym, and went to work out.

P.S. We have a water leak in the bathroom that needs to be fixed. The house smells moldy and musty. There is some mold growing on the wall in the kitchen.

Wednesday, 7 March, 2001

Same morning routine. We watched the 0600 BBC World News. The fighting is still escalating on the border. The news said that NATO is considering allowing Yugoslavian (Serbia) forces to assist Macedonia in fighting the Albanian UCPMB. I think that this would be a very bad move and might spark off a more regional conflict. We went to the British chow hall and there was a sign up talking about food rationing because of the closed border and the fighting. We only had one fried egg, toast and beans. The closed border is already affecting our supply lines. Craig and I need to stock up on food and water just in case this goes on for awhile. We plan to get our next flights home out of Prishtina airport just in case. It takes an extra day because there are no morning flights but we can leave "unofficially" a day early. I taught classes all day. We are having some U.N. high official coming to Station #2 tomorrow because we are doing so well in the mission. I got off at 1600 and went to the gym for a two hour workout. After workout I went back to the office to try and chat with Carnita but the internet was down. I went to the house and watched the BBC news. U.S. KFOR troops were involved in a firefight on the Kosovo/Macedonian border today. Two UCPMB soldiers were killed. Two Serbian troops were also killed today by a land mine near Presevo. It looks like things are getting worse fast. We were told we are having an evacuation drill soon. I hope we don't lose our clean water supply or our free breakfast. I re-packed my evacuation pack today just in case.

Thursday, 8 March, 2001

Same morning routine. Off to chow at 0630. They are still rationing the chow. Got to work at 0715. The internet was still down. I taught Use of Force all morning. The U.N. official and the station commander sat in on our class for a few minutes this morning. Apparently we have the best training program in the mission. Randy and I went down to the company building. I gave the clerk 2,500DM to be include in my next pay. We then went to lunch at the new German restaurant (Ardi's) with the Germans (Joe and Thommy). I had chicken strips in a mushroom and wine sauce with spaetzle and kraut on the side. The Germans do not like more than one food item on the same plate so they have several small plates in front of them. They think I am a heathen because I put everything on one plate just to mess with them. I got home at 1600 and we went for our workout. Craig had to drop his vehicle off at his office because someone needs it tomorrow. That means no British chow hall for us tomorrow. We walked back to the house from DPU. We stopped at the corner market and Craig bought some eggs to boil for breakfast in the morning.

UNMIK POLICE PRESS UPDATE

09 MARCH, 2001
PRISTINA Region
ATTEMPTED MURDER
Orlat Village, Glogovac - 08/03 - 2040 hrs. A known K-Albanian male shot another K-Albanian male once in the abdomen. The victim was transported to a local hospital and then to Pristina hospital where his condition is listed as serious. No arrests were reported yet. The circumstances of the incident are under investigation.
ILLEGAL POSSESSION OF WEAPONS
Stari Rujce Village, Lipljan - 08/03 - 1700 hrs. A K-Albanian male was arrested after a search of his residence resulted in the seizure of a pistol, three hand grenades and an assault rifle with ammunition.
PROTEST
Pristina - 08/03 - 0900 hrs. Approximately 200 K-Albanians protested in front of the District Court Building demanding the release of three detainees who are being held on a pending court case. The protest ended peacefully approximately two hours later.
PEC Region
TRAFFICKING IN WOMEN
Gramocelj Village, Decani - 06/03 - 0900 hrs. A K-Albanian male was arrested for illegal trafficking in women.
MITROVICA Region
SHOOTING
Mitrovica South - 08/03 - 1915 hrs. A K-Albanian female died from injuries sustained after being shot in the head.

Friday, 9 March, 2001

I got up at 0530. Craig was already up, had the coffee made and was in the shower. He has to be in early to serve a warrant. We had boiled eggs and bread for breakfast. I got to work at 0700 and still have no internet. I taught classes all day and got off work at 1530. I went downtown and called home. I talked to Carnita and the kids for about twenty minutes. I got back to the house and Craig and I went to the gym. After our workout we stopped at Reggie's and picked up the vehicle so we can go to the chow hall tomorrow. There was more fighting on the border today. It seems to be getting worse. The U.S. KFOR is right in the middle of it.

UNMIK POLICE PRESS UPDATE
10 MARCH, 2001
GNJILANE Region
INTIMIDATION
Cerevajka Village, Vitina - 09/03 - 0730 hrs. Five K-Serbian males reported that they were stopped and questioned by a group of K-Albanian males wearing UCPMB uniforms. During the questioning, the suspects took the documents belonging to the victims but later returned them.
PRIZREN Region
ATTEMPTED MURDER
Prizren - 08/03 - 2325 hrs. UNMIK Police arrested a K-Albanian male after he fired one round through a window into an occupied shop. The suspect later implicated in his statement to police that he was trying to kill one of the patrons inside.
INDUSTRIAL STRIKE
Prizren - 09/03 - 0855 hrs. Approximately 420 workers employed with the Printex factory staged a peaceful strike in protest of losing the power supply of Kosovo Electric.
PEC Region
THREATS
Dakovica Town - 08/03 - 1600 hrs. A K-Roma male reported that unknown persons left a letter outside his house which stated that he pay an amount of cash by delivering it to a named location or the lives of his family will be at stake. The letter contained information about his family and an empty cartridge.
MITROVICA Region
ASSAULT/CRIMINAL DAMAGE/ARSON
Mitrovica North - 09/03 - 1951 hrs. Approximately 30 K-Serbians attacked a house occupied by two elderly K-Albanians with Molotov cocktails setting the house on fire. The victims sustained unknown type of injuries and were taken to hospital.
ASSAULT/CRIMINAL DAMAGE
Mitrovica North - 09/03 - 2000 hrs. A UNMIK Police vehicle was attacked by a group of 70 K-Serbians who were throwing stones at it while in route to answer a call. The vehicle sustained minor damage. The officers were not injured.

Saturday, 10 March, 2001

Same morning routine. Out to the British chow hall for breakfast and in to the office by 0715. No KPS classes today. I helped Joe do exit interviews for KPS class #9 to release them to independent patrol. I wrote the interview questions. We had a special operation today. One hundred Albanian Prisoners of War from last year's conflict are to be released from Serbia and returned to Kosovo. KFOR and CivPol traffic units are escorting buses from the Serbian border to the BBC compound. Randy, Joe, Thommy and I had to control access to the entrance of the compound at the K.P. highway. The POWs were bused to the BBC compound and released there. There were at least 5,000 family and friends there to greet the POWs. It was a long, miserable duty. There was a lot of dust and vehicle exhaust and lots of stupid drivers. I will write a complete story of the incident. I did not get back to the house until 1800. I did not go to the gym tonight.

Sunday, 11 March, 2001

Same Sunday morning routine today. Nothing new to write about.

UNMIK POLICE PRESS UPDATE
12 MARCH, 2001
PRISTINA Region
SUICIDE / ACCIDENT
Pristina - 11/03 - 1230 hrs. An elderly K-Albanian female was found dead in a well at her residence. No foul play was suspected.
GNJILANE Region
Gnjilane - 11/03 - 1715 hrs. A K-Albanian male was arrested after he assaulted a KFOR Soldier at a checkpoint. Minor injuries were reported.
PEC Region
ILLEGAL POSSESSION OF WEAPONS
Dakovica Town - 10/03 - 2330 hrs. A K-Albanian male was arrested after he was found in possession of an assault rifle during a traffic stop.
UXO FOUND
Cremljane Village, Dakovica - 10/03 - Nighttime. A young K-Albanian girl found an unexploded rocket while playing. KFOR EOD disposed of the device. No physical injuries were reported.
MITROVICA Region
ARMED ASSAULT

Supkovac Village, Leposavic - 10/03 - 2000 hrs. Unknown suspect(s) fired several times with an unknown type firearm at a truck driven by a K-Serbian male. The driver was struck once in the right arm and sustained minor injuries.

Monday, 12 March, 2001

Same routine today as usual. Nothing new to report.

UNMIK POLICE PRESS UPDATE
13 MARCH, 2001
PRISTINA Region
ATTEMPTED MURDER/ARMED ROBBERY
Pristina - 12/03 - 0230 hrs. Three unknown armed persons broke into the home of a K-Albanian male customs officer and robbed him of a large amount of cash after shooting him in his left hand and right calf. When the victim was shot in the right leg, the bullet went through and hit one of the suspects. The victim was transported to Pristina Hospital where he is listed to be in stable condition.
GNJILANE Region
EXPLOSION
Gnjilane - 12/03 - 0111 hrs. A K-Albanian owned grocery store was completely destroyed in an explosion that also damaged ten other businesses in the area. No physical injuries were reported.
EXPLOSION/ASSAULT/CIVIL UNREST
Partesh Village, Gnjilane - 12/03 - 2030 hrs. Approximately 200 K-Serbians became unruly after an abandoned K-Serbian home was the target of an explosion. UNMIK Police responding to the area to quell the situation reported that a KPS Police vehicle was damaged by demonstrators throwing rocks in addition to four civilian trucks being burned. One K-Albanian male received minor injuries after he was pulled from his vehicle and assaulted by the crowd. His vehicle was burned. The K-Albanian victim was transported to a hospital. No arrests were reported.
PRIZREN Region
BOMB EXPLOSION
Prizren - 12/03 - 0020 hrs. Unknown person(s) threw an explosive device into a garden of a K-Albanian house. The explosion caused only damage to the windows of the surrounding buildings.
ATTEMPTED HAND GRENADE ATTACK

Prizren - 12/03 - 2030 hrs. A K-Albanian male threatened to blow up the occupants of a restaurant with a hand grenade. He was quickly seized by the patrons. The subject fled on foot. Neither injuries nor arrests were reported.

PEC Region

ASSAULT

Pec - 11/03 - 2100 hrs. A K-Albanian male was arrested after assaulting an UNMIK Police officer during a traffic stop. No injuries were reported.

UXO FOUND

Decani Town - 11/03 - 1500 hrs. A construction worker at a local site located an unknown type of unexploded ordinance. KFOR EOD responded and disposed of the device.

Pec - 12/03 - 1830 hrs. A K-Albanian male reported finding an anti-tank rocket along a roadside. KFOR EOD responded and disposed of the device. No physical injuries were reported.

MITROVICA Region

BOMB EXPLOSION

Vucitrn Town - 12/03 - 2315 hrs. An unknown type explosion caused minor damage to a K-Albanian owned shop. No physical injuries were reported.

Brent Faulkner- Pristina

Clay working on laptop at the house

Ken McCarty at the house

John Hatchell at Main HQ- Pristina

Riots in Mitrovica- French KFOR

Gas deployed- Mitrovica riot

Grenade explosion- Mitrovica Riots- German KFOR

Ferdinand "Guam" Ibabao
KIA 10-14-2004
Baghdad, Iraq

Tuesday, 13 March, 2001

Same morning routine. I showed the *Surviving Edged Weapons* video for the morning class. After lunch I was part of the selection board to interview candidates for the first KPS First Line Supervisor training. We had eleven candidates to interview and it took until 1800. I got home too late to go to the gym. I stayed at the house and watched the news. The UCPMB agreed to a weeklong cease fire with Serbia. The fighting is continuing on the Macedonian border and that group is now calling itself the "National Liberation Army". The weather was warm and sunny today. It looks like Spring is here.

P.S. The night before last there was a bad accident in front of our old house. Fourteen people were hit by a drunk driver as they were leaving the Red Lion bar. A lot were pinned to the wall and one girl lost her foot.

E-mail home

Hi Hun,
I got back to the office last night and the internet just went off. I got a good workout last night. I may have to miss tonight because I am helping interview candidates for KPS supervisor training. I may get home later than usual. We are still eating breakfast at the British KFOR chow hall. Contact you later.
Love, Clay

E-mail to Libby Press

Hello from Kosovo,
It has been a while since I last wrote an update on my mission here so I thought it time to do so. I have been here for seven months now and things are going as well as can be expected. The water and power situation is better than when I first got here but there still are times when there are problems for a few days. Just last month we had power rationing. The power was on for three hours and then off for three. You just have to get used to it. The water situation may be a problem since there was not much snowfall this winter. The reservoir is low and I expect water problems this summer. I am already stocking up on the bottles of water. The

winter was thankfully pretty mild, although there were days when I could see my breath inside the house. The cold was only a problem for the officers from tropical areas, especially the African countries. They were surprised to see me wearing short sleeve shirts when they were wrapped up in their heaviest coats. That brings up a funny story. One of my police colleagues from one of the African countries was explaining his police duties back home. He is an "Elephant Officer." He explained that it is his job to sit all day in a watchtower and keep a lookout for elephants nearing his village. If elephants come near he is to sound a warning to the village, as elephants are very dangerous and destructive. He is a second-generation "Elephant Officer" as his father before him. I asked him how many times he has spotted elephants and he said that he has never seen one yet. As a point of fact, he doesn't think his father ever saw one either. I am still conducting classroom training for the new Kosovo Police Service (KPS) officers as they are assigned to our station from the police academy. They have to undergo four weeks of classroom training at the station level before being released to their Field Training Officers. The training is going well and the young officers seem eager to learn, especially from U.S. officers. Last week I was involved in the return of one hundred Albanian Prisoners of War from Serbia. They have been in prison since the 1999 war, some of them for no other reason but that they are Albanian. It was quite an experience. American police and military had to escort the buses from the Serbian border to the release point here in Pristina. It was a pretty tense situation because a bus load of Serbian civilians was bombed while under military escort just three weeks ago on the same road. Thankfully there were no problems this time. I was assigned to control traffic at the entrance to the release point. There were over five thousand people at the release point to welcome the prisoners back. I was surprised to see the types of people the prisoners turned out to be. The kind of Prisoners of War you would expect to see would be men of fighting age between 18 and 45. These POWs were men and women, old and young. Some looked very thin and all were in civilian clothes. Not one of them was in uniform. As the prisoners were released they left the area in the company of many of their family and friends. There were a lot of tearful reunions and a steady stream of people leaving the area, waving Albanian flags. The most memorable thing about the whole event for me was being approached by several of the

prisoners as they left. Several of them stopped to shake my hand and thank me just because I was an American. They had seen the American flag on the sleeve of my uniform and wanted to thank me for getting them released. We are still the heroes to these people. I hope it stays that way. On the negative, there has been another outbreak of hostilities. There are two separate groups of Albanian guerilla armies. One is called the UCPMB and is operating on the eastern border between Kosovo and Serbia. They have been attacking Serbian forces in the NATO "buffer zone." The other group, the NLA, is fighting on the southern border between Kosovo and Macedonia. There is a fear that this fighting may escalate into a civil war in Macedonia. Supplies for Kosovo come through the border with Macedonia and there are already shortages and increased prices because of the fighting. Our gasoline is also being rationed now. Things here in Pristina are still fairly safe but the fighting is only fifty miles from here. Time will tell how, or if, the new hostilities will affect the mission here. Well, that's all the Balkan news I have for now. For those of you who can get it, the BBC World News has good coverage of the area. I'll be home again soon. So long for now from Kosovo.
Clay Coker

UNMIK POLICE PRESS UPDATE
14 MARCH, 2001
GNJILANE Region
ATTEMPTED MURDER
Malishevo Village, Gnjilane - 13/03 - 2040 hrs. Two unknown suspects, one armed with an unknown type firearm, demanded money from a K-Albanian male and a K-Albanian female. Suddenly they opened fire at the couple. Both victims sustained minor injuries. The female victim was hospitalized.
THREATS
Gnjilane - 12/03 - 1300 hrs. Four unknown K-Albanian males threatened a K-Roma female as she was walking home.
PRIZREN Region
HARBORING A FUGITIVE
Shadervan Village, Prizren - 13/03 - 0300 hrs. UNMIK Police conducted a raid on a residence where two escaped convicts were located hiding in an attic. Two other K-Albanian males who were in the residence were also arrested for harboring a fugitive.
TRAFFICKING OF WOMEN

Prizren - 13/03 - 1700 hrs. UNMIK Police arrested two K-Albanian males for trafficking of women for prostitution.
PEC Region
ASSAULT
Pec - 10/03 - 2130 hrs. Two K-Albanians were arrested after assaulting an on duty KPS officer.
ILLEGAL POSSESSION OF WEAPONS
Sisman Village, Dakovica - 13/03 - 0900 hrs. A K-Albanian male was arrested after a search of his house resulted in the seizure of five assault rifles, a pistol, a grenade, magazines, ammunition and several meters of explosive fuse.
MITROVICA Region
ARSON
Zvecan Village, Mitrovica North - 13/03 - 2152 hrs. Unknown persons broke the window of a vehicle belonging to the NGO "International Organization for Migration" and threw Molotov Cocktails through the open window setting it on fire.

Wednesday, 14 March, 2001

Same morning routine again. It was raining this morning. The BBC news said the fighting on the Macedonian border is getting worse. Serbian troops have moved into the "buffer zone". I got called away from classes today to interview one more candidate for the First Line Supervisor course. This was the only female KPS officer interviewed. Her name is Isma Muja. She is thirty years old and was an engineering teacher before the war. She joined the KLA and was a combat soldier. It is known that she personally killed two Serbian soldiers. She interviewed very well and made quite an impression. She will definitely be one of the three chosen for promotion. I went to the gym after work. It may be off limits soon. They are under investigation for providing the TMK with all of our photos, names and addresses for their data base.

P.S. My ear is bothering me again.

UNMIK POLICE PRESS UPDATE
15 MARCH, 2001
GNJILANE Region
CRIMINAL DAMAGE

Berivojce Village, Kamenica - 13/03 - 1835 hrs. UNMIK Police detained three K-Albanian males after they cut a main power supply cable, which led to a KFOR camp, with an axe. One suspect was slightly injured by showering sparks, which emitted from the power cable.

PEC Region

DEAD BODY FOUND

Rausic Village, Pec - 14/03 - 1900 hrs. A badly decomposed female body was found in a ditch near the village.

MITROVICA Region

CIVIL UNREST/CRIMINAL DAMAGE

Mitrovica North - 14/03 - 0530 hrs. Three K-Serbs were arrested for illegal possession of weapons. Following the arrest, a crowd of about 150 people gathered in front of the UNMIK Police station and demanded their release. The crowd threw stones at the station causing minor injuries to a KFOR soldier and an UNMIK Police officer. One UNMIK Police vehicle was set on fire. Some of the demonstrators were observed carrying weapons. The situation was brought under control.

GRIEVOUS ASSAULT

Mitrovica North - 14/03 - 0930 hrs. Approximately forty K-Serbians entered a UNMIK Police officer's apartment, hit him with wooden sticks, kicked him in the back and threatened him with a knife. The officer escaped from the mob by jumping out a window. The officer sustained minor injuries.

ROBBERY

Mitrovica North - 14/03 - Morning hrs. A group of K-Serbians confronted a K-Albanian male and his son and threatened to cut their throats after robbing them of cash and identity documents.

ASSAULT / EVICTION

Mitrovica North - 14/03 - 1705 hrs. A K-Albanian male and female were assaulted by a group of K-Serbians who forced them out of their flat. The victims received minor injuries.

Mitrovica North - 14/03 - 0915 hrs. Approximately thirty K-Serbians entered a K-Albanian male's flat, put a gun to his head and assaulted his wife and daughter. The extent of the injuries was not reported.

Mitrovica North - 14/03 - 0910 hrs. A group of ten K-Serbians broke into a K-Albanian female's flat and assaulted her and her brother. The extent of the injuries was not reported.

ILLEGAL POSSESSION OF WEAPONS

Zubin Potok - 13/03 - 1600 hrs. UNMIK Police recovered one machine gun and a shotgun from the home of a K-Serbian male robbery suspect. The weapons were confiscated.

Thursday, 15 March, 2001

I got up at 0600. No van today so no British chow. I had a boiled egg and coffee. I got to the office at 0700. Not much going on today. Class #13 is in their FTUs today. Randy, Cedric and I took a trip to Camp Bondsteel. It is the U.S. KFOR base in the Gnjilane region. We are now allowed on the base. We went to shop at the PX. I bought some American items like vitamins, IcyHot, jalapeño peppers and good tuna. After shopping we went to the AFES Burger King and had lunch. I bought some burgers to take back to Craig. I got back to the office at about 1500 and then to the gym by 1600. After the workout I went back to the office and chatted with Carnita for about an hour. I was surprised that the internet was up. Maybe they have the bugs worked out. I went back to the house and worked on getting my Class A uniform ready for tomorrow night's U.N. "Medal Parade." It is actually a contingent meeting and dinner.

UNMIK POLICE PRESS UPDATE
16 MARCH, 2001
PRISTINA Region
GRENADE ATTACK
Gonia Gusterica Village, Lipljan - 13/03 - 1930 hrs. Unknown person(s) threw a hand grenade at an occupied K-Serbian house causing minor structural damage.
PRIZREN Region
ILLEGAL POSSESSION OF WEAPONS
Sisman Village, Prizren - 15/03 - 1500 hrs. An assault rifle, 2 magazines and 2 hand grenades were recovered by UNMIK Police from the home of a K-Albanian male who was arrested on a prior assault charge. The items were confiscated.
PEC Region
HUMAN REMAINS FOUND
Klina Town - 15/03 - 0755 hrs. A K-Albanian male found human bones while plowing his field. A female neighbor identified the remains as that of her 72-year-old husband who has been missing

since 01-04-99. The subject was identified by personal items on the remains.

GRENADE ATTACK

Brekoc Village, Dakovica - 15/03 - 0045 hrs. A K-Albanian owned petrol station was attacked with a rocket-propelled grenade. Only minor property damage was reported.

POSSIBLE SUICIDE

Omeberde Village, Istok - 15/03 - 1010 hrs. A K-Albanian male was found hanging from a tree in his yard by another K-Albanian male. The victim was removed from the tree and taken to KFOR hospital where the body was examined. The circumstances of the incident are under investigation.

MITROVICA Region

CRIMINAL DAMAGE

Mitrovica North - 15/03 - 1855 hrs. An UNMIK Police vehicle was attacked with stones by a group of K-Serbians. The rocks broke the rear window. No physical injuries were reported.

DEMONSTRATION

Mitrovica North - 15/03 - 1200 hrs - 1247 hrs. Approximately 1,000 K-Serbians held a peaceful demonstration. During the civil unrest twenty-one UNMIK Police officers sustained minor injuries and seven UNMIK vehicles were damaged by K-Serbians.

Friday, 16 March, 2001

We got up at 0500 today when John Nelms from the DPU came by to get Craig's White U.N. van to get to the airport in Skopje. His 0400 ride had failed to show up so he came by for the van and left Craig a "coke". The border is now open to official U.N. and KFOR vehicles only. We went to chow and then in to work for a while. I went to the house at lunch to finish getting things ready for tonight's meeting. I cleaned the house up some and opened all the windows to air out the house. It was warm and sunny today. We walked down to the British Council building for our U.N. "Medal Parade." We had an hour contingent meeting and then got our U.N. mission service medals. The guest speaker was a RUC commissioner from Northern Ireland. The dinner was no more than snacks so Craig and I went to the new American restaurant "Bristol" and ate chicken fried steak, mashed potatoes, mac and cheese and peas. The food is brought in from the states. The rumor is that it was opened by a U.S. CivPol officer who comes from a wealthy family.

UNMIK POLICE PRESS UPDATE
17 MARCH, 2001
GNJILANE Region
ILLEGAL POSSESSION OF A WEAPON
Malishevo Village, Gnjilane- 15/03 - 2230 hrs. UNMIK Police arrested a K-Albanian male after he was found in possession of 5 hand grenades. The items were seized.
PRIZREN Region
ILLEGAL POSSESSION OF WEAPONS
Qollak Village, Prizren - 16/03 - 1500 hrs. UNMIK Police arrested two K-Albanian males after a house search revealed that they were in possession of numerous weapons and ammunition, along with explosives and explosive device detonating equipment.

Saturday, 17 March, 2001

Same morning routine today except we did not go to the British chow hall. Not much going on at the office. Randy and I went to lunch at Ardi's with the Germans. Today is St. Patrick's day so as a joke I gave RUC officer Barry Greene a bar of Irish Spring soap I brought from the states. He said that he had never heard of it. I told him about the "Irish" commercials and he thought it was funny that most American's think it really comes from Ireland. After work Craig and I went to the gym. The fighting in Macedonia is in the news every day. There is talk that the fighting may develop into a full Civil War.

E-mail home

Hi Hun,
How's it going? The parade last night was OK but kind of a disappointment. The dinner was just snacks. I was recognized for the November bombing and the contingent commander wants to get an American Contingent award program. If it happens before I leave he wants to give me some kind of medal. The fighting is still getting worse in Macedonia but the border is open again for official vehicles. Not much else going on. Well I'll go for now. Love, Clay

UNMIK POLICE PRESS UPDATE
18 MARCH, 2001
PEC Region
GRENADE ATTACK
Dakovica Town- 17/03 - 0300 hrs. Unknown suspects threw a hand grenade at a K-Albanian house causing minor structural damage. No physical injuries were reported.
SHOOTING
Pec - 16/03 -2330 hrs. A K-Albanian male security guard at Pec Hospital reported that unknown suspect(s) fired an automatic weapon near the hospital entrance.

Sunday, 18 March, 2001

Same Sunday morning routine as usual. The BBC is still reporting the fighting in Macedonia. Not much going on at the office except for Sunday paperwork. I went to the house for lunch and had a can of chili and some kippered herring I got at the Bondsteel PX. We went to the gym after work and then back to the house for the BBC. We watched a BBC special called *Future Wars*. The episode, called *Rules of Engagement*, was about the training of British Royal Marines for service in the Balkans.

P.S. Craig found out today that he has to stop taking the white U.N. van home at night. This means we will not have any way to get to the British chow hall in the mornings and we will have to walk to and from the gym. Nothing last very long here before it gets screwed up.

UNMIK POLICE PRESS UPDATE
19 MARCH, 2001
PRISTINA Region
UXO FOUND
Kosovo Polje Town - 18/03 - 1650 hrs. A hand grenade was found by workers carrying out repairs of a local residence. KFOR EOD safely recovered the item.
GNJILANE Region
ARSON
Ogoshte Village, Kamenica - 18/03 - 1945 hrs. Unknown person(s) set fire to an unoccupied K-Roma house causing only minor property damage.

ASSAULT
Gnjilane - 18/03 - 1430 hrs. Two unknown K-Roma males assaulted a K-Albanian male.
PRIZREN Region
BOMB EXPLOSION
Adem Jasheri Village, Prizren - 18/03 - 0525 hrs. An unknown type explosion occurred in front of a K-Albanian owned shop causing extensive structural damage to it and other nearby shops. A security guard working in the area received minor injuries from the blast.
MITROVICA Region
UXO FOUND
Mitrovica South - 18/03 - 1430 hrs. Two K-Albanian juveniles found a rocket propelled grenade launcher in a field. KFOR EOD disposed of the device.

Monday, 19 March, 2001

I got up at 0530. Craig was using the head so I made coffee. I took my turn for the "Triple Sierra" routine. We could not go to chow this morning because we found that someone had slashed both tires on the right side of the van. Craig had to walk to DPU to get help to fix the tires. I got to the office at 0720 and checked my e-mail. I was supposed to start the First Line Supervisor orientation this morning but one of the officers, Isma Muja, was accused of breaking the chain of command. I had to interview her and find out what happened. There is apparently some jealously about a female being promoted. It turned out that she was falsely accused. I don't think I would want to be the one to piss her off. Orientation will begin tomorrow. I got off work at 1530 and Craig and I went to the gym at 1600. Same evening routine.

P.S. I got a "bad feeling" about the tires being slashed and our security in general. I made sure my early warning booby traps and trip wires were all set outside my window and our front door.

UNMIK POLICE PRESS UPDATE
20 MARCH, 2001
GNJILANE Region
UXO INJURY

Ljukar Village, Likove Macedonia - 18/03 - 1400 hrs. An Albanian male was brought to the Gnjilane Hospital for treatment of an injury he sustained to his left foot. The victim was apparently working in his garden when a grenade exploded.

Tuesday, 20 March, 2001

Same morning routine today. Craig and I walked down to DPU to get the U.N. van to go to the chow hall. It is worth the fifteen minute walk to get that good British chow. I spent the morning at work giving orientation to the First Line Supervisor training course. Station #2 was selected for the very first KPS supervisor's course because of our excellent training reputation. That was apparently the reason for the visit from the U.N. "big wig" a couple of weeks ago. I taught class #13 in the afternoon and got off at 1600. Same evening routine tonight. We ran out of bottled water this evening and need to go buy some at the corner market. We don't get our water supply from the company for two more days.

P.S. There was a bomb scare on Ramiz-Zudiku street near the internet café. Someone left an explosive device outside a shop. EOD came and disposed of the device.

UNMIK POLICE PRESS UPDATE
21 MARCH, 2001
PRISTINA Region
SUSPECTED UXO
Pristina - 20/03 - 1400 hrs. Three separate incidents of suspicious objects were reported. KFOR EOD carried out investigations that included a controlled explosion in order to ascertain the items. No injuries were reported.
PRIZREN Region
DEATH FROM APPARENT LAND MINE EXPLOSION
Suva Reka Town - 20/03 - 2210 hrs. A K-Albanian male's body was found in a minefield after an explosion.
HUMAN REMAINS FOUND
Orahovac Town - 20/03 - 1430 hrs. A K-Albanian male reported that he found skeletal remains.
PEC region
UXO FOUND

Marmull Village, Dakovica - 19/03 - 2300 hrs. A K-Albanian male reported that he found an anti-tank rocket near his residence. KFOR EOD safely disposed of the device.
Pec - 19/03 - 2305 hrs. A hand grenade was located on the roadway. KFOR EOD safely carried out a controlled explosion.

Wednesday, 21 March, 2001

Same morning routine as yesterday. The BBC news reported that there is a twenty-four hour cease-fire agreement in Macedonia. They gave the NLA rebels an ultimatum to surrender or withdraw to Kosovo or they would launch a major offensive against them. I don't think the Albanian NLA will back down. Craig and I took a day off from the gym. Two Macedonian police officers were shot today. One was killed and the other is in critical condition. The cease-fire/ultimatum deadline is midnight.

UNMIK POLICE PRESS UPDATE
22 MARCH, 2001
PRISTINA Region
DEMONSTRATION
Lipljan Town - 21/03 - 1000 hrs. Approximately 80 K-Serbians gathered to voice their concern against the security situation in the area following a shooting incident that occurred on 20/03 (unknown male fired several shots with an assault rifle; no injuries).
DEMONSTRATION
Pristina - 21/03 - 2200 hrs. Approximately 4,000 people staged a march in support of Macedonian Albanians and the insurgents in Macedonia. The event, which was witnessed by UNMIK Police, ended peacefully without incidents.
GNJILANE Region
EXPLOSION
Vrbovac Village, Vitina - 21/03 - 2147 hrs. An unoccupied K-Serbian home was completely destroyed in an unknown type explosion.
UXO FOUND
Binac Village, Vitina - 21/03 - 1950 hrs. A K-Serbian male found an anti-tank mine behind his home. KFOR EOD responded to the scene and disposed of the device. No damage or injuries were reported.

PRIZREN Region
DEMONSTRATION
Prizren - 21/03 - 1300 hrs. Approximately 3,000 people attended a demonstration in support of the insurgents in Macedonia.

Thursday, 22 March, 2001

Same morning routine today except we skipped the trip to the British chow hall. I was in to work at 0700. I started a three day in-service training session with class #10 today. I taught Police Ethics all morning and did not get finished before lunch. I went to the KFOR restaurant near Station #2 with Randy and Alban. I finished up my ethics class after lunch and got off work about 1600. Randy is going to go to the gym with Craig and I and is thinking of joining. I started to feel strange during the work out and had to stop and sit in the locker room. I was nauseous and had some sinus/allergy issues going on. On the way back to the house I got sick and had to take a cab back to the house. I lay down for a while then got a shower and went to bed. I hope I didn't eat something bad at the KFOR restaurant today. I had fish.

P.S. The fighting in Macedonia is spreading to other towns. The NLA did not surrender or withdraw. There was footage on the BBC of two Albanians being shot and killed while attempting to throw a grenade

UNMIK POLICE PRESS UPDATE
23 MARCH, 2001
PRISTINA Region
DEMONSTRATION
Pristina - 22/03 - 1700 hrs. Approximately 4,000 people, mostly university students, staged a march in support of the ongoing events in Macedonia. No incidents were reported.
GNJILANE Region
EXPLOSION
Drajkovce Town - 23/03 - 0140 hrs. An unknown type of explosive device detonated causing slight damage to a K-Albanian owned home.
PEC Region
GRENADE ATTACK

Dakovica Town - 21/03 - 2000 hrs. Unknown person(s) threw a grenade at a K-Albanian owned house causing damage to a vehicle and the front door of the residence.

ILLEGAL POSSESSION OF WEAPONS

Pec - 19/03 - 0700 hrs. Two K-Albanian males were arrested after a search of their residence resulted in the seizure of 2 assault rifles, a shotgun, knives, masks, a telescope, military maps, chemical detectors and ammunition.

Pec - 19/03 - 0700 hrs. A search of a house conducted by UNMIK Police resulted in the seizure of mines, masks, maps and various military items.

MITROVICA Region

SUSPECTED MURDER

Rudare Village, Mitrovica North - 22/03 - 1300 hrs. An unidentified male body was found. The apparent cause of death seems to be a gunshot wound.

Friday, 23 March, 2001

I got up at 0530. I feel a little better today. We walked and got the van to go to chow. I got to work and checked my e-mail. I sent a message to Carnita that I was sick and could not chat. I started class at 0830. I showed the *Surviving Edged Weapons* and the Trooper Coates shooting tapes. I went to the house for lunch and started feeling sick again. I had a guest speaker for the afternoon Domestic Violence class so I took a nap. I woke up when Craig brought in our water supply at about 1430. I skipped the gym tonight. The weather is partly cloudy and cool today.

P.S. We got an order today from the head of all UNMIK personnel that we are required to wear our U.N. beret while in uniform. The U.S. CivPol are the worst offenders. We hardly ever wear the stupid, baby blue thing.

UNMIK POLICE PRESS UPDATE

24 MARCH, 2001

PRISTINA Region

UXO FOUND

Lipljan Town - 23/03 - 1435 hrs. A hand grenade was located near the railway tracks. KFOR EOD safely carried out a controlled explosion.

GNJILANE Region
DEMONSTRATION
Gnjilane - 23/03 - 1200 hrs. Approximately 7,500 K-Albanians staged a peaceful demonstration against the violence in Macedonia. The rally ended peacefully

Saturday, 24 March, 2001

I feel better this morning but have a headache. We skipped the chow hall and had oatmeal. The sun is out today. The internet was down at the office. I taught Use of Force all morning. We broke for lunch and I went to the house to hang out my laundry. The washing machine is having trouble and not spinning out the water. I hand wrung the clothes in the tub and hung then out on the balcony. I went back to the office and finished classes. I got off at 1530. The internet was still down. I went to the gym and had a good workout but still don't feel right. I went home and ate, took a hot shower and went to bed.

UNMIK POLICE PRESS UPDATE
25 MARCH, 2001
GNJILANE Region
ATTEMPTED BOMBING
Gnjilane - 23/03 - 2345 hrs. A K-Albanian male shop owner reported finding a plastic trash bag in the rear of his store, which contained an unknown object. UNMIK Police along with KFOR responded to the scene where the device was found to be an unexploded bomb. KFOR EOD disarmed the device. No damages or injuries were reported.
DEMONSTRATION
Ferizaj Town - 24/03 - 1200 hrs. Approximately 400 K-Albanians staged a demonstration in support of Albanian solidarity in Macedonia.
PRIZREN Region
TRAFFICKING IN WOMEN
Prizren - 21-22/03. Three K-Albanian males were arrested for buying and illegally confining two Moldavian females for use as prostitutes.
Prizren - 23/03 - 1700 hrs. A K-Albanian male was arrested after he was found with a Moldavian female who he used as prostitute.
UXO FOUND

Prizren - 24/03 - 1730 hrs. An unexploded bomb, which had no fuse, was discovered by construction workers who were repairing public drains. EOD safely removed the device.
MITROVICA Region
DEMONSTRATIONS
Mitrovica South - 24/03 - 1125 hrs. Approximately 200 K-Albanians demonstrated in front of the Battery Factory commemorating the death of a K-Albanian female.
Mitrovica South - 24/03 – 1300 hrs. Approximately 500 K-Albanians protested the incident inside Macedonia during which two Albanian males died at a checkpoint.
ASSAULT
Mitrovica North - 24/03 - 1500 hrs. An unknown K-Serbian male assaulted a K-Albanian male.

Sunday, 25 March, 2001

I got up at 0530. I could not sleep in today. Craig and I had coffee and watched the BBC news. Macedonia launched its big offensive against the NLA in the hills above the town of Tetovo. The shelling started about 0600. I got to work and discovered that the time changed today. Kosovo observes Daylight Savings Time. Spring forward. I started feeling sick again. I was dizzy and light headed. I don't know what is wrong with me. I went to the house at 1300 and went to bed. I have no appetite but I know I need to eat. I stayed in bed until 1600. I got up and made myself eat some tuna and noodles and a banana. I could not make the gym with Craig. If I do not feel better by tomorrow I will of see Doc.

UNMIK POLICE PRESS UPDATE
26 MARCH, 2001
GNJILANE Region
ARSON
Urosevac Town - 25/03 - 1430 hrs. A wooden shed belonging to the Brown and Root company was totally destroyed by fire. No injuries were reported.
Vrbovac Village, Vitina - 25/03 - 1015 hrs. A KFOR vehicle was involved in an accident with a civilian vehicle. No injuries were reported.
FOUND UXO

Dramnjak Village, Urosevac - 25/03 - 1050 hrs. Three juveniles (gender and ethnicity not reported) located an anti-personnel mine. KFOR safely disposed of the device.
Urosevac Town - 25/03 - 1145 hrs. A K-Albanian male reported finding a grenade. KFOR safely disposed of the device.
Urosevac Town - 25/03 - 1630 hrs. A K-Albanian male reported finding a rocket-propelled grenade near his residence. KFOR safely disposed of the device.
PRIZREN Region
MEMORIAL CEREMONY
Bela Crkva and Celina Village - 25/03 - Time not reported.
Approximately 2,000 persons attended two peaceful gatherings in memory of those who died during the war.
Prizren - 25/03 - 1200 hrs. Approximately 500 persons attended a TMK organized ceremony in memory of those who died during the war.
PEC Region
UXO FOUND
Dakovica Town - 24/03 - 1700 hrs. UNMIK Police received information regarding the sighting of a cluster bomb near a roadway. KFOR EOD responded and disposed of the device.
Papracane Village, Decani - 24/03 - 1700 hrs. A K-Albanian male reported finding an unexploded hand grenade in his farm field. KFOR EOD responded and disposed of the device.
Junik Village, Decani - 25/03 - 1030 hrs. While on patrol, UNMIK Police located a mortar shell. KFOR EOD responded and disposed of the device.
MITROVICA Region
SHOOTING INCIDENT/GRIEVOUS INJURY
Mitrovica South - 25/03 - 1300 hrs. A K-Albanian male was admitted to KFOR hospital with a gunshot wound. No further information available.

Monday, 26 March, 2001

I slept until 0600. I am feeling a little better. Same morning routine. I did not go with Craig to chow this morning. I had a banana and oatmeal. I went to work and taught classes all day and got off at 1600. I could not see Doc today because of the lack of an available vehicle and there was a large demonstration downtown today. They were protesting about the war in Macedonia. The new war is really starting to affect our supplies. Our U.N. fuel station is out of fuel and the border is closed again. The weather today was in the 60s but was overcast.

P.S. The fighting in Macedonia is still heavy. There was an infantry attack against the rebel positions in Tetovo. There were heavy casualties. Many civilians were found hiding in basements from the shelling.

UNMIK POLICE PRESS UPDATE
27 MARCH, 2001
PRISTINA Region
DEMONSTRATION
Podujevo Town - 26/03 - 1200 hrs. A crowd of about 1,000 people attended a peaceful demonstration organized by the War Veterans Association in support of Macedonia Albanians.
MEMORIAL CEREMONY
Kosovo Polje - 26/03 - 2000 hrs. Approximately 1,000 K-Albanians attended a peaceful ceremony in memory of those who died during the war.
GNJILANE Region
FOUND UXO
Ferizaj Town, Urosevac - 25/03 - 2033 hrs. A K-Albanian male reported finding an unexploded 73mm rocket. KFOR EOD safely disposed of the device.
DEMONSTRATION
Kamenica Town - 26/03 - 1630 - 1800 hrs. A group of approximately 1,200 K-Albanians gathered to peacefully protest the recent conflict in Macedonia.
PRIZREN Region
ILLEGAL POSSESSION OF WEAPONS
Prizren - 26/03 - Time not reported. UNMIK Police arrested a Macedonian male for being in possession of 2 rifles, 5 hand grenades and 500 rounds of ammunition.
Prizren - 26/03 - 1630 hrs. Ten Macedonian refugees (gender not reported) were arrested for illegal weapons and ammunition possession after they attempted to cross the border into Kosovo.
Zaplujze Village, Prizren - 26/03 - 2030 hrs. UNMIK Police arrested six Macedonian males after they were found in possession of miscellaneous military items and ammunition.
MEMORIAL CEREMONY

Velika Krusa Village, Prizren - 26/03 - 1000 hrs. Approximately 3,000 K-Albanians gathered for a memorial service in memory of those who died during the war. There were no incidents reported and the event ended peacefully.

PEC Region

FOUND UXO

Lluka Village, Decani - 26/03 - 0840 hrs. A K-Albanian male reported finding unexploded ordinance. KFOR EOD safely disposed of the device.

Pec Town - 26/03 - 1100 hrs. An unexploded grenade was located under a kiosk. KFOR EOD safely disposed of the device.

DEMONSTRATION

Pec Town - 26/03 - 1200 - 1300 hrs. A crowd of approximately 500-600 K-Albanians gathered to demonstrate their solidarity with the ethnic Albanians of Macedonia. The demonstration was peaceful and no incidents were reported.

MITROVICA Region

ATTEMPTED MURDER

Zubin Potok - 25/03 - 1400 hrs. A K-Serbian male was shot several times by an unknown person. The condition of the victim was not reported.

Mitrovica South - 26/03 - Time not reported. A K-Albanian male was shot by an unknown suspect and transported to Pristina Hospital. The present condition of the victim was not reported.

UXO FOUND

Vucitrn - 26/03 - 1840 hrs. A K-Albanian male reported that he found a hand grenade near his residence. KFOR EOD responded to the location and disarmed the device.

Tuesday, 27 March, 2001

Up at 0530. Same morning routine. I am feeling better but not 100%. I had oatmeal and a banana for breakfast. I taught ethics today. This is the last full day of classes for class #13. Tomorrow we have a short review and a test. I have to take Randy to Prishtina airport at 1100 tomorrow. I will try and see Doc then. I started feeling bad again about noon. I went to the house at 1600. I am still not feeling up to working out so Craig and I went to check out a new gym closer to the house. It is only a three minute walk and costs 100DM per month. We may switch to this new gym in April.

P.S. There was a big demonstration again today because of a high profile murder trial. The owner of Golak Towing is on trial for killing a municipal official over a construction site disagreement. There is also going to be some kind of war crimes trial in a couple of days here in Prishtina. It could be bad. Some more Albanian POWs were released from Serbia today.

UNMIK POLICE PRESS UPDATE
28 MARCH, 2001
PRISTINA Region
DEMONSTRATION
Pristina - 27/03 - 1030 hrs. Approximately 3,000 K-Albanians, most of them elderly, gathered in front of the Government building and staged a peaceful protest against the non-payment of their pensions.
Glogovac Town - 27/03 - 1200 hrs. Approximately 2,000 K-Albanians, consisting mostly of school children, assembled near the Municipal building, to show their solidarity with Macedonia Albanians.
MEMORIAL CEREMONY
Kosovo Polje - 27/03 - 1200 hrs. About 800 K-Albanians attended a peaceful ceremony in memory of those who died during the war. The event started inside the railway station and then ended at the cemetery.
PRIZREN Region
CELEBRATION
Malisevo Town - 27/03 - 1800 hrs. A crowd of approximately 400 K-Albanians gathered to celebrate the release of prisoners from Serbia.
MITROVICA Region
DEAD BODY FOUND
Mitrovica South - 27/03 - 1400 hrs. A body of a male (ethnicity unknown) believed to have been the victim of the industrial accident that occurred in Pec region was found lying in a truck.
UXO FOUND
Leposavic Town - 27/03 - 1400 hrs. A K-Serbian male reported that he had found a hand grenade. KFOR EOD disposed of the device.

Wednesday, 28 March, 2001

I got up at 0530. I did my morning routine and then walked down to get the DPU van. We went to breakfast at the British chow hall. I had a good, British military breakfast. I got to work at 0715 and check my e-mails. I gave the review and then the final exam for the classroom training. Everyone did well on the test. At 0930 Randy and I went to get our MSA. I then took Randy to his house to change clothes and then drove him to Prishtina airport. I went to the company building to pay for my plane tickets and to see Doc Donovan. He checked my BP and it was up but he said that he could not get an accurate reading because the cuff was too small for my arm. Doc checked my blood sugar and it was pretty low. Doc said that I need to eat more and drink more juices. I went to the gym but could not get past two exercises. I took a cab home, ate and went to bed.

E-mail home

Hi Hun,
Sorry for not e-mailing. I have been sick and the internet has been down. I went to see Doc today and my blood sugar level was really low. I need to eat more. My blood pressure may be a little high too but he could get an accurate reading because my arm was too big for the cuff and he hasn't got a thigh cuff here with him. He wants me to get it checked when I am home. I may be borderline. I am feeling better today. I got some food at the store and making myself eat more. I need your good cooking to make me well. Talk to you soon, Clay

UNMIK POLICE PRESS UPDATE
29 MARCH, 2001
PRIZREN Region
ABDUCTION
Lubizda Village, Prizren - 27/03 - 1320 hrs. A K-Albanian female reported that she was abducted by two unknown male suspects and forced to work as a prostitute. The victim managed to escape after being held for three days.
TRAFFICKING IN WOMEN
Prizren - 28/03 - Time not reported. UNMIK Police arrested a K-Albanian male after an investigation revealed his involvement in the trafficking of women for prostitution.

HUMAN REMAINS FOUND

Musutiste Village, Suva Reka - 28/03 - 1230 hrs. A K-Albanian male reported to UNMIK Police that he had found what appeared to be human skeletal remains.

DEMONSTRATION

Malishevo Town - 28/03 - 1250 hrs. Approximately 350 K-Albanian students from the primary and secondary schools staged a peaceful demonstration in support of the ethnic Albanians in Macedonia. The event ended peacefully and there were no incidents reported.

MEMORIAL CEREMONY

Zur Village, Prizren - 28/03 - 0900 hrs. Approximately 2,000 K-Albanians participated in a memorial ceremony. The service ended peacefully.

MITROVICA Region

ILLEGAL POSSESSION OF WEAPONS

Duboka Village, Leposavic - 28/03 - 1500 hrs. A K-Serbian male was arrested after a house search discovered a machine gun, shot gun, detonators, fuses, assorted weapon parts and ammunition.

Pantina Village, Vucitrn - 27/03 - 2305 hrs. A KFOR search of a vehicle (whose occupants fled from the scene) resulted in the recovery of mortar shells, mines, and rockets.

ASSAULT

Mitrovica South - 27/03 - 1230 hrs. A German national employee of the OSCE reported that two K-Albanian males attacked his vehicle while it was occupied by two K-Serbians passengers. No injuries or damage were reported.

MEMORIAL SERVICE

Izibica Village, Srbica - 28/03 - 1230 hrs. Approximately 4,000 K-Serbians attended a service in memory of people who died during the war.

Thursday, 29 March, 2001

Same morning routine. Got to work at 0800. I helped get the office ready for an audit today. At about 1000 I had to take one of the L.A.s to the emergency room. He had a diabetic incident. I saw some U.S. Army airborne troops at the emergency room. I am not sure why they were there. I went back to work and e-mailed Carnita that I would not be on the chat or phone tonight.

P.S. The fighting in Macedonia spilled over into Kosovo today. The village of Krivenik came under mortar attack. A British journalist and two Albanian civilians were killed and sixteen were wounded. The weather was cool and cloudy today. The U.S. troops I saw at the ER were escorting the wounded from Krivenik.

UNMIK POLICE PRESS UPDATE
30 MARCH, 2001
PRISTINA Region
PROSTITUTION
Lipljan Town - 29/03 - 0230 hrs. UNMIK Police detained a K-Albanian male who was found in the company of four Ukrainian female prostitutes.
DEMONSTRATION
Pristina - 29/03 - 1900 hrs. Approximately 600 people, mostly K-Albanian students, protested against the ongoing conflict in Macedonia.
Pristina - 29/03 - 1000 hrs. Approximately 70 K-Albanians demonstrated outside the courthouse in support of three K-Albanians currently on trial.
GNJILANE Region
MORTAR ATTACK
Krivenik Village, Kacanik - 29/03 – 1155 hrs. Two K-Albanians and a British journalist were killed, in addition to sixteen people injured (ethnicities not confirmed), during a mortar attack on the village. The injured persons were transported to the hospital for treatment of their injuries.
GRENADE ATTACK
Prelez Village, Urosevac - 29/03 - 2300 hrs. Unknown person(s) threw a grenade into a petrol station that is under construction. Minor damage and no injuries were reported.
PRIZREN Region
FOUND WEAPONS
Prizren - 29/01 - 1100 hrs. While on patrol, KFOR reported locating two unoccupied vehicles on a roadway that contained 38 machine guns, 1 AK-47 rifle and miscellaneous ammunition.
PEC Region
MURDER
Pec Town - 29/03 - 1045 hrs. The body of an unknown male approximately 40 years of age was found partially buried. The victim was reported to have head injuries.

DEAD BODY FOUND
Jabllanica - Vogel Village, Pec - 29/03 - 1800 hrs. The body of a newborn female infant was found in a stream.
DEMONSTRATION
Istok Town - 29/03 - 1200 - 1300 hrs. A crowd of approximately 1,500 K-Albanians peacefully demonstrated in support of ethnic Albanians in Macedonia.

Friday, 30 March, 2001

Same morning routine. We went to the British chow hall for breakfast. I was in the office by 0720. I checked and sent e-mails. I went to KFOR hill with Thommy. I bought a new diary book because this one is almost full. I bought some stuff for Thommy at the U.S. PX because Germans are not allowed to shop there. U.S. CivPol are allowed now. We went and had coffee at the German KFOR coffee shop. I thought how strange it was to be hanging around and drinking coffee with German soldiers when just 56 years ago my grandfather was fighting their grandfathers. After KFOR hill we stopped at the Norwegian (Maxi) PX and bought some more food. I went to the house, ate and went to bed.

E-mail home

Hi Hun,
I am feeling a little better. Trying to get enough calories in me each day. I haven't worked out for a few days. The fighting has moved into Kosovo, just in one village so far. There was a mortar attack where three civilians were killed and 16 wounded. One of the dead was a British journalist. I had to take one of the L.A.s to the hospital for a diabetic incident and there was a squad of U.S. Army Airborne troops there. I think they were escorting some of the wounded from the village. Several Macedonian insurgents have been caught entering Kosovo also.
Things here are still safe. Don't worry. I am counting the days until I can come home. March has been a real bummer and a hard month, probably the hardest yet. I can't wait to see you. Love always, Clay

UNMIK POLICE PRESS UPDATE
31 MARCH, 2001

PRISTINA Region

SKELETAL REMAINS

Obrija Village, Gllogovac - 30/03 - 1900 hrs. Three K-Albanian males reported that they had found the remains of a fully clothed male skeleton.

PUBLIC UNREST

Glogovac Town - 30/03 - 1000 hrs. Approximately 1,000 people protested against the demolition by Municipal workers of illegally built structures. Four K-Albanian males were arrested.

DEMONSTRATION

Pristina - 30/03 - 1420 hrs. Approximately 2,000 people protested against the ongoing conflict on the border with Macedonia.

GNJILANE Region

DEMONSTRATION

Kacanik Town - 30/03 - 1500 hrs. A demonstration was held to protest the recent mortar attack in the village of Krivenik.

PRIZREN Region

ARMED ASSAULT

Prizren - 30/03 - 0043 hrs. Three K-Albanian males were arrested after KFOR soldiers conducted a traffic stop on the vehicle they were in for a curfew violation. During the incident, one of the suspects opened fire with an AK-47 rifle from the moving vehicle at the pursuing KFOR soldiers. The suspects then halted their vehicle and fled on foot. They were later apprehended by KFOR and UNMIK Police.

ILLEGAL POSSESSION OF WEAPONS

Donje Ljubinje Town - 27/03 - 0930 hrs. 38 Macedonian Albanians and 6 K-Albanian males were arrested after they were observed crossing the border illegally into Kosovo. Two pistols, eighteen AK-47 rifles, one mortar and several rounds of ammunition were confiscated.

UXO FOUND

Prizren - 30/03 - 1945 hrs. UNMIK Police located an unexploded hand grenade that was disposed of by KFOR EOD.

MEMORIAL CEREMONY

Retimnje Village, Prizren - 30/03 - 1100 hrs. Approximately 200 K-Albanians attended a memorial ceremony in honor of those who died during the war.

DEMONSTRATIONS

Orahovac Town - 30/03 - 1220 hrs. Approximately 1,000 K-Albanians attended a public gathering in support of ethnic Albanians in Macedonia.
Suva Reka Town - 30/03 - 1200 hrs. Approximately 2,000 K-Albanians attended a public gathering supporting the "Association of War Invalids."
MITROVICA Region
PROSTITUTION
Skenderaj Town - 29/03 - 2300 hrs. A K-Albanian male and two Bulgarian females were arrested for their involvement in prostitution.

Saturday, 31 March, 2001

I slept in until 0600 today. I got up and made the coffee. "Triple Sierra" and then breakfast. Craig slept in until 0700. I was in to work at 0730 and finished working on my PowerPoint presentation on Police Ethics. I hope to have it translated into Albanian by Tuesday's class. I went to the company building with Cedric Stephens (U.S. CivPol) to get water and a couple of movies. I went home early.

P.S. The BBC news today reported about a raid on Slobodan Milosevic's residence early this morning in Belgrade. There was a big gun battle with his body guards. Today is the U.S. imposed deadline to bring Milosevic in or Serbia loses 100 million dollars in aid.

UNMIK POLICE PRESS UPDATE
01 APRIL, 2001
PRISTINA Region
SKELETAL REMAINS
Kamoran Village, Glogovac - 31/03 - 1000 hrs. A K-Albanian male found a human skull while working in his field.
PRIZREN Region
MEMORIAL CEREMONY
Pusto Selo Village, Prizren - 31/03 - 1200 hrs. Approximately 1,000 K-Albanians gathered for a memorial ceremony honoring those who died in the war.
PEC Region
FOUND WEAPONS

Kusnin Village, Dakovica -28/03 - 0415 hrs. A Carabinieri unit found a backpack containing two assault rifles, one anti-troop mine, two gas masks and ammunition near the Albanian border.

Sunday, 1 April, 2001

I slept in until 0630. I got up and did my morning routine and then watched the BBC. Our living room heater went out and blew out our extension cord and tripped out our breakers. I had to move the TV closer to the plug to be able to use the shorter extension cord. The outlets in our rooms will not work now. We went to chow at the British KFOR chow hall at 0830 and then to work at 0900. I finished my PowerPoints and then checked e-mails. Cedric and Thommy got in at 1100. Craig picked me up at noon and we went to Camp Bondsteel. We went to Burger King first and then to the PX. We stayed on the base about an hour. I bought a *Newsweek* and the April *Reader's Digest*. (Score!) We were back in Prishtina by 1530. We went to the gym today. After about an hour, Craig got a bad headache and I got sick and puked. We went home to no power. We read by candlelight until 2000 when the power came back on. We watched the BBC news and then went to our rooms.

P.S. The weather turned off cool today. The temperature dropped into the upper thirties today. The outlets in our rooms are out and we can't use our heaters. I had to turn on the propane heater to get some heat into the house.

P.P.S. Slobodan Milosevic is now in custody.

UNMIK POLICE PRESS UPDATE
02 APRIL, 2001
MITROVICA Region
MURDER
Mitrovica North - 01/04 - 2100 hrs. During a dispute a known K-Serbian male shot at three other K-Serbian males, killing one and wounding two before fleeing from the scene. The injured were taken to a hospital for medical treatment.

Monday, 2 April, 2001

I got up at 0530, "Triple Sierra" and made coffee. I was in to the office by 0730. Alban came in and I had him work on translating my Ethics PowerPoint into Albanian. I took Cedric and Thommy downtown to a meeting at Regional HQ. After dropping them off I went to the Bristol and ate some eggs and hash browns. I went back to the office and waited for Thommy to call for me to come and pick them up. I went to get them at 1130 and then we went to lunch at Ardi's. It took Alban until 1600 to finish the translations and it took me another hour to finish the overhead slides. Craig came by to get me at 1700 and we went to the gym. Toward the end of the workout I got sick again. We took a cab home and I went to bed. I had a bad night. I woke up at 0200 from nightmares and anxiety.

P.S. I am going to go see "Doc" Donovan again tomorrow to check my BP and blood sugar.

P.P.S. A U.S. "spy" plane collided with a Chinese fighter jet and had to land in China.

UNMIK POLICE PRESS UPDATE
03 APRIL, 2001
PRISTINA Region
MEMORIAL CEREMONY
Glogovac Town - 02/04 - 1100 hrs. A group of approximately 2,500 K-Albanian students gathered in memory of students killed in the war.
PRIZREN Region
MURDER
Kijevo Village, Malisevo - 02/04 - 2200 hrs. The dead body of a K-Albanian male was found by his family members in his residence. The victim had sustained two bullet wounds to the head.
SHOOTING
Trnje Village, Suva Reka - 02/04 - 2330 hrs. Unknown suspect(s) shot an automatic weapon towards a gas station causing minor damage to the building and a vehicle.
MEMORIAL CEREMONY
Mala Hoca Village, Orahovac - 02/04 - 1100 hrs. Approximately 700 K-Albanians gathered in memory of those killed in the war.
MITROVICA Region
ASSAULT

Mitrovica North - 02/04 - 1040 hrs. A small group of K-Serbians assaulted a K-Bosnian male employee of the NGO "ACTED".

Tuesday, 3 April, 2001

I got up at 0600 and I feel bad already. I had a bad night with nightmares and interrupted sleep. I made myself eat some fruit for breakfast. I went in to work at 0730. No KPS showed up for class today. I feel too bad to teach anyway. Cedric took me to the company building to see Doc. He was not there so Cedric took me to the British KFOR field hospital to have my BP checked. My BP was 210/120. The Brits said that I had to get a referral from the company Doc before they could give me a full physical. Cedric took me back to the company building but Doc was not there. I had to go to the UNMIK clinic. I saw an Albanian female doctor who took my BP and then gave me a nitro pill and told me to come back on Thursday. I did not take the pill and I went back to the company. Doc is gone teaching a class. I got to feeling really bad so the company got a UNMIK referral to the British KFOR field hospital. They gave me a physical. Everything except my BP was OK. A British doctor gave me a note to give to Doc in the morning.

UNMIK POLICE PRESS UPDATE
04 APRIL, 2001
GNJILANE Region
EXPLOSION
Donje Livoc Village, Gnjilane - 03/04 - 2100 hrs. An unknown device exploded in an unoccupied K-Serbian owned residence. The house was completely destroyed.
PRIZREN Region
MURDER
Prizren - 02/04 - 2250 hrs. The dead body of a K-Albanian male was found by his family members in his residence. The victim died of apparent gunshot wounds.
PEC Region
ILLEGAL POSSESSION OF WEAPONS
Dakovica Town - 02/04 - 1500 hrs. A K-Albanian male was arrested after a search of his residence resulted in the seizure of a machine gun.
MITROVICA Region

ASSAULT/CRIMINAL DAMAGE
Mitrovica North - 03/04 - 2100 hrs. A British male employed by the NGO "American Friends Service Community" and a K-Albanian male, were assaulted by a group of unknown K-Serbians who then stole a mobile phone, cash and damaged the windscreen of their vehicle. The K-Albanian male victim was transported to the hospital. The extent of the injuries were not reported.

Wednesday, 4 April, 2001

I walked down to the company building to see Doc at 0900. My BP was still very high. He wanted me to go to see the German doctors in Prizren. The Germans have the biggest field hospital in the theater. A local Albanian employee of the company named Chumly drove me to Prizren. When we got there I met with the Prizren company "Doc". His name was Jim Hulitt. He took me to the German KFOR hospital to get checked in. I started the check in process but was told to return at 1500. I ate at the German KFOR chow hall. The food was good but different from the British. I went to the company building in Prizren and was taken on a tour of the town. Prizren is the oldest town in Kosovo. I saw the old Turkish fort that overlooks the city. This is where the Germans have sniper positions. At 1500 I was taken back to the hospital and saw the internal medicine doctors. My BP was still very high, 240/160. They drew blood and did an EKG and then decided to admit me to the hospital. The hospital is a collection of tents. It looks a little like the *M*A*S*H* television series. My area has four beds in one tent. Our meals are served in the next tent and the head is a trailer connected to the tent complex. The head is about a 40 yard walk from my bunk. They gave me some BP medications and a sedative to calm me down. They take my BP every half hour. Only the doctors can speak a little English. The nurses and other patients only speak German.

P.S. Doc Jim notified Prishtina that I had been admitted and made arrangements for Station #2 and Craig to be notified.

UNMIK POLICE PRESS UPDATE
05 APRIL, 2001
GNJILANE Region
EXPLOSION

Livoc Village, Gnjilane - 03/04 - 2100 hrs. An explosion occurred in an unoccupied Serbian owned residence. Extent of damage was not reported.
Vitina Town - 04/04 - 2113 hrs. An explosion occurred in an unoccupied Serbian owned residence. Extent of damage was not reported.
PEC Region
FOUND HUMAN REMAINS
Svrhe Village, Klina - 04/04 - 1800 hrs. A K-Albanian male, who was searching for a cave, found human remains. UNMIK Police responded to the scene and found the human remains of three to four bodies.
MITROVICA Region
Mitrovica North - 02/04 - 1200 hr. A known K-Albanian male threw stones at a K-Serbian male's bus causing damage to the windshield.

Thursday, 5 April, 2001

Lights on here at 0700. It is also the shift change time. They distributed the morning medications and took vitals. My BP is still high but not as bad. I had a breakfast of bread, jam and a boiled egg in the next tent. No one speaks English so I just grunt and smile. The doctors came around about 0900 and said that I would have to stay for several days so they could run some tests and get my medications adjusted. I found out that the German soldier in the bed next to me is Causten Hausen. He is twenty years old and speaks a little English. He is in for a tooth extraction. He traded me two German KFOR key rings for one of my U.N. patches. I had lots of BP checks today and it is still too high. Jim brought a November 1999 *Time Magazine* for me to read. Craig and Bekim came by later and brought me a bag of clothes, toiletries and books. Doc Donovan and Jim came back later to check on me. They had the Prizren Regional Commander with them but I don't remember his name. Later in the evening I could tell that I was having an anxiety episode and my BP was elevated. One of the German doctors checked it and it was high enough that he gave me a sedative and a spray of Nitro under my tongue. They put a monitor on me that takes my BP automatically every half hour. My BP started to come back down. I had my evening meal in bed because I was hooked up. Lights out at 2200.

P.S. Today is Carnita's 38th birthday. I had flowers delivered to her.

UNMIK POLICE PRESS UPDATE
06 APRIL, 2001
GNJILANE Region
MURDER
Klokot Village, Vitina - 05/04 - 1430 hrs. Unknown suspect(s) shot and killed a K-Serbian male. No further information given.
ARMED ASSAULT
Gnjilane - 05/04 - 1730 hrs. An UNMIK and KPS officer were assaulted by a group of unknown K-Albanian male subjects who were armed with clubs. One K-Albanian male was arrested.
EXPLOSION
Vitina - 05/04 - 2115 hrs. An unknown type of explosion occurred in front of a K-Serbian male's residence. Neither injuries nor the extents of damage were reported.
PRIZREN Region
MURDER / ARSON
Orahovac Town - 05/04 - 0100 hrs. Three K-Albanian males were arrested for an arson that resulted in the death of a K-Roma female.

Friday, 6 April, 2001

Lights on at 0700. I got a shave today. I started a 24 hour urine collection this morning. I did not get any breakfast this morning. When the doctors made their morning rounds they said I was scheduled for an ultrasound of my internal organs and I could not eat. I spent most of the morning reading the new book I had just bought on my last trip to the Camp Bondsteel PX; *The Red Baron.* It is kind of funny reading this book in a German military field hospital. All I did today is read and piss in a bottle. My BP is still high and they are increasing my medications. I had another bad spell around 1500 when they finally came and got me for my ultrasound. Doc Donovan and Jim showed up to be with me. The German doctor said that everything looked fine on the ultrasound. I finally got to eat something for the first time today. They gave me my medications and I tried to rest. Lights out at 2200.

P.S. We are very near the Macedonian border. I can hear the fighting from here. I am not too worried about it, being with the German KFOR. They even have tanks (panzers).

UNMIK POLICE PRESS UPDATE
07 APRIL, 2001
PRISTINA Region
MURDER
Lipljan Town - 06/04 - 1730 hrs. A K-Roma female died of injuries sustained in a fight between two gypsy families. No further information given.
EXPLOSION
Glogovac Town - 04/07 - 0027 hrs. A grenade explosion occurred in front of two kiosks damaging their windows.
GNJILANE Region
EXPLOSION
Kamenica Town - 05/04 - 2230 hrs. An unoccupied K-Serbian owned residence was the target of a second explosion, which caused only property damage.
PRIZREN Region
ATTEMPTED ARSON
Orahovac Town - 06/04 - 0500 hrs. Unknown person(s) attempted to set a K-Bosnian shop on fire by throwing a petrol bomb in it, which didn't explode.
PEC Region
ACCIDENTAL DEATH
Grebnik Village, Klina - 06/04 - 1550 hrs. A K-Albanian male employed by the NGO "Halo Trust" was killed when a mine he was attempting to remove exploded.
MITROVICA Region
DEMONSTRATION
Leposavic Town - 06/04 - 1330 hrs. Approximately 300 K-Serbians demonstrated in front of the Municipality Building in protest of future tax collection sites.

Saturday, 7 April, 2001

Lights on at 0700. They increased my medications today. I finished my first 24 hour urine collection and started on another one. Craig came in at 0930 to visit. He said that he had called Carnita and let her know that I was in the hospital and that so far all the tests were good. He talked to her on the 5th. This was not a good birthday present for her. I had more exams today and everything except my BP looks normal. I am passing the time by lying in bed and reading. I finished my *Red Baron* book and read the April, 2001 *Readers Digest* from cover to cover, even the advertisements. Jim was in twice today. My BP is still up but I am sleeping well. Lights out at 2200.

E-mail to Carnita

Hi Carnita,
I spent about an hour with your husband this morning, he's
fine. They did an EKG and everything was great, no problem. They also did an ultrasound on his stomach and chest. Everything was fine there, right size and right place, no problems. He had to collect urine in a bottle for 24 hours from Friday morning until this morning for some type of urinalysis test. They do not have the results back on that yet because they sent it to Germany. He's bored but doing fine. Take Care, Craig

E-mail from Carnita

Hi my hunny,
I know you won't get this right away, but wanted to send it anyway. First off I want to tell you the birthday flowers are BEAUTIFUL! It really made my day to get them. Craig told me you went into the hospital the same day as I got the flowers, so it was nice getting them the same day. I feel so much better knowing you went to get a good checkup. Please let me know right away how you are doing. I didn't tell your parents because I didn't want your mom to be upset. Love you, Carn

UNMIK POLICE PRESS UPDATE
08 APRIL, 2001
PRISTINA Region
EXPLOSION
Glogovac Town - 07/04 - Time not reported. A hand grenade explosion was reported. No injuries were reported.
FOUND UXO
Pristina - 07/04 - 0830 hrs. A hand grenade was located along a

roadside. KFOR EOD responded and disposed of the device. No injuries or damages were reported.

GNJILANE Region

EXPLOSION

Korbulic Village, Kacanik - 07/04 - 1900 hrs. A seventy year-old K-Albanian male was seriously injured when he stepped on a mine.

PEC Region

FOUND HUMAN REMAINS/POSSIBLE MASS GRAVE

Klina Town - 07/04 - 1100 hrs. A gravesite containing numerous skeletal remains was located between the villages of Volljak and Severka.

Sunday, 8 April, 2001

I got up at 0600 and finished my second 24 hour urine collection. I finally got a hot shower, shave and clean clothes. I finished my "Triple Sierra" routine before the lights came on at 0700. I took my morning medication and had breakfast. My first BP of the day was closer to normal, 150/80 but still up. They are increasing the dose again. During the morning rounds one of the doctors said that I would be seeing Dr. Braas sometime today. He is a neurologist/psychologist. I wrote out a statement for Doc Donovan about how I was treated by the UNMIK clinic. I read until time to see Dr. Braas. Dr. Braas said that they have found no physical reason that is causing my BP to be so high. He interviewed me about traumatic events in my life. I told him about my "friendly fire" incident in the USMC where I was shelled for several minutes and hit in the helmet by a shell fragment from a 155mm HE artillery round. I told him about crashing my patrol car and injuring my leg during a high speed pursuit in 1988. I recounted the details of the 1997 "Wolf Creek shootout" where I shot and killed the man who was trying to kill us with a 12 gauge. I also told him how shortly after the shooting I had to fight a man for a .44 magnum revolver inside a vehicle as he tried to shoot me. Finally I told him about my most recent brush with death in the November bombing in Prishtina. After hearing about all the critical incidents that I had been involved in Dr. Braas was sure that my BP problem was caused by PTSD and that I should end my mission and return home. He said that my staying so long has shown toughness but that continuing to stay in mission would show stupidity. He was not surprised that I have been having nightmares and anxiety episodes. Craig came by to visit and I told him about what Dr. Braas had said. Craig agreed that I should go home.

P.S. Heavy rain started today. The sound of the rain on the tent helped me sleep.

E-mail to Carnita

Hi Carnita,
I just got back from seeing your husband. He's fine, bored and tired of being there. All the tests are coming back normal. The two 24-hour urine tests he did have to be sent to Germany to be analyzed, so we do not know the results on them. But I'm guessing they will be normal like the rest of the test. He will be in the hospital for another three or four days, but there is a good reason for it. They put him on medication to bring his high blood pressure down, but they started it out at a real small dosage, which is good. They are very slowly, gradually increasing it to get his blood pressure down to normal. It's come down a lot, it's not near as high as it was, but it's not down to the normal range yet. I know that's not the news you wanted to here, that he's going to be there that long, but, I'm glad they're doing it this way, the right way, instead of just pumping him full right away. The doctors are saying that since all of his test are normal it's probably PTSD that's causing it. If that's the case I would guess that they're going to send him home. I do not know when though. Take Care, Craig

UNMIK POLICE PRESS UPDATE
09 APRIL, 2001
PEC Region
MEMORIAL SERVICE
Koshare Village, Decani - 08/04 - 1000 hrs. Approximately 3,000 K-Albanians attended a peaceful memorial service in memory of those killed in the war. No incidents were reported.
Sverke Village, Pec - 08/04 - 1230 hrs. Approximately 300 K-Romas attended a peaceful memorial service in memory of three local villagers who died last year. No incidents were reported.

Monday, 9 April, 2001

I got up at 0700. I slept well. My morning BP was 140/85. The doctor came by and said that I need to continue with the mediations for a while and that I should be sent back to the states in a few days. He said that they want to do a stress test sometime today or tomorrow. It is still raining hard today. Nothing to do but lie in bed and read. Lights out at 2200.

UNMIK POLICE PRESS UPDATE
10 APRIL, 2001
PEC Region
THREATS/INTIMIDATION
Dakovica Town - 09/04 - 0700 hrs. An UNMIK police officer received a note on the door of his accommodation threatening death if he did not leave the village.
MITROVICA Region
ROBBERY
Mitrovica North - 08/04 - 1755 hrs. Three unknown male suspects attacked an off-duty UNMIK Police officer and stole his jacket, sunglasses and cash. The victim sustained minor injuries.

Tuesday, 10 April, 2001

I got up at 0600 and showered and shaved before everyone else got up. Lights on at 0700. The doctors made their rounds. Nothing new. BP was 140/85. Jim came in at 0900 and brought me some more books to read. There is no word yet on when I can be released. Craig came to visit and brought me some clothes and another book. Dr. Braas came by while Craig was there. He said that I definitely have PTSD and will be going home soon. Jim came by and talked with Dr. Braas to arrange getting me checked out of the hospital and arranging a medevac flight out. They said I should be back home by Sunday or Monday if all goes well.

P.S. Still having heavy rains.

Wednesday, 11 April, 2001

Same morning routine again. The doctors made their rounds. Everything is still Ok and improving. Jim came in and said that I would have to pay my hospital bill today and leave at 0900 in the morning. He said that I would be reimbursed by the company. I paid the bill at 1700. It cost 3,564DM for the eight days I was here. I am ready for my final check out in the morning. Lights out at 2200. It is still raining.

P.S. I was woken up a little after 0200 by several explosions nearby. I'm sure the German KFOR has it under control.

UNMIK POLICE PRESS UPDATE
12 APRIL, 2001
PRIZREN Region
GRENADE ATTACK
Zerze Village, Orahovac - 11/04 - 0215 hrs. Unknown persons attacked three separate businesses owned by the same K-Albanian family with hand grenades at the same time. Minor property damage at each bar was reported.
PEC Region
SUICIDE
Crnce Village, Istok - 11/04 1600 hrs. A K-Albanian male committed suicide by hanging.
MITROVICA Region
THREAT/INTIMIDATION
Srbica Town - 11/04 - 1918 hrs. A K-Albanian male was arrested after he threatened a UNMIK Police officer.

Thursday, 12 April, 2001

I got up at 0600 and did my morning routine and got packed. I had breakfast and morning meds and waited for the doctors to make the rounds. I checked out at 0900. I got all my paperwork together and about a two week's supply of medications. I was met outside the hospital by a local Albanian employee of the company for the ride back to Prishtina. His name was Timmie. He said that "timmie" in Albanian means "smoke." We drove directly to the company building in Prishtina. I started the check out process. The clerk rescheduled my CTO flights for 16 April. I was refunded my money for the tickets because it is a medevac out of mission. I got a ride to the house and gathered up all my company gear that needed to be turned in. I went back to the company and turned everything in and finished checking out. I went back to Station #2 and chatted with Carnita for half an hour and gave her my flight details. I went home and went to bed by 2130.

UNMIK POLICE PRESS UPDATE
13 APRIL, 2001
PRISTINA Region
THREATENING BEHAVIOR
Pristina - 12/04 - 1215 hrs. An unknown K-Albanian male threatened another K-Albanian male by placing a hand grenade in the victim's mouth.
GNJILANE Region
ARSON
Kacanik Town - 10/04 - 1200 hrs. Unknown person(s) set approximately one hectare of land owned by a K-Albanian female on fire.
PEC Region
MURDER
Dakovica Town - 12/04 - 1955 hrs. Three unknown male suspects, all of them armed with assault rifles, entered a boutique and tried to rob the owners. Suddenly the suspects opened fire at the persons in the shop. One K-Albanian male was killed and three other K-Albanian males were injured (two seriously). The injured persons were brought to the hospital for treatment.

Friday, 13 April, 2001

I went in to the office today at 0830. Randy was assigned to help me get checked out. We started the U.N. check out process and had to go to several offices and get a check out sheet signed off. Just like the military. We stopped by the U.S. Contingent Commander's office. I spoke with Deputy Commander Allen Davis. He said that they were planning to give me a State Department medal for valor for the bombing in November. Secretary of State Colin Powel visited Macedonia yesterday and was supposed to come to Kosovo today. The visit was cancelled because of the heavy rains. I finished checking out with the U.N. except for my final MSA payment. They will mail it to me. It should be around $800. They only pay one third pay for days in the hospital. I got back to the house at 1700 and went to bed.

UNMIK POLICE PRESS UPDATE
14 APRIL, 2001
GNJILANE Region
MURDER

Vitina Road, Urosevac - 13/04 - 0735 hrs. A 57-year-old K-Albanian male was found shot to death in his motor vehicle. No suspect has been arrested yet.
PRIZREN Region
GRENADE ATTACK
Prizren - 14/04 - 0020 hrs. Unknown person(s) threw two hand grenades at an occupied K-Serbian owned house causing only minor damage to the exterior.
MITROVICA Region
ASSAULT
Mitrovica South - 14/04 - 0014 hrs. A K-Albanian male was arrested after assaulting an UNMIK Police officer during a traffic check.
THREAT/INTINMIDATION
Vucitrn Town - 12/04 - 1930 hrs. A K-Albanian male was detained after threatening UNMIK Police officers at a checkpoint.

Saturday, 14 April, 2001

Up at 0600. I did my morning routine. I took my meds and ate breakfast. I watched the BBC news and saw where they finally released the U.S. aircrew of the "spy plane incident." China is still holding the plane. Two British KFOR soldiers were killed when their vehicle struck an anti-tank mine near the Macedonia border. They were in the Gnjilane region near Camp Bondsteel. The fighting is still sporadic and the mine was freshly planted. I went to the office at 0900 after spending the morning packing. I went to lunch at Ardi's with Randy, Joe, Alban and Vjosa. I had the Chicken Schnitzel. I started to feel anxiety coming on. It may have something to do with being around so many people. I got to the house about 1500. I have plans to go to the Indian Inn with Brent, Craig and John around 1800. The weather is still very cool and windy with rain turning to snow. We got to the Indian Inn and had a good meal of hot chicken curry. Brent gave Craig and I a ride back to the house. We watched a movie until the power went off. I went to bed.

E-mail home

Hi Hun,
I got the doctor's info. Thanks. Counting down! Just two more days. I am all checked out and packed. My only concern is having

two heavy bags to drag through the airport. I hope it doesn't cause me to miss any connections. The only problem may be in Chicago. I can't wait to get home. I want to get checked out and back to normal. Love, Clay

UNMIK POLICE PRESS UPDATE
15 APRIL, 2001
PRIZREN Region
FOUND SKELETAL REMAINS
Orahovac Town - 14/04 - 1520 hrs. The skeletal remains of a human body were found in the yard of a K-Albanian residence.
ATTEMPTED SUICIDE
Prizren - 14/04 - 1200 hrs. A K-Albanian male attempted to commit suicide by cutting his throat. The victim was transported to a local hospital where he is listed in serious condition.
MITROVICA Region
ATTEMPTED ARSON
Mitrovica South - 14/04 - 1104 hrs. Unknown suspect(s) threw a petrol bomb onto the pedestrian walkway. No injuries were reported and the fire self extinguished.

Sunday, 15 April, 2001

I got up at 0600. I slept pretty good. I took my morning meds and ate. I watched the BBC news and finished the movie from last night. The rain turned to snow and there is about two inches in the yard. I hope the snow does not affect my flight out tomorrow. I went to the office at 0900 to check e-mails but the internet was down. I finished all my packing and left some stuff, toiletries and medicines, for Craig. I ate lunch, watched TV and napped most of the day. We found out today that three Russian KFOR soldiers have been killed by snipers in the border fighting. Our landlord, KPS officer Bekim Huseni, came over to visit about 2000. He is a very nice guy but he doesn't speak English. He brought over three beers, bananas and Fig Newton's. We noticed that the beer bottles had twist off caps instead of the usual standard caps that require a bottle opener. We have noticed that the twist off type caps are not common here. Craig took a beer and twisted the cap off. Bekim's eyes got big and he was obviously very surprised (and apparently has never seen a twist off cap). Craig did not miss a beat. He made a muscle, pointed to his bicep and said "American!" Bekim was amazed. He stayed and watched a movie with us. I went to bed at 2200. This is my last night in the house.

P.S. Thommy Erdmenger got back from CTO today and was able to come and say goodbye.

UNMIK POLICE PRESS UPDATE
16 APRIL, 2001
ATTEMPTED SUICIDE
Orahovac Town - 15/04 - 1810 hrs. A K-Albanian female attempted suicide by hanging herself.
PEC Region
DEMONSTRATION
Pec and Dakovica Towns - 15/04 - 1240 hrs. Approximately 250 K-Albanians participated in a march called EXODI-99 to commemorate the second anniversary of the exodus of K-Albanian persons from Kosovo. The event was staged peacefully and was held without incidents.
MITROVICA Region
MURDER
Turicevac Village, Srbica - 15/04 - 1800 hrs. A K-Albanian male was killed and his brother wounded after they were shot by unknown suspect(s). No further information given.
DEMONSTRATION
Mitrovica South - 15/04 - 0830 hrs. Approximately 75 K-Albanians participated in a march called EXODI-99 to commemorate the second anniversary of the exodus of K-Albanian persons from Kosovo. The event was staged peacefully and was held without incidents.
FOUND UXO
Brabonic Village, Mitrovica South - 15/04 - 1115 hrs. An UNMIK Police patrol unit located a land mine along a roadway. KFOR EOD responded to the location and took control of the scene.
FOUND DEAD BODY
Leposavic Town - 15/04 - 0820 hrs. The body of an infant child was found dead near a Gypsy Camp.

Monday, 16 April, 2001

I got up at 0600. This is my last morning in Kosovo. I went to the office to send my final e-mail home and arrange my ride to the airport. Thommy Erdmenger, Joe Massing and Station Commander Pete Anderson gave me a ride to Prishtina airport about noon. I had to pay $175 for overweight luggage. The company will reimburse me. I had coffee with the guys until my flight left at 1345. My flight to Vienna took about two hours. I got all my boarding passes taken care of with Austrian Air for tomorrow's flight. I have a layover here in Vienna. I checked in at the hotel across from the airport. The room is included in the price of my ticket. I had a fish sandwich for supper at the McDonald's in the airport. After supper I went to the room and watched the only English channel available; the BBC. I got to sleep early.

Final e-mail home

Last Message from Kosovo! I will be leaving for the airport in a couple of hours to fly to Vienna where I will spend the night. I will be home at 2359 on Tuesday night if I don't run into any trouble. I hope that the flights go as scheduled and that I will have no problems. Love, Clay

Tuesday, 17 April, 2001- End of Mission

I got up in Vienna at 0600 and ate at the breakfast buffet in the hotel restaurant. My flight left for Chicago at 1000. The meals and service on Austrian Air were great. I got into Chicago on time and had to claim my bags and go through customs. I flew United from Chicago to Seattle and arrived to find my bags were missing. One bag arrived on the next flight in from Chicago but the second was on another flight. I flew Horizon Air from Seattle to Kalispell. Carnita was waiting for me. None of my luggage arrived. They told me to come back at noon tomorrow and check. Carnita and I drove to the motel and got to bed about 0200. Even without my luggage it is great to be back!

P.S. I arrived at my airport of origin so my mission is officially over after 240 days.

EPILOUGE

After a month's medical leave I returned to duty as the Chief of Police of the Libby, Montana Police Department. Then, on September 11, 2001, the world changed forever. The United States was thrust into its next armed conflict which continues to this day. The United States, along with Great Britain, invaded Afghanistan in October of 2001 and then Iraq in March of 2003. In 2004 I was preparing to deploy on another civilian police mission in Iraq. I had traveled to Virginia for pre-deployment training, again with the support of my wife. On October 14, 2004 four employees of the company I had worked for in Kosovo were killed in Iraq. Suicide bombers had made it into Baghdad's fortified "Green Zone" where I was about to venture. My wife immediately "recalled" me home. It would be another two years before I learned that one of the men killed was Ferdinand Ibabao. Ibabao had deployed with my group to Kosovo in 2000. Ibabao's death was the reason that I did not go to Iraq. It is possible that his death may have saved my life. You just never know. I finally retired from the department in 2009 and signed onto another mission with the company in Afghanistan. I served as a professional mentor to the commanding general of the Afghan National Civil Order Police (ANCOP), which is the tactical arm of the Afghan National Police. While in Afghanistan I met up with several people that I had served with in Kosovo. Ken McCarty was in the group I deployed with. Randy Stensaas and Cedric Stephens were working at Camp Gibson in Kabul. Shannon Leary and Randy Wilson were also there working with the Department of State's Bureau of International Narcotics and Law Enforcement. I had stayed in contact with Brent Faulkner over the years. He stayed with the company in various missions until 2010 when he returned to Montana law enforcement. In 2010 I began working for the State of Montana, began a private consulting business, and started writing books.

GLOSSARY

AAK – Alliance for the Future of Kosovo
AOR – Area of Responsibility
AAFES – Army & Air Force Exchange Service
BRH – Brain Reducing Hat-AKA- Brimless Stetson
Burek – Spinach, meat & cheese filled pastry
Coca Cola/Coke – Red and White Toyota 4x4 patrol vehicle
CTO – Compensatory Time Off
DM – Duetsche Mark
DPU – Downtown Patrol Unit
DU – Depleted Uranium
EOD – Explosive Ordinance Disposal
EOM – End of Mission
Fli – Traditional Albanian pastry
FRY – Federal Republic of Yugoslavia
GIG – Citizen's Initiative of Gora
KFOR – Kosovo Force (NATO)
KLA/UCK – Kosovo Liberation Army/ Ushtria Çlirimtare e Kosovës
Kosovo/Kosove – Serbian/Albanian
Kosovo Krud – local cold and flu
KP – Kosovo Polje (Serbian) Fushe Kosove (Albanian)
KPS – Kosovo Police Service
L.A. – Language Assistant
LDD – Democratic League of Dardania
LDK – Democratic League of Kosovo
LNDSH – National Democratic Party of Albania
NATO – North Atlantic Treaty Organization
NLA – National Liberation Army
MSA – Mission Subsistence Allowance
OSCE – Organization for Security and Co-operation in Europe
PDK – Democratic Party of Kosovo
PFTO – Primary Field Training Officer
PLK – Liberal Party of Kosovo
PQLK – Party of the Liberal Center of Kosovo
PRK – Republican Party of Kosovo

PSHDK – Albanian Christian Democratic Party of Kosovo
Pristina/Prishtina – Serbian/Albanian- Capitol city of Kosovo
Rakia – Kosovo moonshine- distilled fermented fruit
RUC – Royal Ulster Constabulary
SDK – Slavic Democratic Coalition
SFRY – Socialist Federal Republic of Yugoslavia
SRSG – Special Representative of the Secretary General (UN)
Triple Sierra – Shit, Shower and Shave
TMK – Kosovo Protection Corps
UCK/KLA – Ushtria Çlirimtare e Kosovës/ Kosovo Liberation Army
UCPMB – Liberation Army of Presevo, Medveda, and Bujanovac
U.N. – United Nations
UNHCR – United Nations High Commission for Refugees
UNMIK – United Nations Mission in Kosovo
VCP – Vehicle Check Point

References

(2000, November) Bomb Hits Yugoslav Lawmaker's Home. *Associated Press.* Retrieved 11 October, 2008 from http://www.unmikonline.org/press/wire/im231100.html

(2000, November) Albright Condemns Kosovo Violence. *Associated Press.* Retrieved 11 October, 2008 from http://www.unmikonline.org/press/wire/im231100.html

Answer.com (2008) *Political Biography: Josip Broz Tito.* Retrieved 09 November, 2008 from http://www.answers.com/topic/josip-broz-tito

Answer.com (2008) *Politics: Kosovo War.* Retrieved 09 November, 2008 from http://www.answers.com/topic/kosovo-war

Answer.com (2008) *Political Biography: Slobodan-Milosevic.* Retrieved 09 November, 2008 from http://www.answers.com/topic/slobodan-milosevic

Buza, S. (2000, November) Balkans Blast: One Man Dies in Kosovo Explosion. *Reuters.* Retrieved 11 October, 2008 from http://www.unmikonline.org/press/wire/im231100.html

Coker, C. (2000, November) *United Nations Officers Report No. 23638.*

Gall, C. (2000, November) Strife Flares in Kosovo. *New York Times.* Retrieved 11 October, 2008 from http://www.unmikonline.org/press/wire/im231100.html

Inderwisch, M. *UNMIK Police Mission Presentation.* (2001, January) UNMIK Police Press and Public Information.

Kelmendi, A. (2003, July) *Balkan Crisis Report.* Retrieved 09 November, 2008 from http://www.iwpr.net/?p=bcr&s=f&o=156596&apc_state=henib cr2003

Smith, J. (2000, November) Yugoslavia Asks U.N. to Restrain Kosovo Militants. *Washington Post.* Retrieved 11 October, 2008 from http://www.unmikonline.org/press/wire/im231100.html

Wood, N. (2000, November) Kosovo Killing. *The Guardian.* Retrieved 11 October, 2008 from http://www.unmikonline.org/press/wire/im231100.html